IMAGES
of America

EDGEWATER

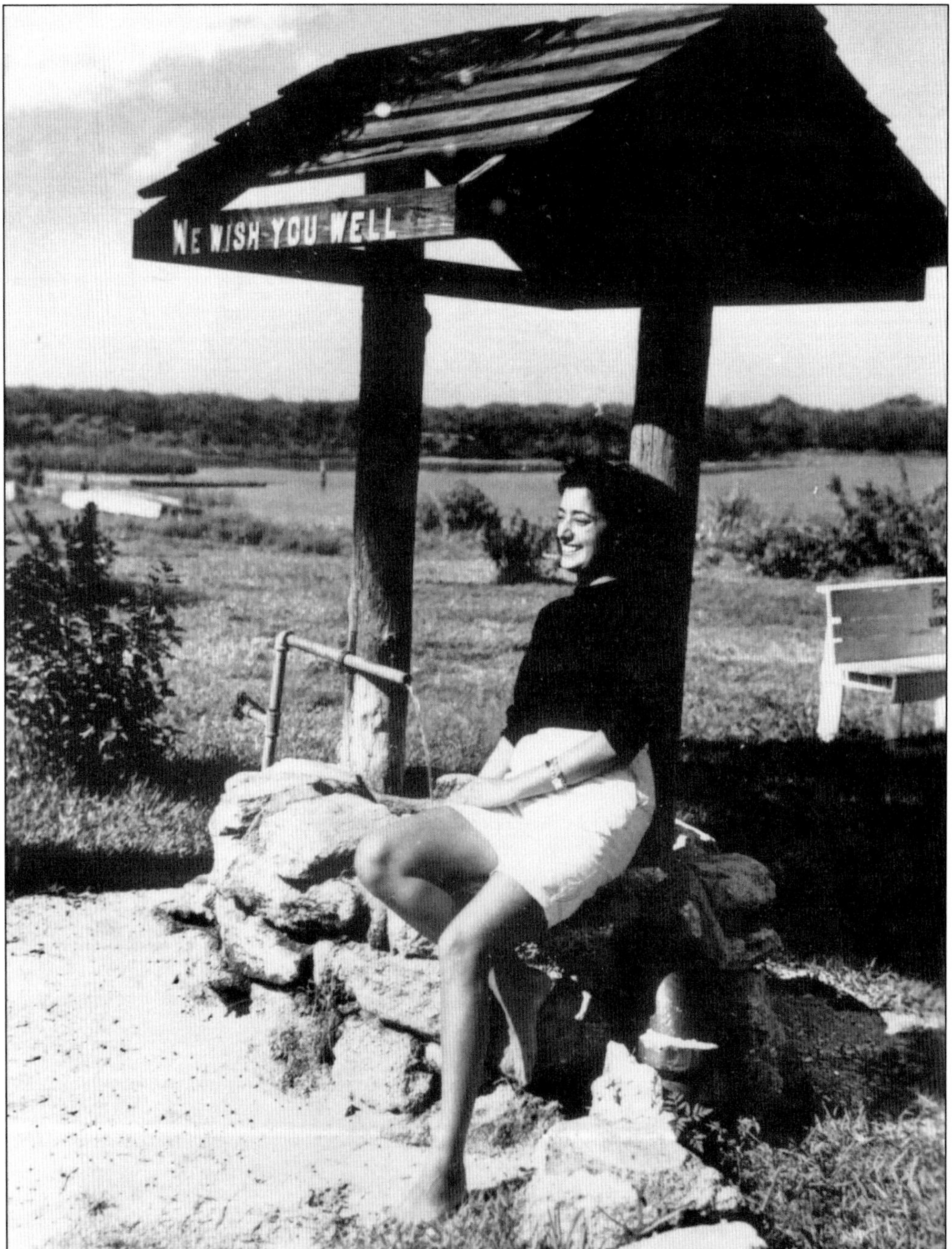

DELORES TOMARELLI ON THE OLD FLOW WELL, C. 1950S. The well was driven in the 1870s, and a pipe in the ground provided free-flowing sulphur water to the new community. Despite the odor and the taste, settlers in early Hawks Park traveled from throughout the area to get water from this source.

On the Cover: The *Wantah* was a touring and party boat owned by the Wilkinson family in early Hawks Park days. It would take you anywhere you "wantah" go.

IMAGES
of America

EDGEWATER

Sandra Wallus Sammons and Jo Anne Sikes

ARCADIA
PUBLISHING

ISBN 978-0-7385-1844-2

Published by Arcadia Publishing
Charleston, South Carolina

Printed in the United States of America

Library of Congress Catalog Card Number: 2005924477

For all general information contact Arcadia Publishing at:
Telephone 843-853-2070
Fax 843-853-0044
E-mail sales@arcadiapublishing.com
For customer service and orders:
Toll-Free 1-888-313-2665

Visit us on the Isnternet at www.arcadiapublishing.com

Dedication

To my husband, Bob Sammons, who found Edgewater for us.

—Sandy Sammons

To Gayle Harmon, who stirred my interest in Edgewater history.

—Jo Anne Sikes

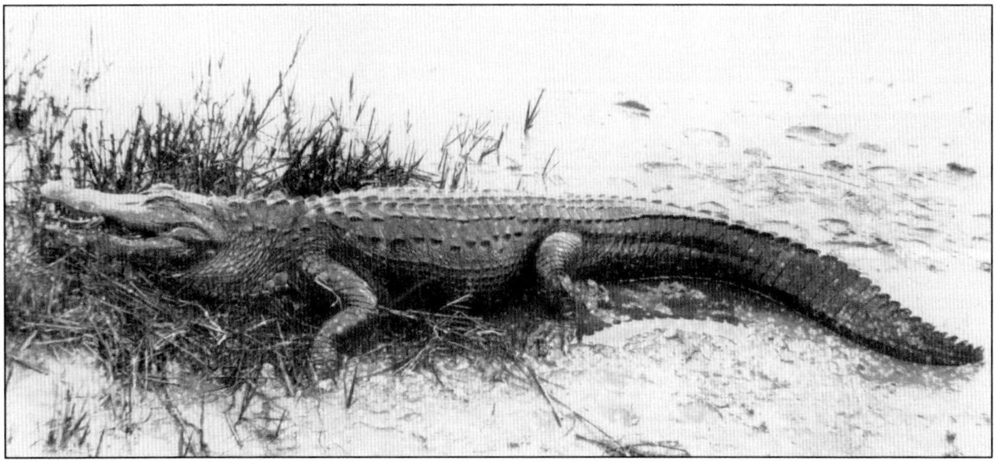

AN ALLIGATOR IN HAWKS PARK, C. 1880. Early Hawks Park was a frontier community. Occasionally an alligator would swim over to a wet area near Dr. Hawks's house and would be fed fish by the doctor and others. The settlement was full of wildlife, and according to Dr. Hawks, "The river teems with fish and the shores abound with game. . . . deer are abundant, bear not uncommon. . . . Besides game birds there is an immense variety of other land and water birds."

CONTENTS

The title of each chapter is part of Dr. Hawks's advertisement for Hawks Park (see page 16).

ACKNOWLEDGMENTS

The authors are particularly grateful to Dr. John Milton Hawks, founder of Hawks Park, who, through his books and carefully kept records, left us much information about the early days of his settlement. Since the current residents of Edgewater are still interested in and proud of their history, this compilation of photographs, postcards, and memories of Hawks Park/Edgewater has been a community project. The authors wish to acknowledge the contributions of the following: the City of Edgewater and Susan Wadsworth, city clerk; the Edgewater Museum and Lynne Plaskett, curator; and the Edgewater Public Library and Gayle Harmon and Ruth McCormack, librarians. Others who made excellent contributions were Phillip and June Currier, Rod Dinnen, Melissa Loveland Fowler, Marie Goodrich, Alfred and Anne Gray, Gary Luther, David McCallister, Annie McDevitt, the family of David and Helen McGinnis, Steven Chase and the Marshall family, Doris Massey, Lee and Heather Metchick, Dot Moore, A. Stephen Patrick, Harvey Petersen Jr., Leon and Frances Robitsch, Larry Sweett, Michael and Bridget Visconti, Ed and George Wilkinson, and Hazel Wilkinson.

INTRODUCTION

The city of Edgewater, Florida, was founded as Hawks Park by Dr. John Milton Hawks over 130 years ago. The small frontier settlement grew steadily through the years to become a thriving community along the water's edge.

Dr. Hawks had always been a dreamer. Graduating from public schools at age 16, he immediately went into teaching and determined to "do something with his life." Going on to college, he graduated with medical degrees from Ohio and Vermont schools and started a medical practice and pharmacy in New Hampshire. He also spoke out very clearly against slavery and for women's rights.

Esther Hill, a teacher, married Dr. John Hawks in 1854. On their honeymoon in Florida, while he was out getting "Florida sand in his shoes" (getting hooked on life in the Southern state), she was teaching African American children at a church in the town of Manatee, a practice that was against the law at that time in some states.

Becoming fascinated with her husband's medical books, Esther went on to become a doctor herself, helping to break another barrier. She also was a devoted wife to her husband as he built up two communities in the sparsely settled state of Florida.

The couple worked together and separately during the Civil War for the Union forces. Although Esther was not at first allowed to formally help out as a doctor or a nurse, she went as a teacher and contributed her doctoring skills as needed. John Milton Hawks was a doctor in the field, became head of General Hospital No. 10 (the first Union hospital for African American soldiers), and was an educator when needed. He was also one of the first voices to speak out in favor of allowing blacks to volunteer in the army.

Dr. John Milton Hawks's first venture in Florida failed. He and other officers in the Union Army had tried to create a haven for emancipated slave families at Port Orange, just north of Edgewater. The town is still there today, but it was not successful as a freedmen's colony. After that outcome, Dr. Hawks was only more determined that his next community would not only survive but thrive. And thrive it did.

His choice of location for this next venture certainly was a smart one. On leave from their duties during the Civil War, the two doctors explored part of the east coast of Florida. In 1865, John Milton Hawks bought what was called the Geronimo-Alvarez Grant, which dated back to Spanish days. By 1871, he settled on that property, built a house, and became the first postmaster and real estate agent. Hawks served as president of the Hawks Park Company, a group of investors in the new Florida project that advertised their Southern paradise in Northern newspapers.

The town grew. The Marshall, Wilkinson, and Hubbell families all were early entrepreneurs. A hotel and rooming house were needed and so they were built. A wharf built far out into the river allowed steamboats to stop at Hawks Park, bringing not only mail and supplies but visitors and new settlers. Harry Mitchell, George Durfee, and George Mendell brought their families and built houses and businesses.

Soon record quantities of honey, oranges, and other produce were leaving the Hawks Park wharf, bound for faraway markets. The number of acres in citrus groves increased, more and more pleasure and work boats were seen traveling up and down the river, and simple little frontier cabins were replaced by bigger, sturdier homes. One large hotel was turned into a four-story hospital—the only hospital on the east coast between St. Augustine and Key West at the time. Henry Flagler's railroad reached the thriving town just before Dr. John Milton Hawks's death in 1910. The founder of the little town was thrilled to finally have the mail delivered by rail. That really put his town on the map!

In the midst of all the growth in Hawks Park, the two doctors were very busy as well. Dr. Esther Hawks moved to Lynn, Massachusetts, where she continued her successful medical practice and was very active in that community. She was such a highly respected citizen that she was nominated to be on the Lynn School Board—by both political parties! Dr. John Milton Hawks worked for a time as engrossing clerk in Tallahassee and wrote up an early law for woman suffrage. He also compiled and published the *Florida Gazetteer*, a volume of more than 500 pages that listed the geographical locations of businesses found in each county of Florida at that time. He took a trip down the east coast of the state, which he wrote about in his book, *The East Coast of Florida*, published in 1887, providing us much information about the area at that time.

John and Esther's final thoughts were of the community that was named for them. They made it quite clear in their wills that they believed education was the key to a successful community. Esther, even though she was in the North most of the time, bequeathed $1,000 to be used by the Village Improvement Association for a new library and town hall in Hawks Park. When John died four years later, he left the land for the building site.

With a firm foundation, Hawks Park did thrive, with just a change in name. The city of Edgewater today has a modern library with 52,000 volumes, a city hall, a community center, many parks, and a scenic river walk along which joggers and cyclists can enjoy what is now called the Indian River, a part of the Intracoastal Waterway.

In Dr. Hawks's words, "The river here is a mile and a half wide, interspersed with mangrove islands, with no marsh in front of the village." Edgewater is no longer a community to spend only the winter months or retirement years. It is growing as more people move here to make it their home. The Atlantic Ocean nearby, the Indian River along the water's edge, the Florida sunshine, the old twisted oak trees, and the variety of land and water wildlife are all natural assets to the area and attract more people each year. Truly Dr. John Milton Hawks's dream has become reality. This is Florida at its finest. It is a community of people from all over the United States, and one of the friendliest towns on the east coast!

One

NEW ENGLAND VILLAGE

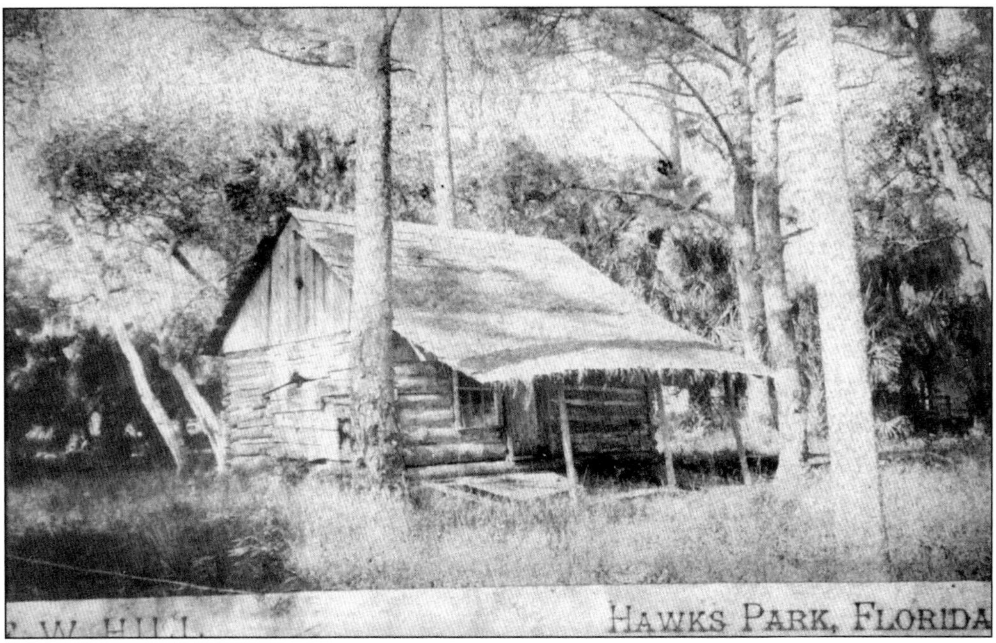

OLD LOG CABIN IN HAWKS PARKS AREA, C. 1870. This cabin may have been standing before Hawks Park was founded in 1871. It could have been built while the area was still part of Mosquito County and the river it overlooked was called the Mosquito River. The county name changed to Volusia in 1854. The river's name would also be changed, to the Hillsborough (or Hillsboro) and, years later, to the Indian River.

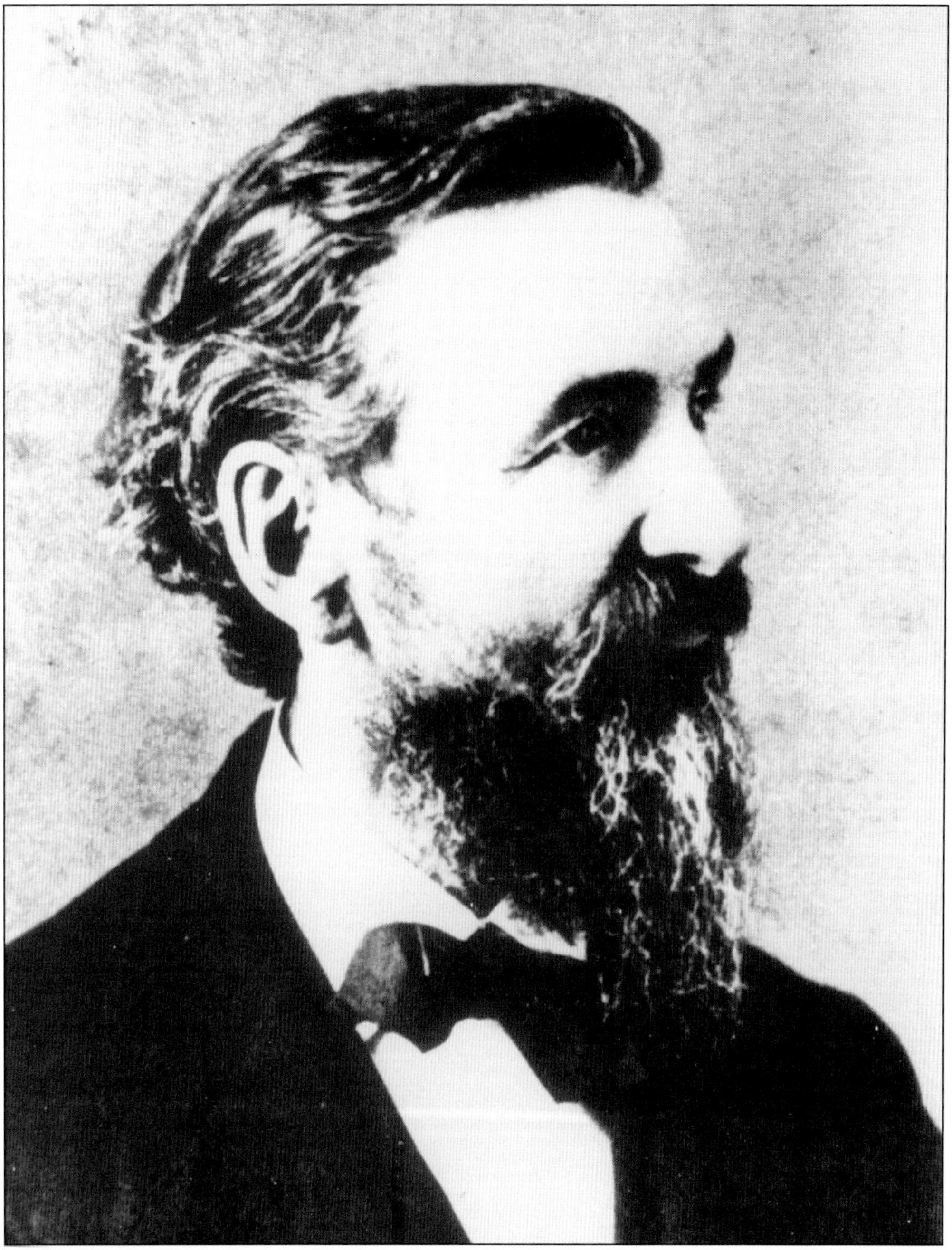

DR. JOHN MILTON HAWKS, C. 1864. Born on November 26, 1826, John Milton Hawks became a teacher and a surgeon but also dreamed about creating his own community in Florida. He became president of the Hawks Park Company and did his best to interest Northern investors and settlers in the venture. A quote about the Hawks Park Company states, "Our stockholders are wide-awake businessmen. There are no salaried officers in the company to eat up profits, and the business will be done as economically as possible. We think we have got a good thing, to say the least, and that there is no chance for loss, as our land is paid for and will increase in value without regard to improvements."

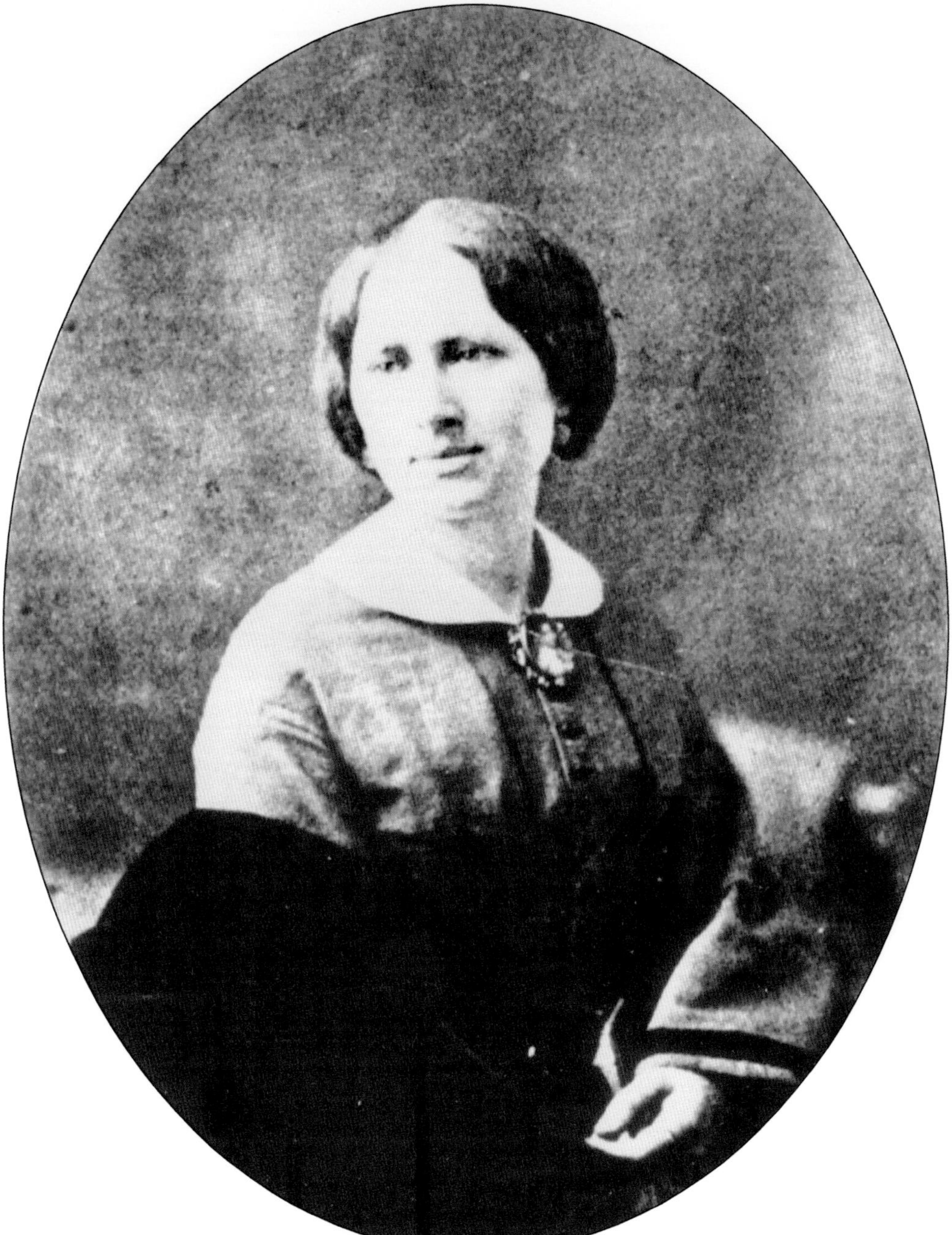

DR. ESTHER HILL HAWKS, C. 1864. Born on August 4, 1833, Esther Jane Hill did not just "go with the flow." She became a successful teacher, principal, general superintendent of schools, and woman doctor, at a time when all of her talents were badly needed. She was also a devoted wife to her husband, encouraging him in his Florida endeavors.

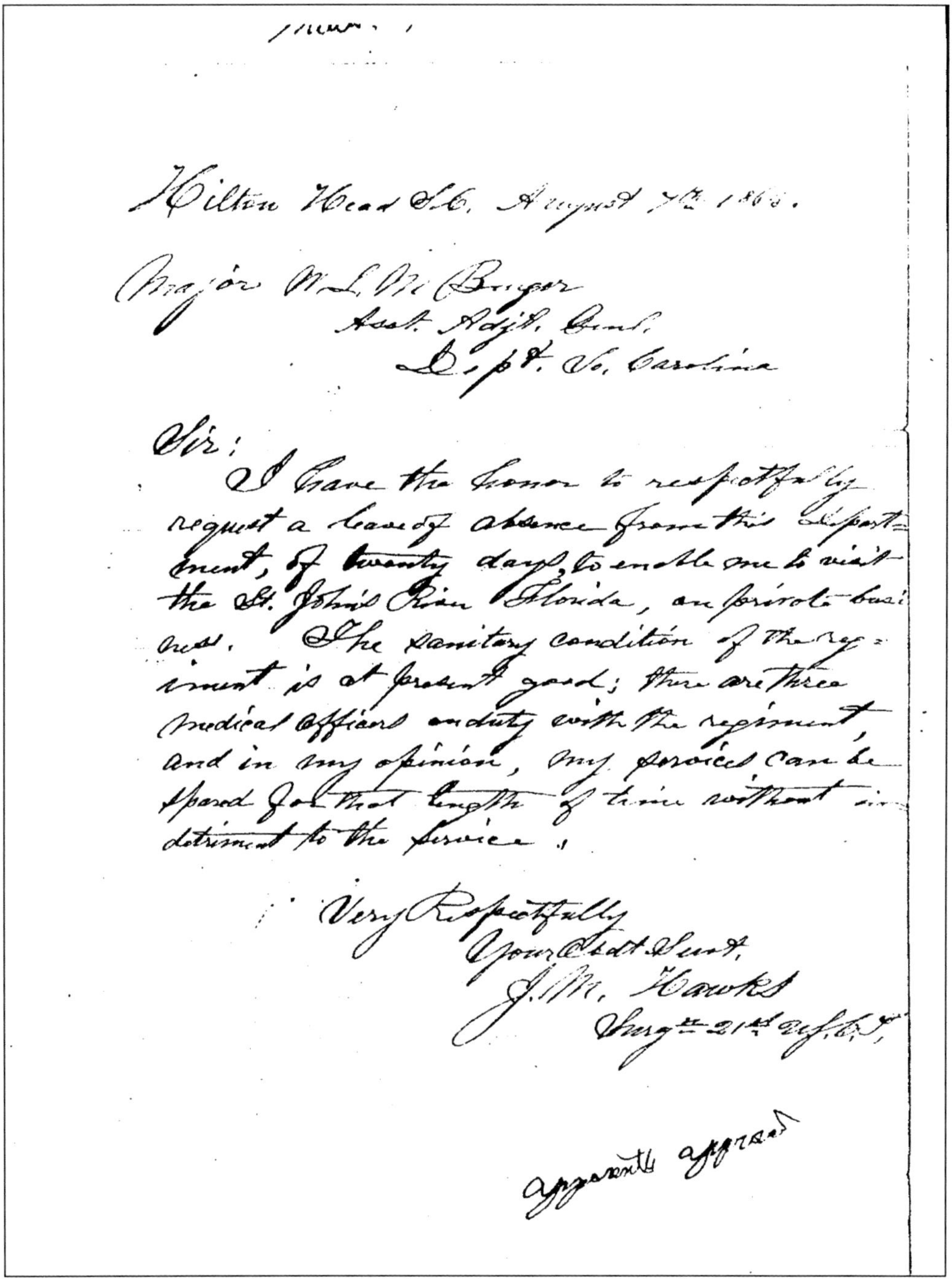

Hilton Head S.C. August 7th 1865.

Major W. L. M. Burger
Asst. Adjt. Genl.
Dept. So. Carolina

Sir:

I have the honor to respectfully request a leave of absence from this Department, of twenty days, to enable me to visit the St. John's River Florida, on private business. The sanitary condition of the regiment is at present good; there are three medical officers on duty with the regiment, and in my opinion, my services can be spared for that length of time without detriment to the service.

Very Respectfully
Your Obdt Servt,
J. M. Hawks
Surg. 21st U.S.C.T.

apparently approved

LETTER, DATED AUGUST 7, 1865. The Civil War was just coming to a close, and Dr. John Milton Hawks was looking to the future. When he was given permission for a 20-day furlough, he and his wife looked at land in the state that so intrigued him—Florida. As a result of this search, he found two sites on which he would attempt to build the communities of Port Orange and Hawks Park. When the first failed, he was determined that Hawks Park would survive. This letter is signed by John Milton Hawks, surgeon, 21st United States Colored Troops. "Apparently approved" is written on the bottom of the letter.

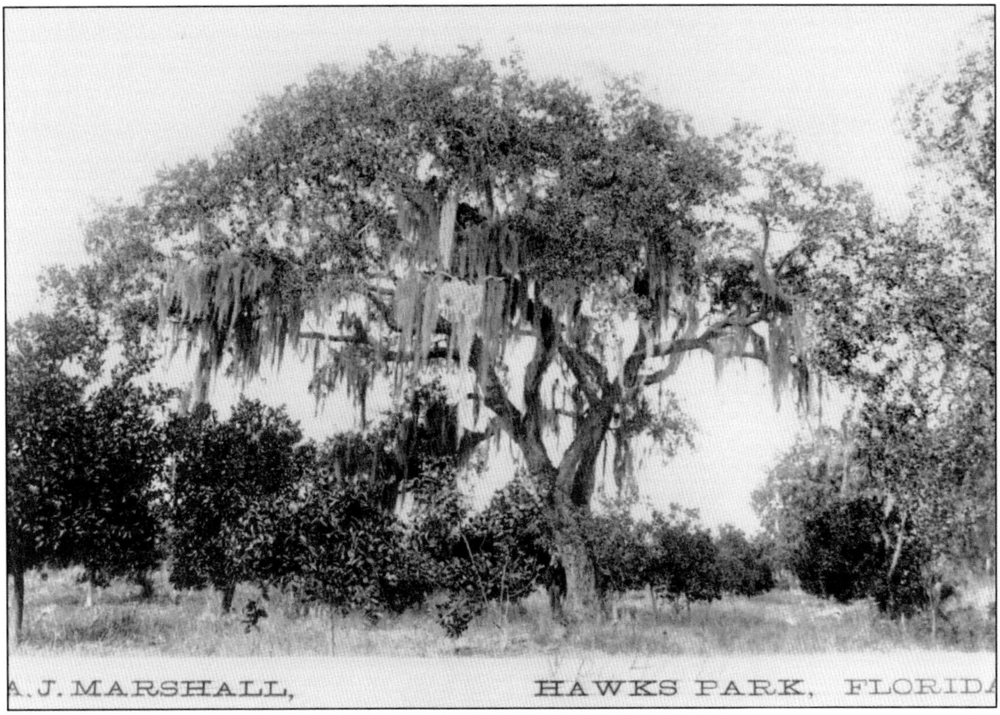

A. J. MARSHALL'S PHOTOGRAPH OF A LIVE OAK, C. 1880. John Milton Hawks is photographed standing under an old live oak in one of his orange groves. The photographer is Addison J. Marshall, one of Hawks Park's early settlers. Hawks was certainly multi-talented—he started orange groves in the area to show the new settlers that it could be done. It is believed that this old oak still stands.

EAST COAST OF FLORIDA VIEWS.

Published by FRED W. HILL, Hawks Park, Fla.

LARGE LIVE OAK,

Draped in Spanish moss, in Dr. Hawks' orange grove, at Hawks Park. About 50 yards from this tree, on a high shell mound on the bluff of the Hillsboro River, are the ruins of a stone floor of an ancient house; the chimney of hewn coquina rock, with a fireplace on both sides of it, was made to do service for a modern, rough dwelling house until 1871. At the foot of the mound there still stands a stone structure called the "Old Minorcan Oven;" it may have been a burial place. A few orange trees are shown in the picture.

DESCRIPTION OF MINORCAN FIND, C. 1880. An archaeological dig conducted in 2002 near the live oak tree in the previous photograph unearthed remnants of an 18th-century structure. These findings allowed researchers to establish that a Minorcan dwelling had been on that site, a part of the original settlement of the failed Turnbull colony at New Smyrna *c.* 1768.

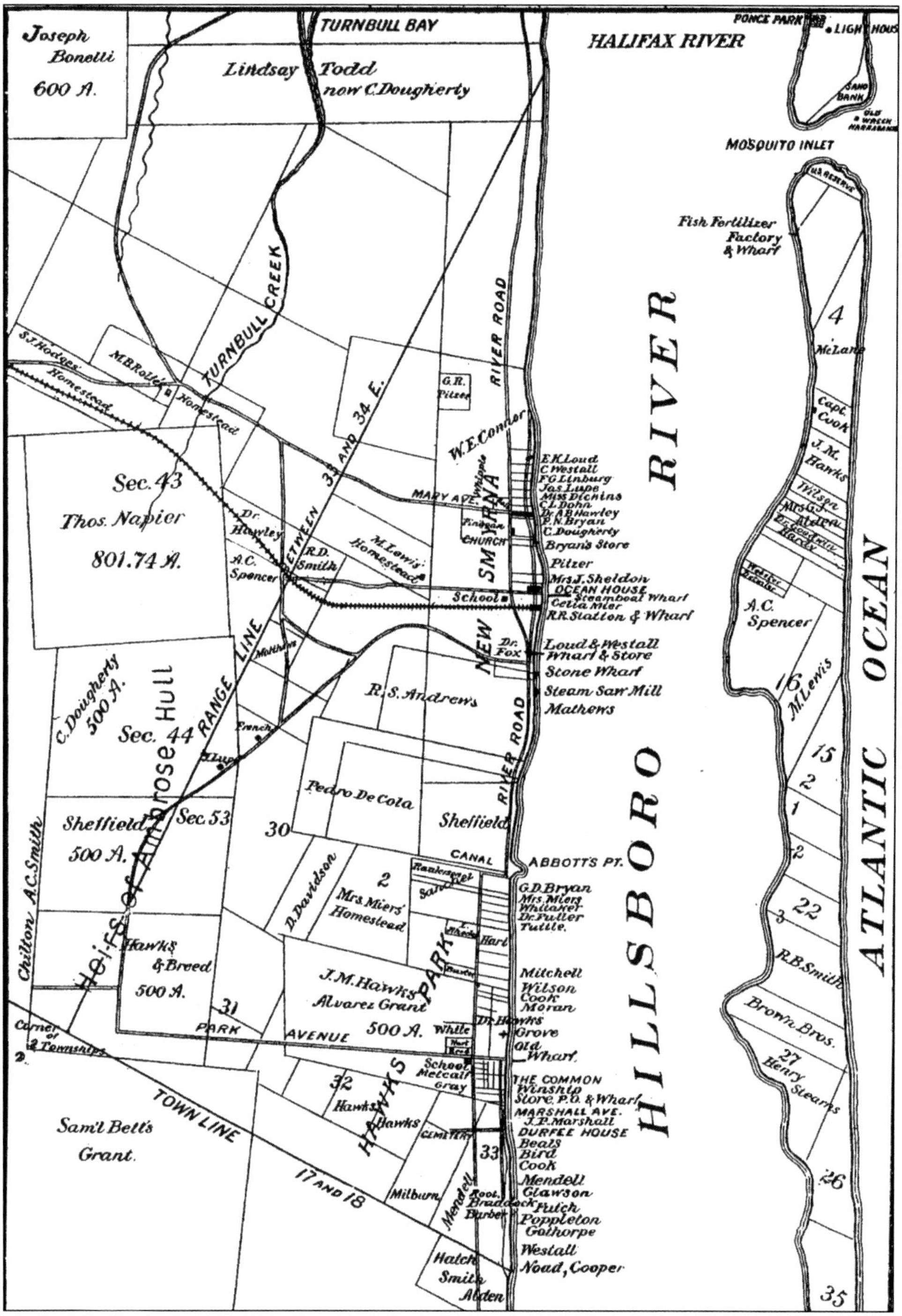

MAP OF THE HILLSBORO RIVER AREA, 1887. John Milton Hawks knew good real estate when he saw it and bought the Geronimo-Alvarez property, an old Spanish land grant of 500 acres, from Charles and Henrietta Lincoln for just $1 an acre. But the Lincolns did well in the deal—just five days before, they had bought the same 500 acres for 50¢ an acre! This map appears in Dr. John Milton Hawks's *The East Coast of Florida* (1887).

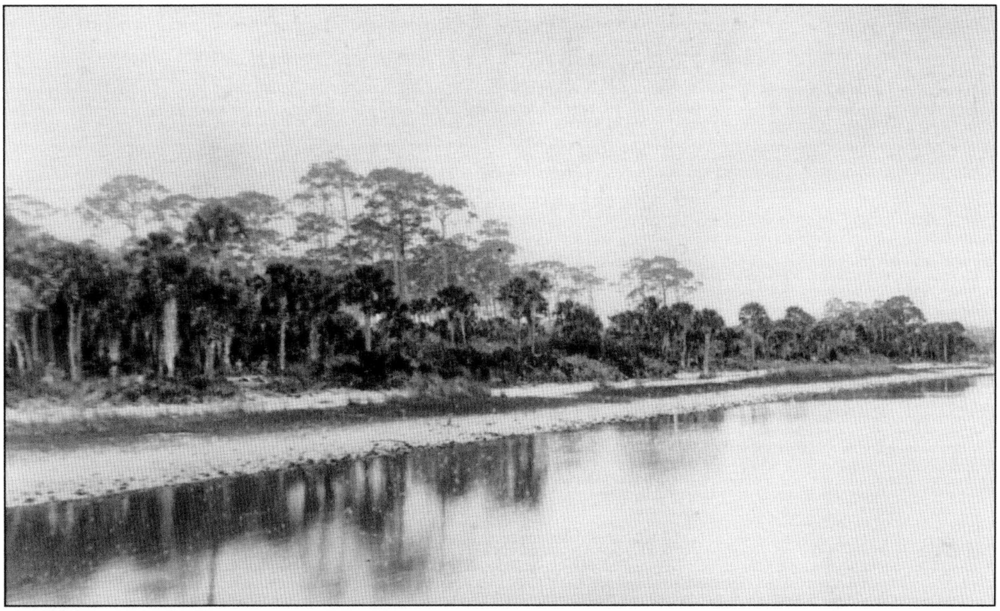

OVERLOOKING EARLY HAWKS PARK, C. 1875. A. J. Marshall, the photographer, took this picture while looking northeast, with the Hillsboro River in the foreground. In his *The East Coast of Florida*, Dr. Hawks described the scene: "The village is located on an elevated ridge of land, once covered with hard wood and pine timber; it is high, well drained, and healthy, with good water from wells 20 feet deep."

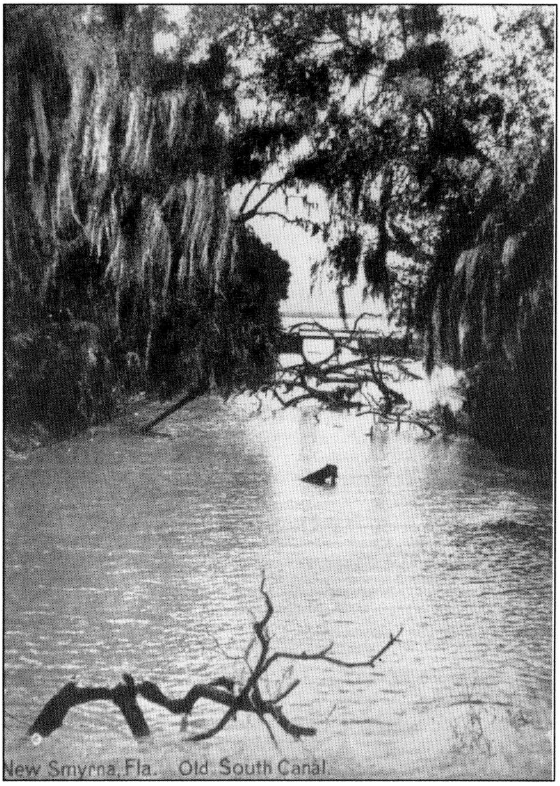

VIEW OF THE SOUTH CANAL, C. 1880. Also known as the Gabordy or Gabardy Canal, the South Canal was, and still is, the southern limit of New Smyrna and the dividing line between New Smyrna and Hawks Park. A survey map dated as far back as 1766 shows a creek here, and an 1835 survey map shows the "Gabordy Canal." The identity of Gabordy is unknown.

Hawks Park,

(SEE MAP AND DESCRIPTION.)

NEW ENGLAND VILLAGE ON THE

ATLANTIC COAST OF

South ❋ Florida

Two miles from New Smyrna R. R. Depot.

On deep water navigation, on the west bank of Hillsborough River. Land high and dry; location healthy; Hotels and Boarding houses, School of 30 pupils; a school house and public hall. Town regularly laid out; streets fifty feet wide. Every variety of soil. Prices reasonable.

Don't settle in Florida until you have seen the "East Coast," Being on the East Coast, dont purchase until you have seen Hawks Park.

Address

J. M. HAWKS,

Hawks Park, - Florida,

—— OR ——

LYNN, - - MASS.

ADVERTISEMENT FOR HAWKS PARK, C. 1871. John Milton Hawks probably wrote this ad, hoping to interest Northerners in coming to Hawks Park. To convince people that his new settlement was truly paradise in the South, Dr. Hawks also wrote, "The Atlantic Coast is, all things considered, the most desirable part of Florida for a residence throughout the whole year. . . . The ocean breezes are invigorating, and ensure a good appetite, and give rosy cheeks to the children."

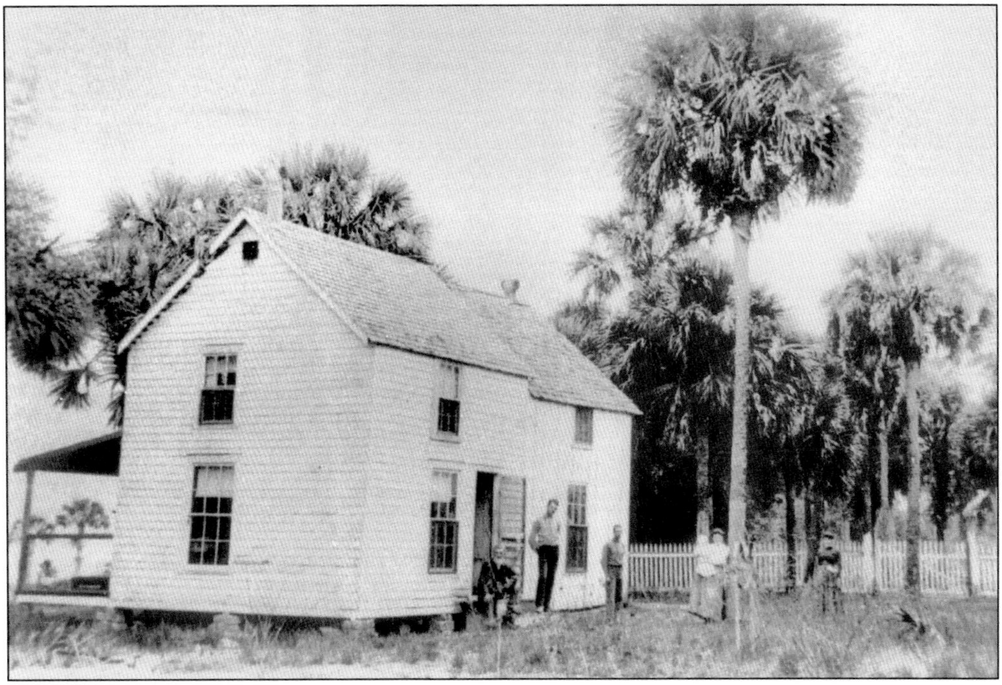

JOHN MILTON HAWKS HOME, C. 1875. Dr. Hawks is seated on the back step. Others are identified from left to right as Fred Hill, W. R. Scribner, Nellie Durfee, and Georgia Scribner. The photograph is looking southeast, and the palms in the distance on the left are along the river road, called the Strand.

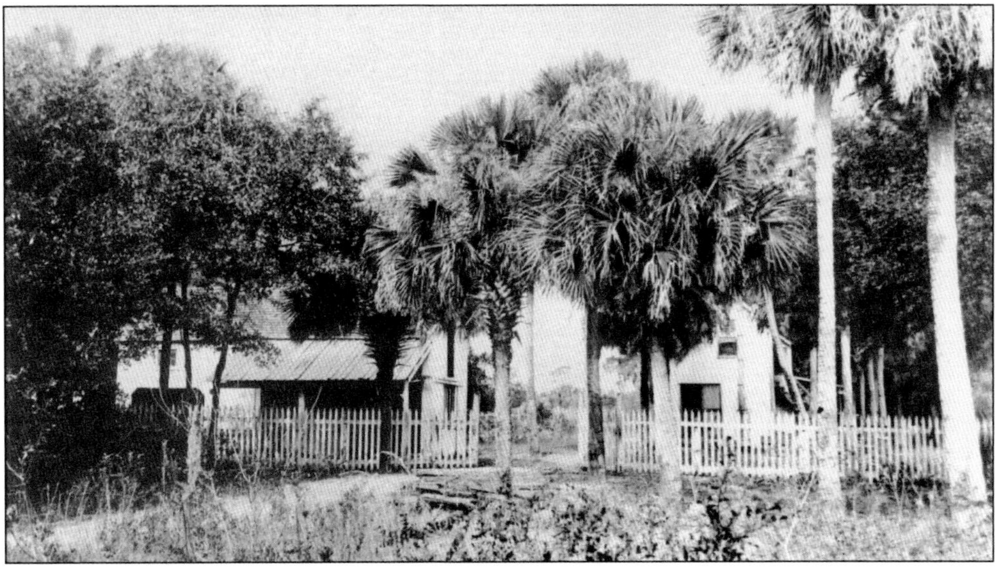

JOHN MILTON HAWKS HOME WITH BARN, C. 1875. The founder of Hawks Park had his home built on a shell mound facing the river. Dr. Esther Hawks visited during the winters, and she was impressed that their home had running water inside the house, two rooms upstairs and two rooms down, with a partial cellar under the house. Since there was no air conditioning, Dr. Hawks's home was built a few feet up from the ground to let air circulate. The home still stands, just north of Edgewater City Hall.

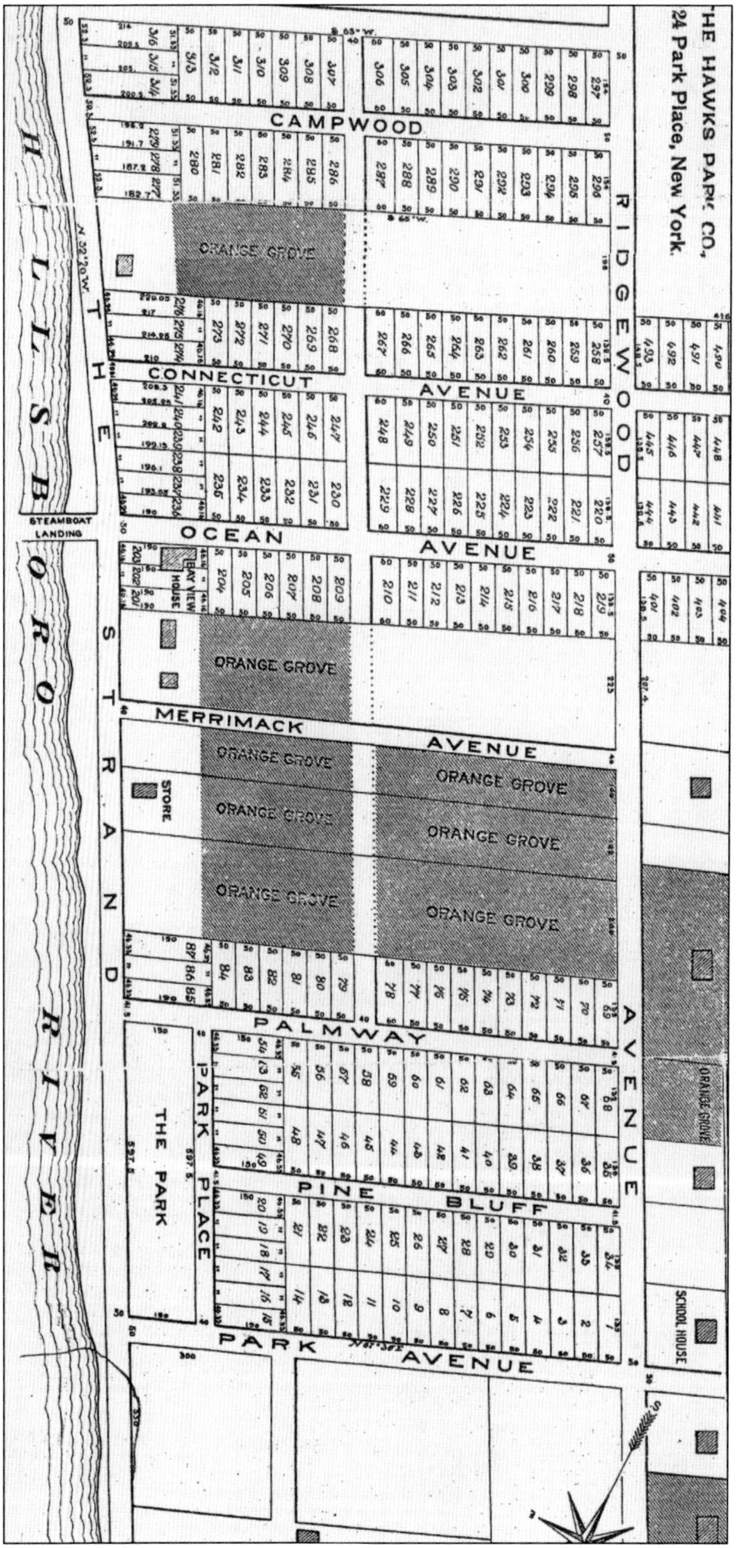

SURVEY MAP OF HAWKS PARK, C. 1880S. The Hawks Park Company hired a surveyor, Alfred Howard, to plan out the community. He created 493 lots, each 100 by 200 feet, surrounding a central park, and with streets 50 feet wide. This early map, which ran as an advertisement in a New York newspaper, shows 13 citrus groves (shaded areas). There was a road along the river called the Strand, and Ridgewood Avenue was the road to Miami.

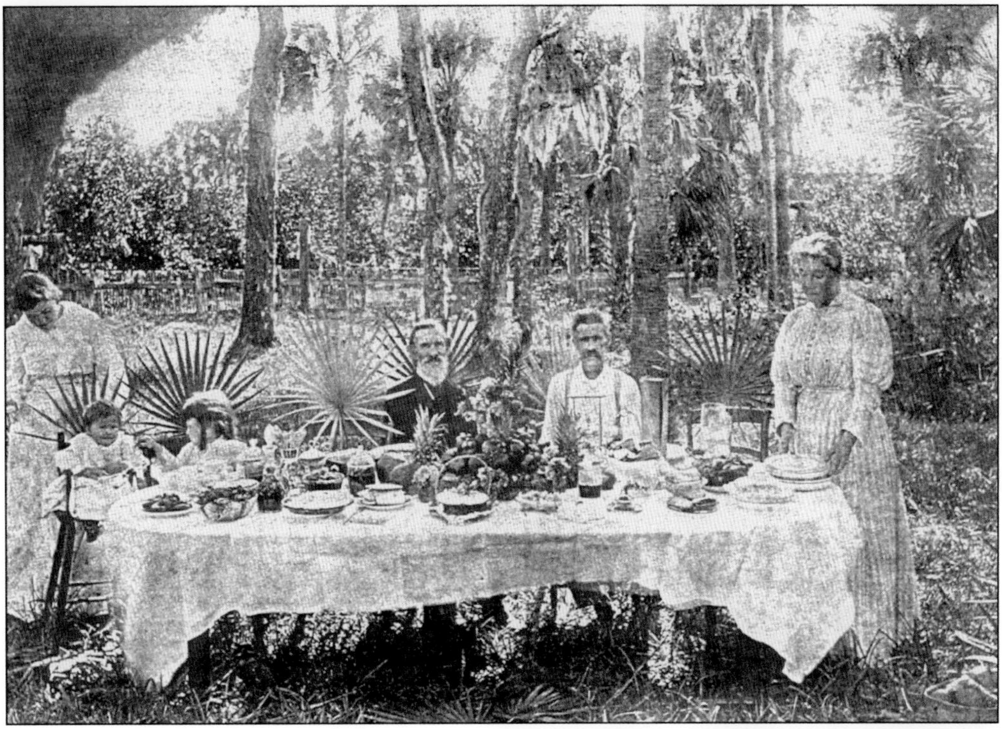

DINNER AT HAWKS PARK, C. 1875. Pictured are John Milton Hawks (with beard, center) Harry Mitchell (to the right of Hawks in photograph), and Alice (Mrs. Harry) Mitchell (standing, right). The other people are unidentified. The scene was well-decorated for this dinner, since someone took great care to place palmetto fronds on the backs of each chair. (Photograph by Hawks Park photographer Royal Hubbell.)

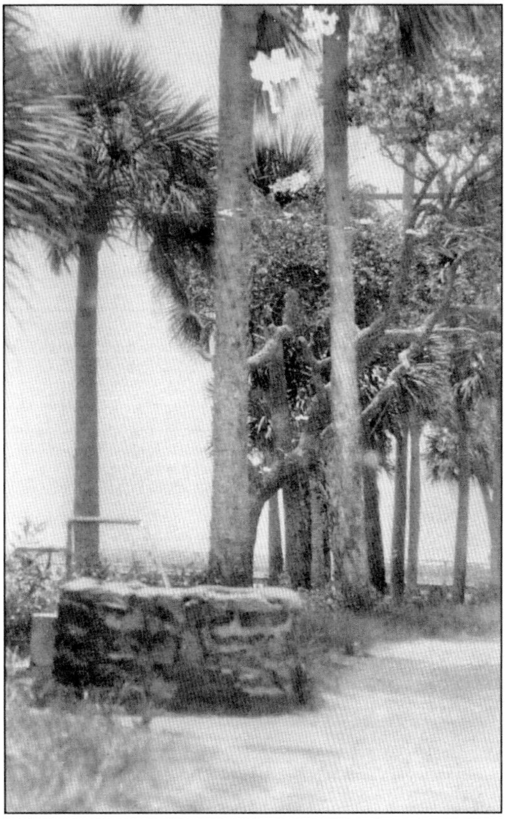

THE OLD FLOW WELL AND THE STRAND, C. 1910. Fresh water was needed for the new settlement, so a free-flowing sulphur well had been drilled at the east end of Park Avenue along the Strand. Since there were few wells at individual home sites then, the flow well became a gathering place for the community, as people came to fill their glass water jugs.

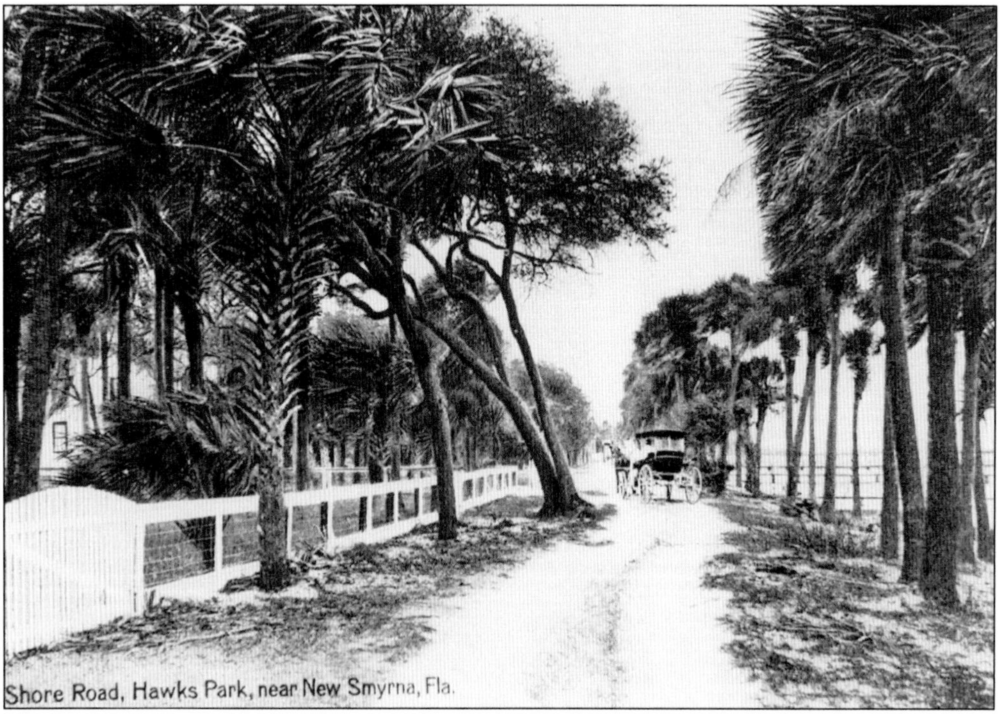

The Strand with Buggy, c. 1886. Following the easy curves of the Hillsboro River, the Strand followed an old Timucuan Indian trail from long ago. From a path, it became a one-way washboard road for horses and buggies, with beautiful views of the river through the moss-draped trees. This photograph, a postcard showing the "shore road," was taken in front of the Harry Mitchell home.

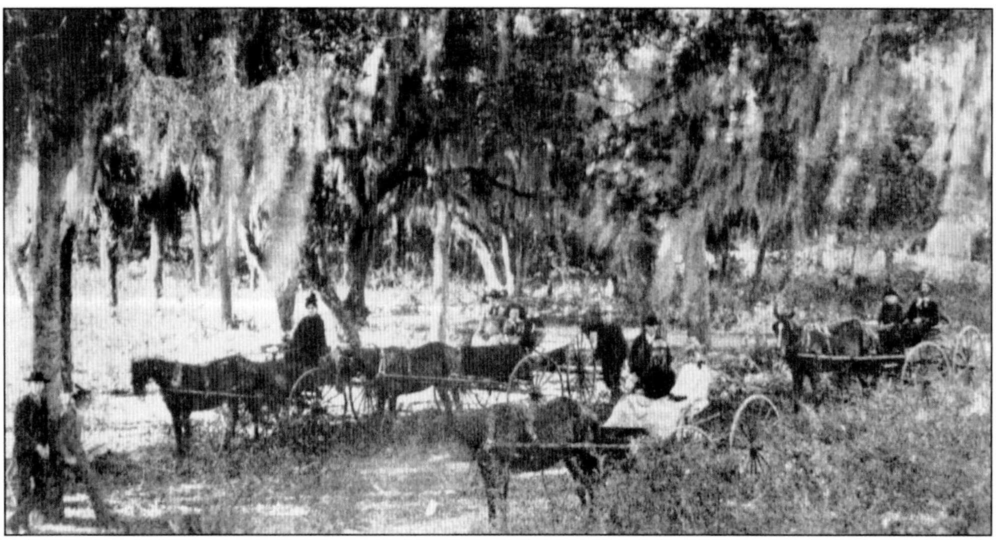

Wagon Turn-around Along the Strand, c. 1887. The story is told of a woman who encountered a wildcat along the road and had to back up the horse until she could get help. The turn-around at Boston Road was a place for friends and neighbors to sit and visit under the moss-covered live oak trees. By 1887, Hawks Park had 115 permanent residents, 41 houses, 160 acres of citrus trees, a general store, hotel, post office, and a school with 32 students.

H. P. WILKINSON WITH RATTLESNAKE, C. 1900. Mr. Wilkinson is about six feet tall, and this rattlesnake was killed among the saw palmettos just southeast of Hawks Park. Rattlesnakes, alligators, and mosquitoes abounded in this wild frontier land. One member of the Wilkinson family remembered, "My grandmother said she didn't know when it was sunup, the mosquitoes were so thick on the window screens."

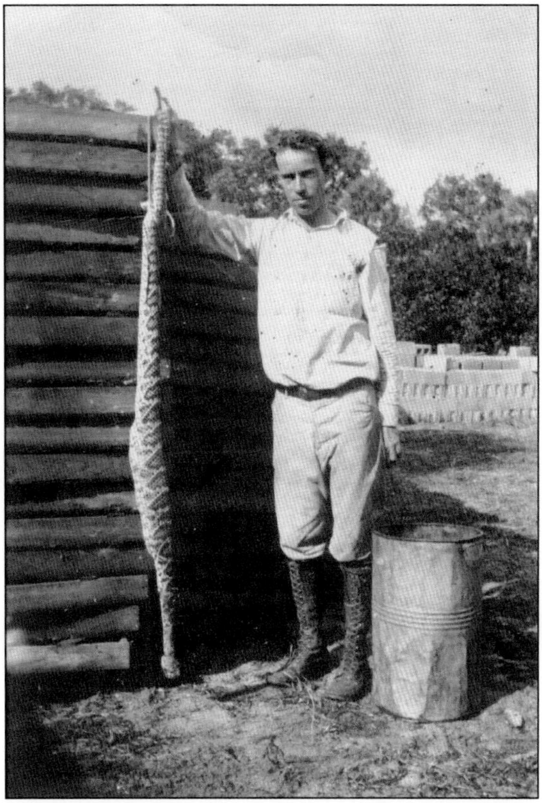

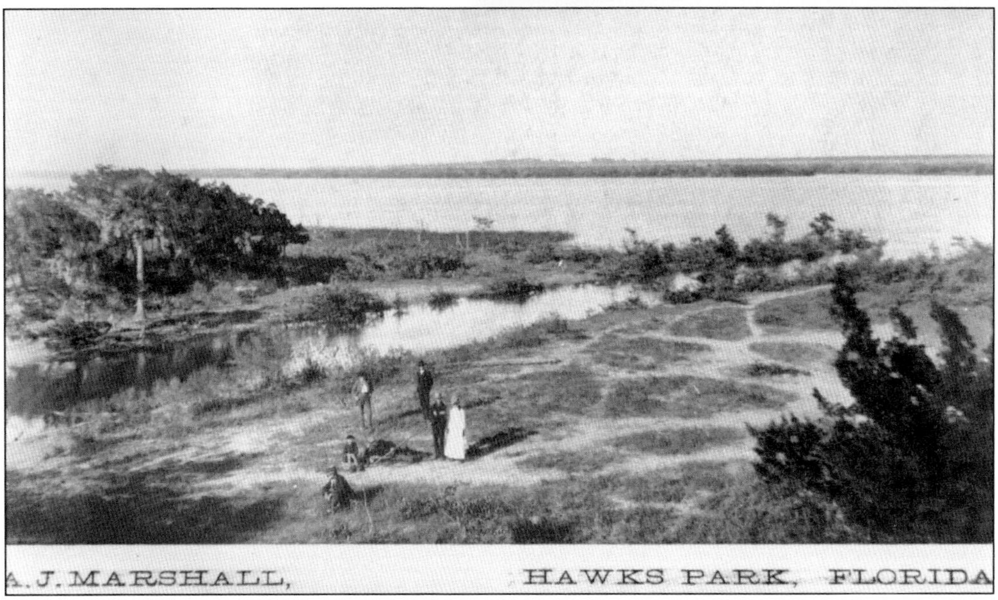

VIEW OF THE SOUTH CANAL, C. 1880. Although the land was generally flat along the river, there were some higher areas because the early Native Americans had created mounds, or middens, from discarded shells. This photograph was taken from the top of one of these mounds. The people shown are unidentified but seem to be either having a picnic or preparing to fish along the river's edge.

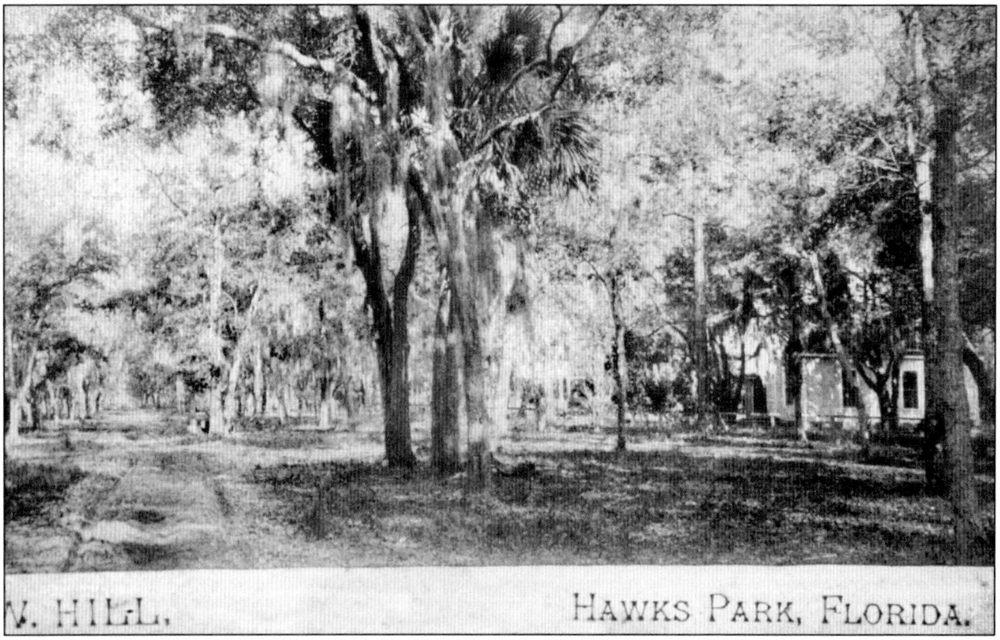

A TYPICAL WINTER COTTAGE IN HAWKS PARK, C. 1880. John Milton Hawks described one house built before his town started: "No useless floor covered the ground of the kitchen and sitting room, and . . . a hen with young chickens was tied by a string in one corner of the room." This was not like the houses built in Hawks Park. Fred W. Hill (who took the photograph above), A. J. Marshall, and Royal Hubbell were three photographers who did much to document the beautiful houses, like the one seen above, in the early settlement.

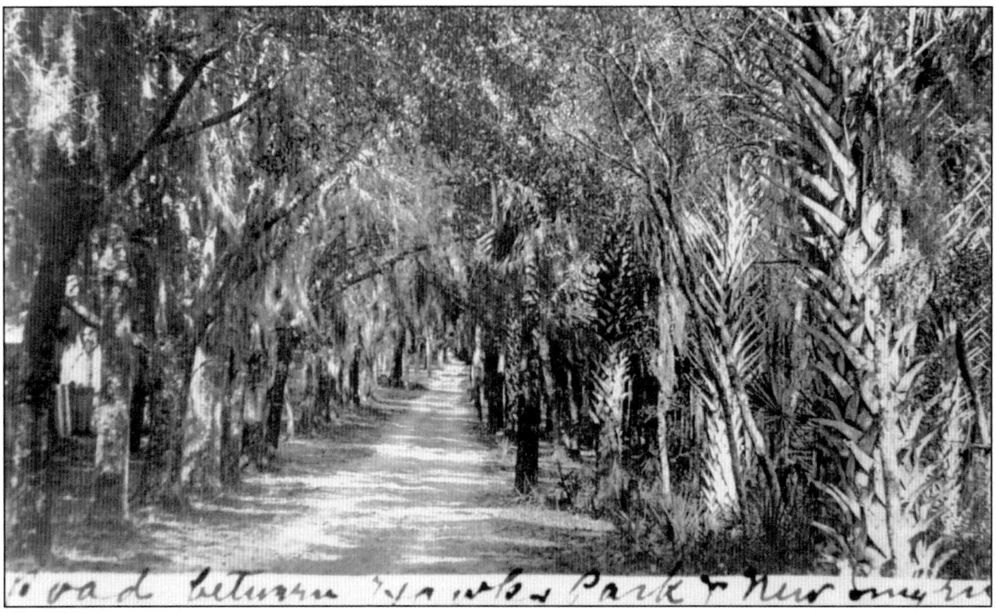

THE ROAD TO NEW SMYRNA, C. 1880. The New County Road connected by land the communities of New Smyrna, Hawks Park, and Oak Hill. It was a two-rut sand road and so bumpy that it was much easier to go by boat to one's destination. Later paved with oyster shells from the Native American mounds nearby, it was named Ridgewood Avenue and then U.S. 1.

Two

Hotels and Boarding Houses

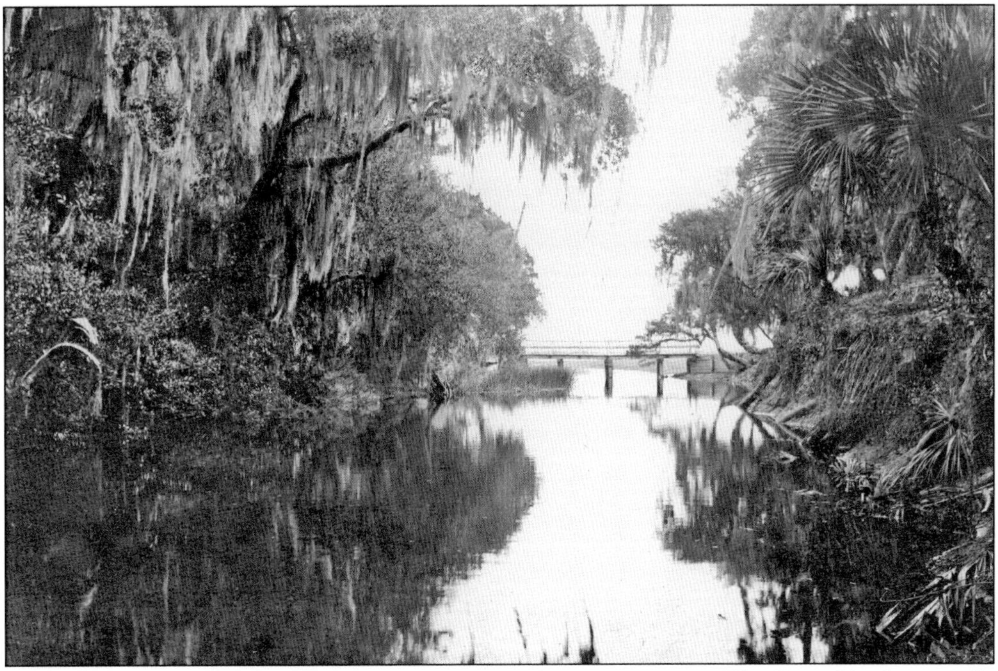

First Horse and Buggy Bridge over South Canal, c. 1890. The Strand had originally ended at the South Canal. The first bridge, a wooden structure, was built in the 1890s so that one could travel through to the New Smyrna settlement on the Strand. Since New Smyrna was Hawks Park's closest neighbor, it was important to have convenient horse-and-buggy access to the businesses and people there. Note the shell mound on the right of this photograph.

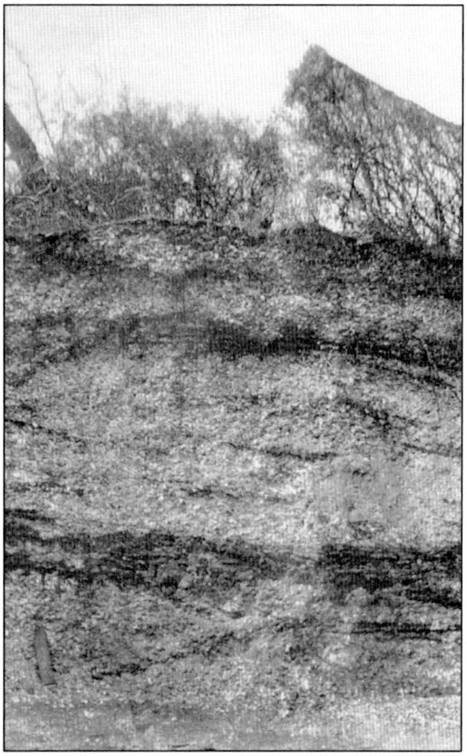

SHELL MOUND, C. 1880. Native Americans lived in the area for several thousand years before the European setters came, and they ate the clams and oysters from the river. Accumulated leftover shells created large mounds along the shore. The mounds, or middens, were then used as guideposts while traveling along the river.

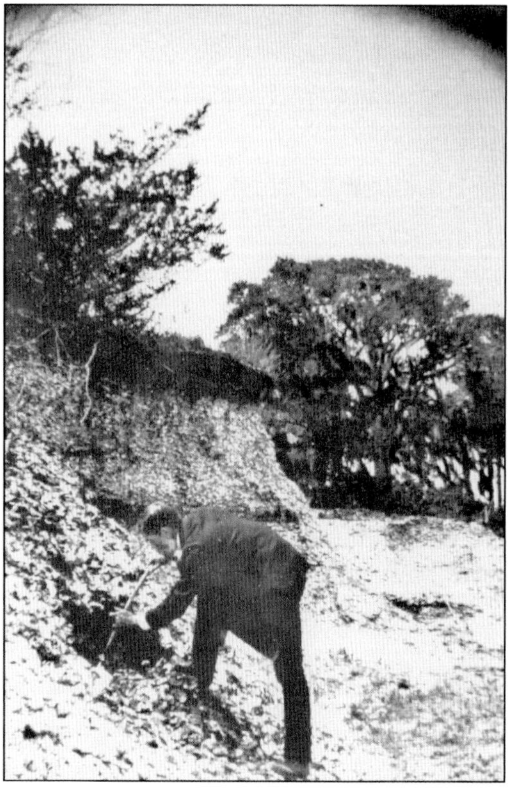

MAN DIGGING IN SHELL MOUND, 1880. The midden in this photograph was in Hawks Park, near the South Canal. Most of the area's shell mounds were largely destroyed, taken shovelful by shovelful to create sturdier road beds and for other purposes. One mound that was preserved was Turtle Mound, along the Canaveral National Seashore to the southeast of Hawks Park. The man is unidentified.

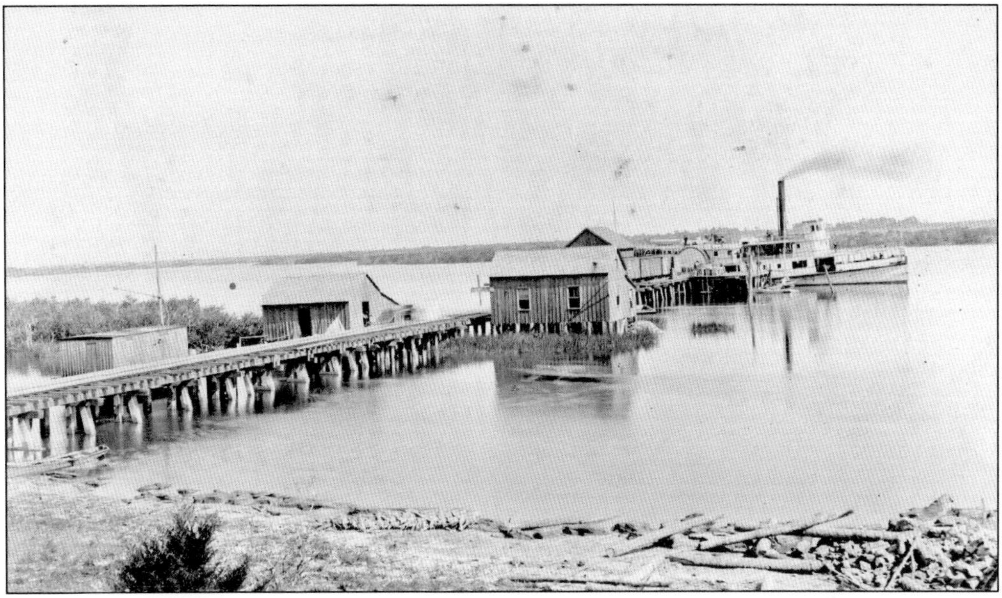

STEAMBOAT AT NEW SMYRNA WHARF, C. 1890. Flat-bottomed steamboats were vital to life along the river. Carrying supplies, mail, and passengers, they might stop at the New Smyrna dock near Canal Street, shown here, before coming farther south to Hawks Park. A wharf, or long dock, at Hawks Park was built out into the deep water so that the steamboat could load and unload its cargo.

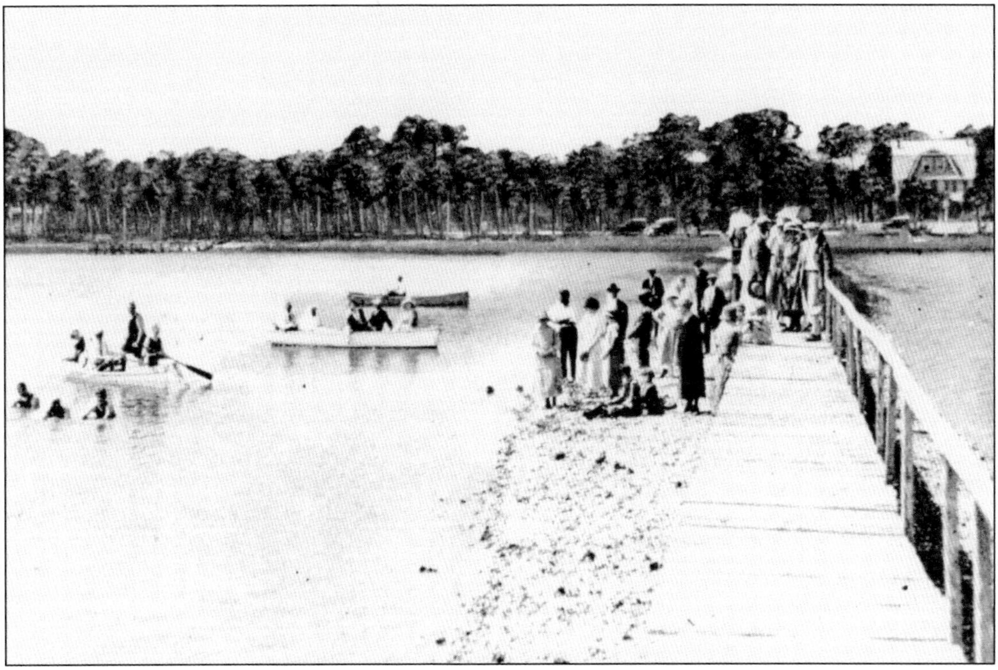

HAWKS PARK WHARF, OR "LONG DOCK," C. 1880. When Hawks Park was platted, a main road of the community was Ocean Avenue. It was at the foot of that street that the steamboat landing was built, and it became another favorite gathering place for the townspeople. The Bayview Hotel is on the right. The people are unidentified.

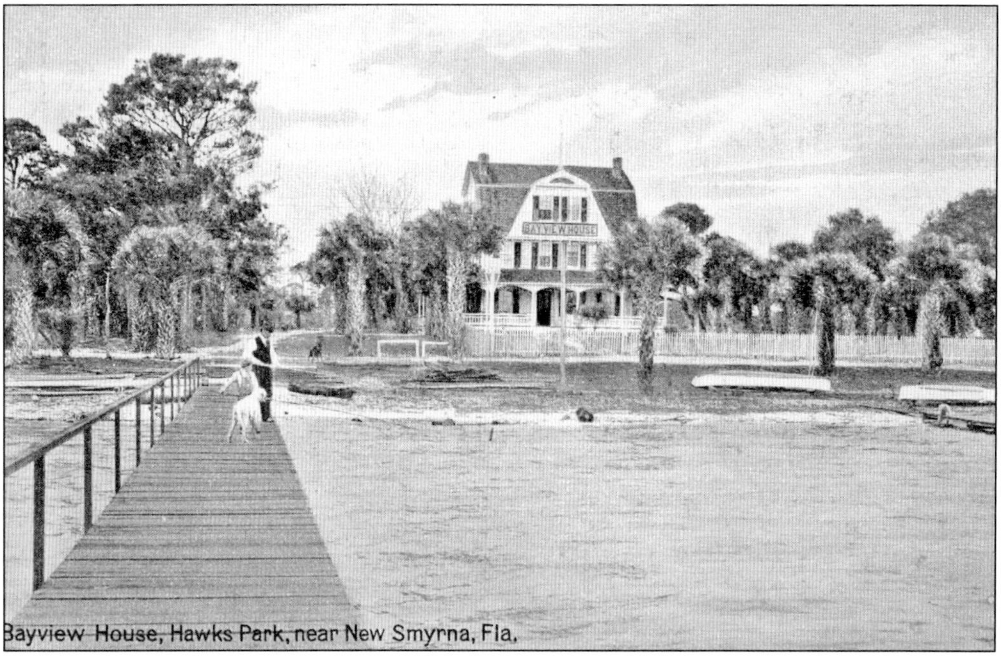

BAYVIEW HOUSE, c. 1917. George Durfee was the manager of this first hotel in Hawks Park. Visitors arriving by steamboat would be picked up at the long dock; those arriving by railroad line at New Smyrna were picked up in a buggy to bring them the two-and-one-half miles back to the hotel. The Bayview House was probably the tallest structure in early Hawks Park. The building was demolished in the 1920s. This is a postcard, which could be mailed for 1¢.

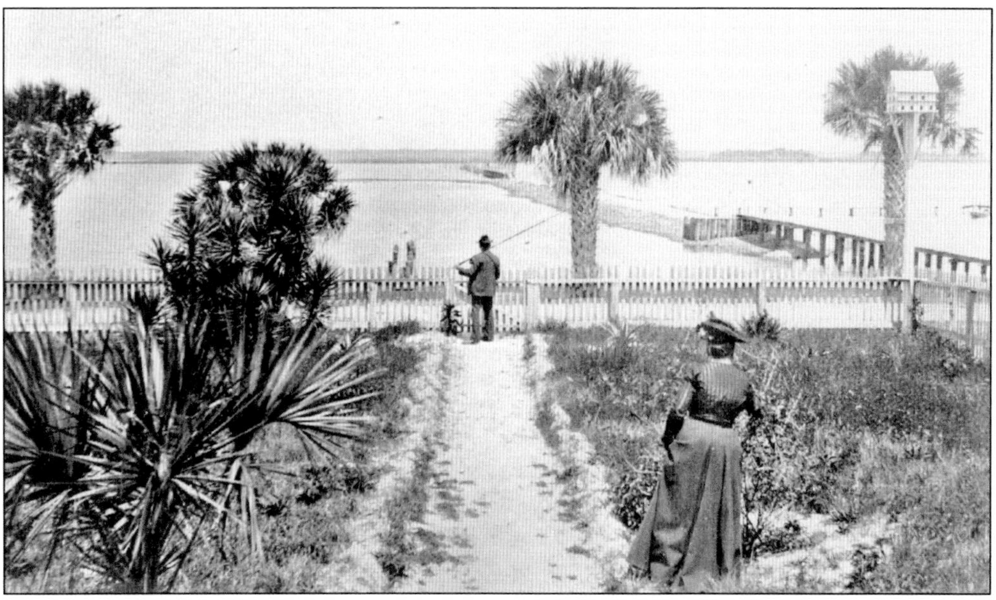

VIEW FROM BAYVIEW HOUSE OUT TO THE LONG DOCK, c. 1885. The Bayview House and the long dock were busy places in Hawks Park. Wagons loaded with lumber, vegetables, honey, citrus, and more would be ready for the steamboats. Hawks Park was growing into a busy, vibrant, hard-working community. The people are unidentified.

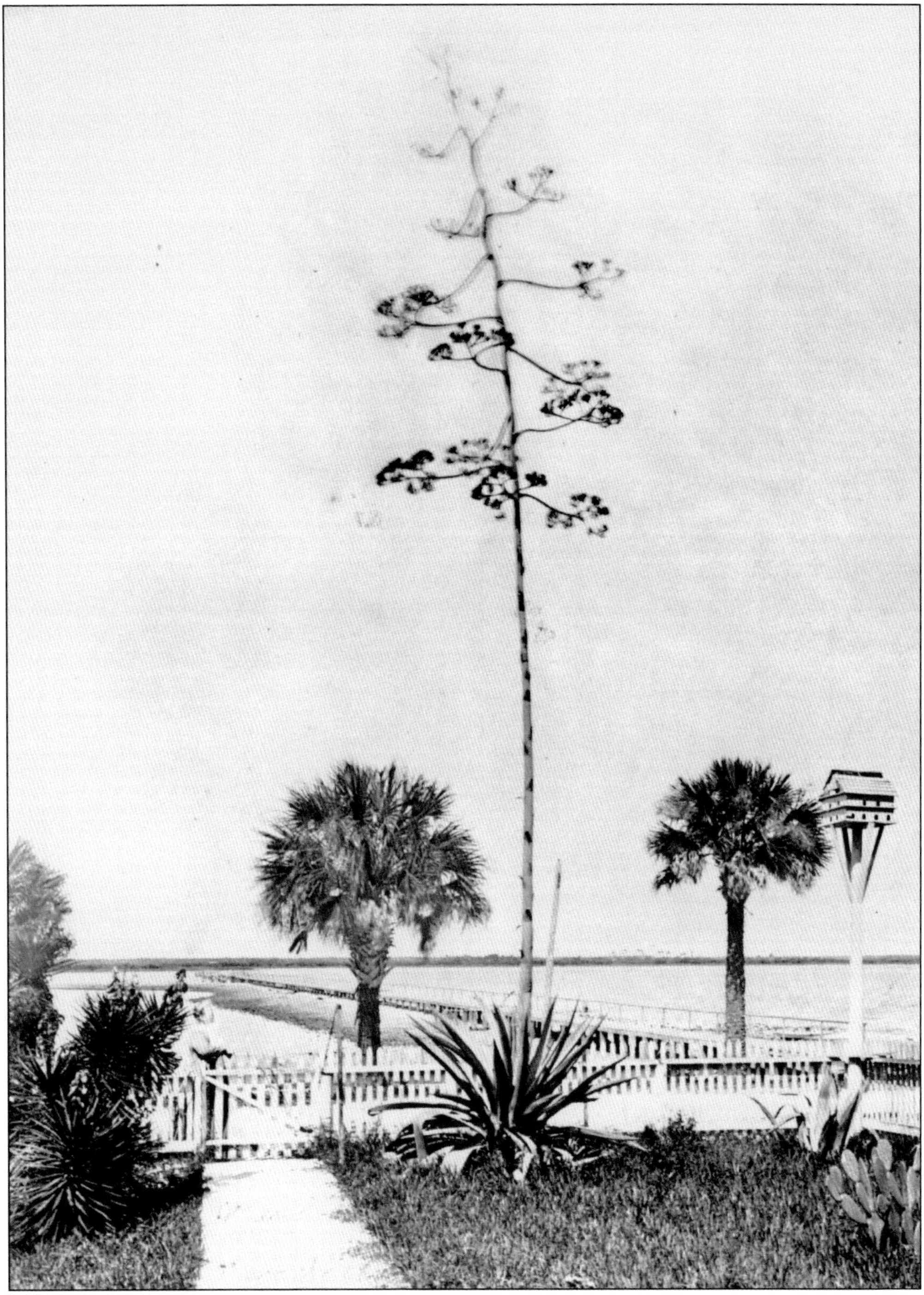

CENTURY PLANT AT THE LONG DOCK, C. 1885. There was natural beauty everywhere. The century plants grew up to 6 feet tall, with flowers at the top of a huge stem, sometimes 20 feet tall. John Milton Hawks had said that he wanted to develop a community where everyone would get along, where there was no need for police, and where people worked together for the good of all. The person is unidentified.

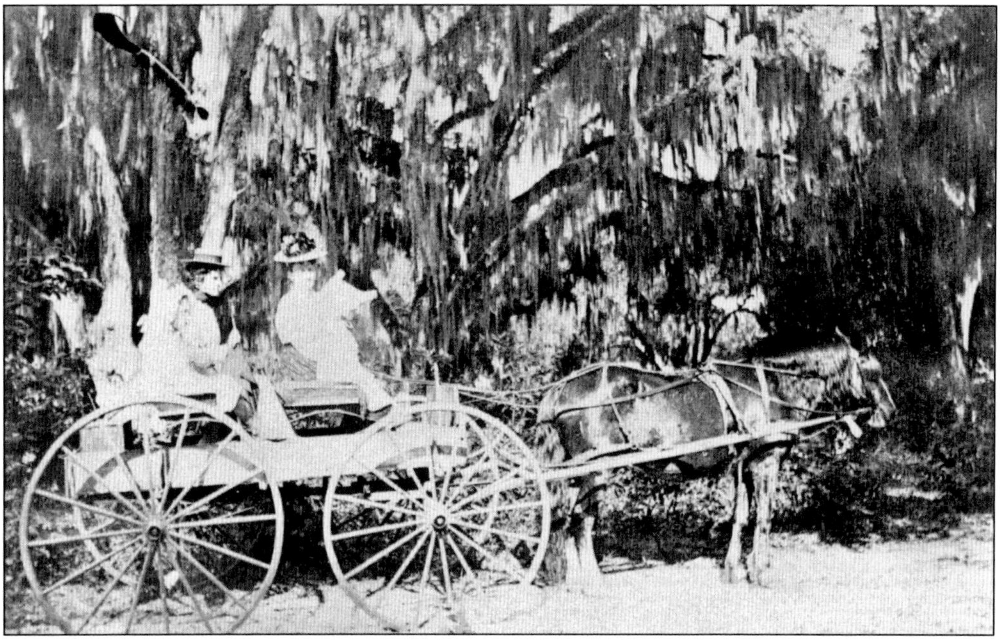

"Going Visiting," c. 1890. These people are unidentified, but John Milton Hawks thought it important to keep a record of people in the area. He kept information in his *Register of Unmarried Persons in the Town of Hawks Park, State of Florida Who are not Members of Families residing in the Town*, starting in the 1880s. He also kept a family record book of early families living in southeast Volusia County from the 1800s to 1900, which listed people and their occupations. These registers are now kept in the Edgewater Museum.

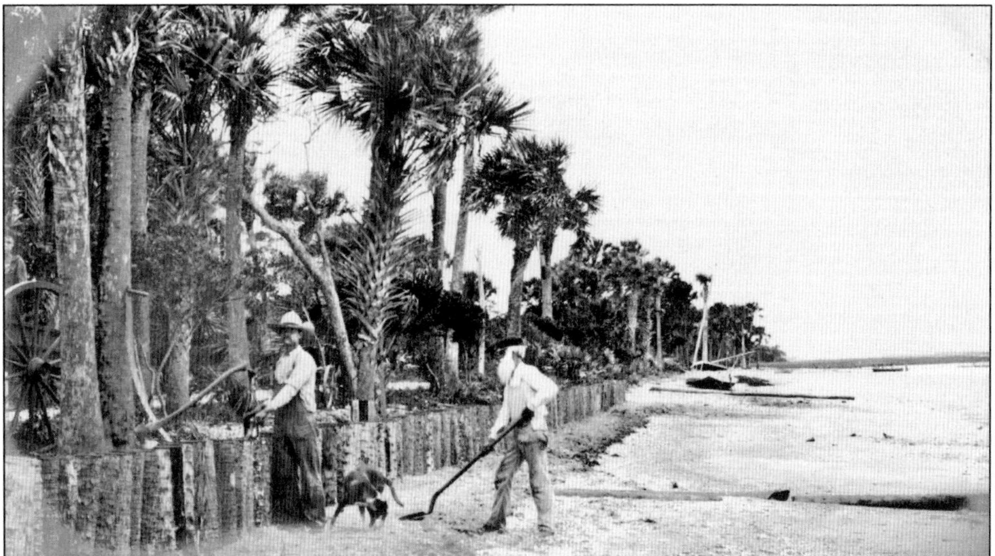

Palm Logs along the Strand, c. 1880. The Hillsboro River was actually a tidal lagoon, and at high tide, there was danger of water flowing over onto the Strand. Sturdy logs were cut from the abundant palms in the area to create a barrier between the water and the roadway. This photograph, taken by Royal Hubbell, was made into a postcard. The men are unidentified.

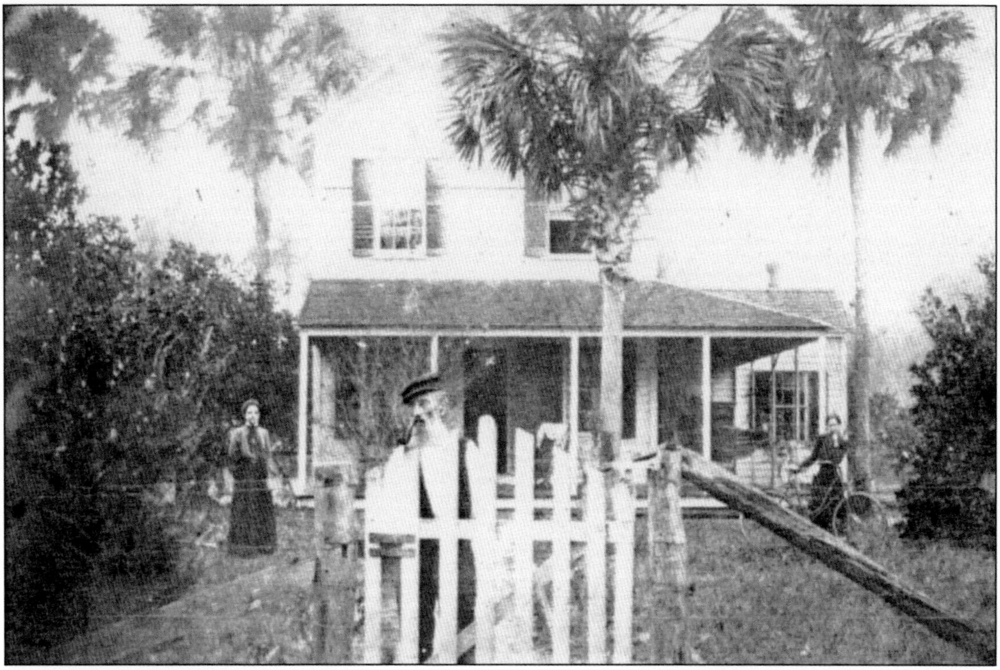

JOHN PLAYTERS WILKINSON, JANUARY 1903. Also pictured are Wilkinson's daughters, Emmy (left) and Nell. The Wilkinson family was living in the area, near Turtle Mound along the river. Steamboats could reach them there with mail and supplies since they were on deep water. The Wilkinsons later had a home in Hawks Park, to be closer to school for the children.

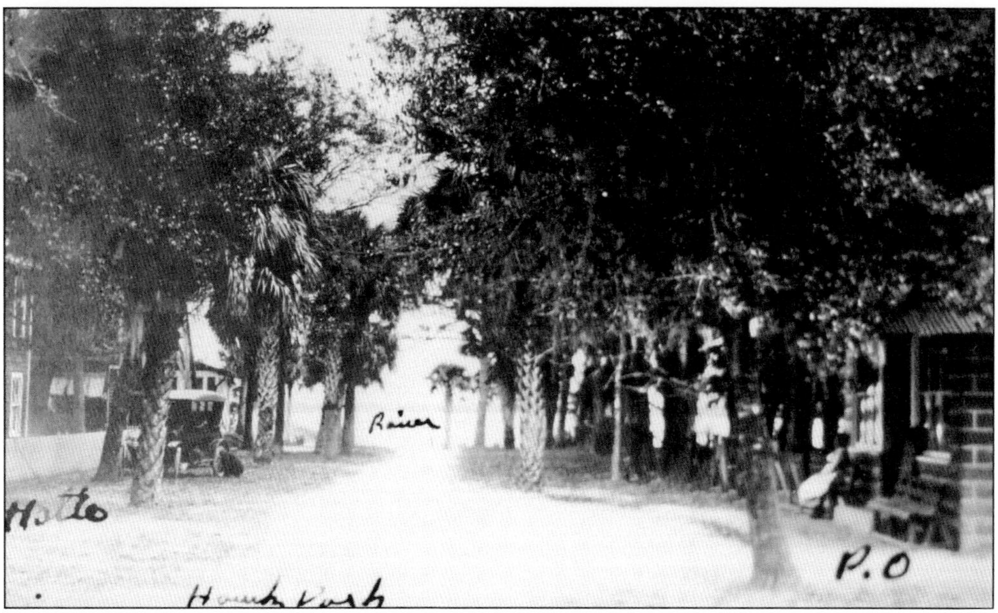

THE HOTEL ("HOTLE"), OCEAN AVENUE, AND THE POST OFFICE, C. 1910. John Milton Hawks was the first, unofficial, postmaster in Hawks Park. Everyone had at least one job. Hawks stated, "Questions needing attention in the interest of happiness and prosperity are the moral, intellectual, and industrial training of the young—and habits of industry inculcated and enforced: 'if a man will not work, neither shall he eat'. . . . This is the best training for the races of men."

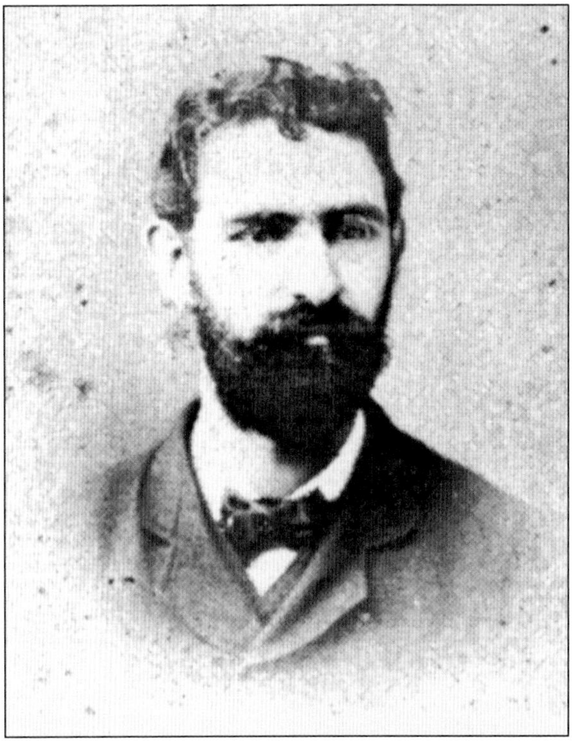

ROYAL WILLIAM HUBBELL PORTRAIT, C. 1890. Royal Hubbell was born in 1860 in Indiana. He moved to Red Wing, Minnesota, to become a professional photographer, married Kate Theodocia Woodley, and then moved to Hawks Park. One of Kate's sisters was Alice Woodley, who married Harry Mitchell. Royal Hubbell would live more than 30 years in Hawks Park and chronicled much of the town's growth.

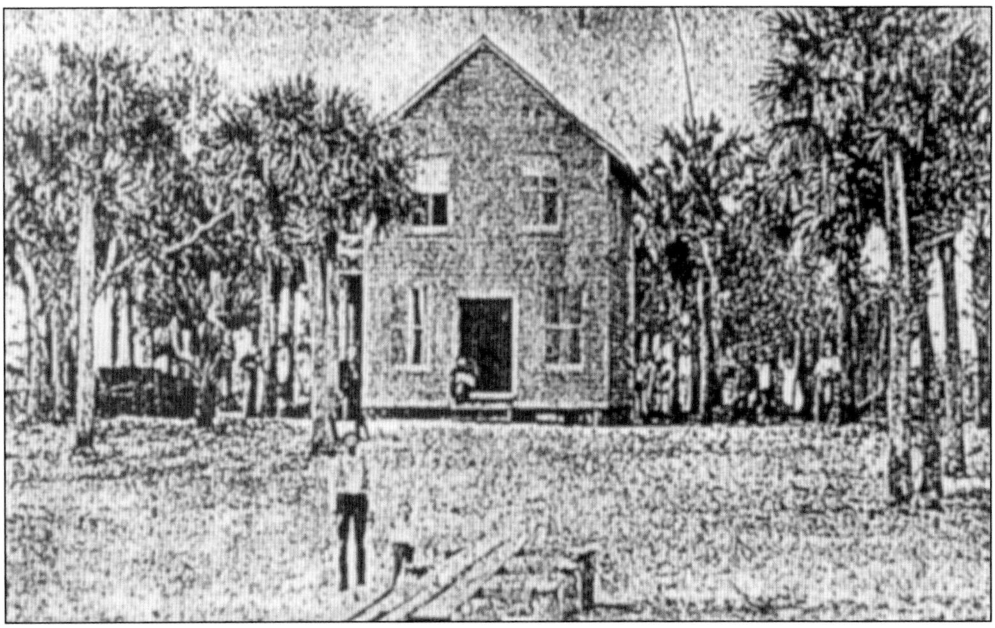

ROYAL HUBBELL HOME, C. 1890. This home is still standing, and Hubbell Street is two blocks to the west. Hubbell's photographs often recorded family events, and many of his scenes were reprinted as postcards. In 1906, he produced a charming souvenir of Hawks Park—a folio of pictures entitled *Ancient and Modern New Smyrna, Fla. and Vicinity*. Containing 136 scenes of the area, it was an easy item to take home as a remembrance and has since been reprinted. The people are unidentified.

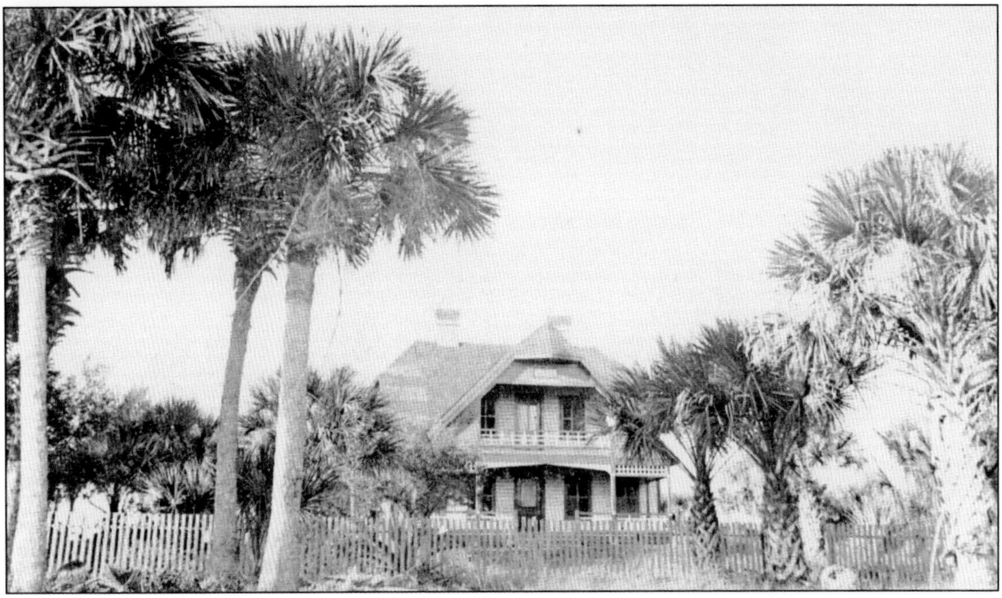

ADDISON J. MARSHALL HOME, C. 1897. A. J. Marshall came to Hawks Park from Bradford, New Hampshire. His Florida home was built in the mid-1890s, right next door to the busy Bayview Hotel. The living room in the Marshall home became the first store, official post office, and library in the fledgling community. This yellow house is still standing, carefully preserved by descendants of the Marshall family. (Photograph by F. W. Hill.)

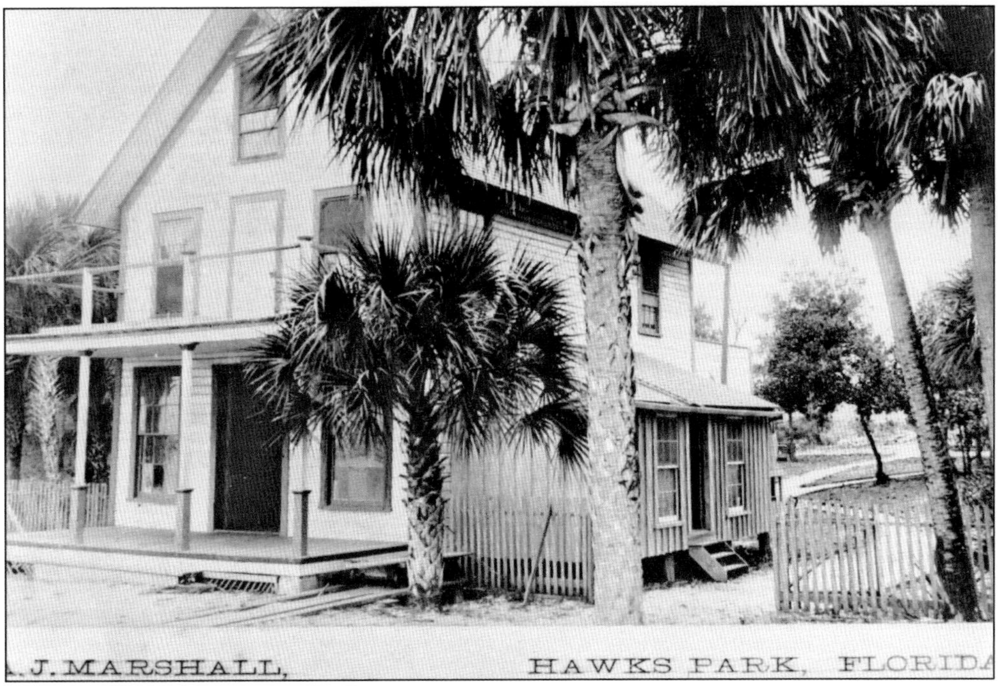

WINTER COTTAGE ON EAST CONNECTICUT AVENUE, C. 1890. Most of the houses in the earliest days had fences surrounding them to keep any wild hogs from getting under the house and rooting around the floor supports. This house is still standing in Edgewater. (Photograph by A. J. Marshall.)

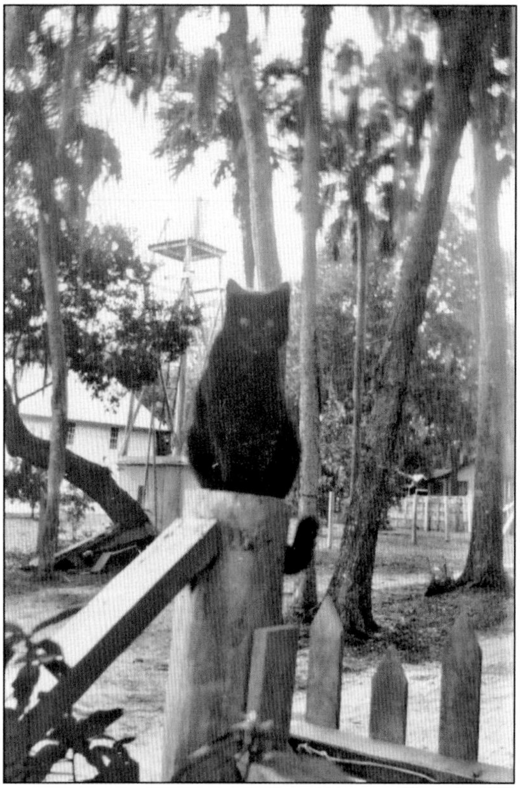

Black Cat on the Porch, c. 1895. Note the water tower in background, which was built by the Wilkinson family. The tower furnished fresh water not only to the Wilkinsons, but also to several of their neighbors. The tower collapsed several years ago.

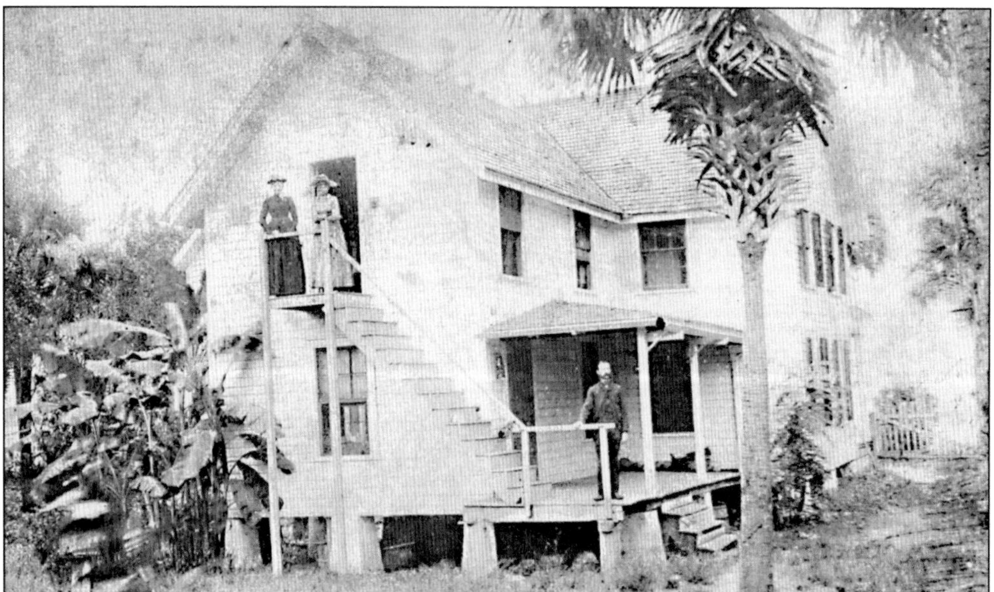

Mendell Boarding House, 1890. Built in the 1880s along the Strand, this first boarding house in town boasted a dumbwaiter. Owner George Mendell is standing on the porch; the other people are unidentified. Mattresses in the early days were made from dried Spanish moss and palm fronds—they had found out the hard way not to use fresh Spanish moss, with all its insects! The home still stands at the corner of New Hampshire Avenue and Riverside Drive.

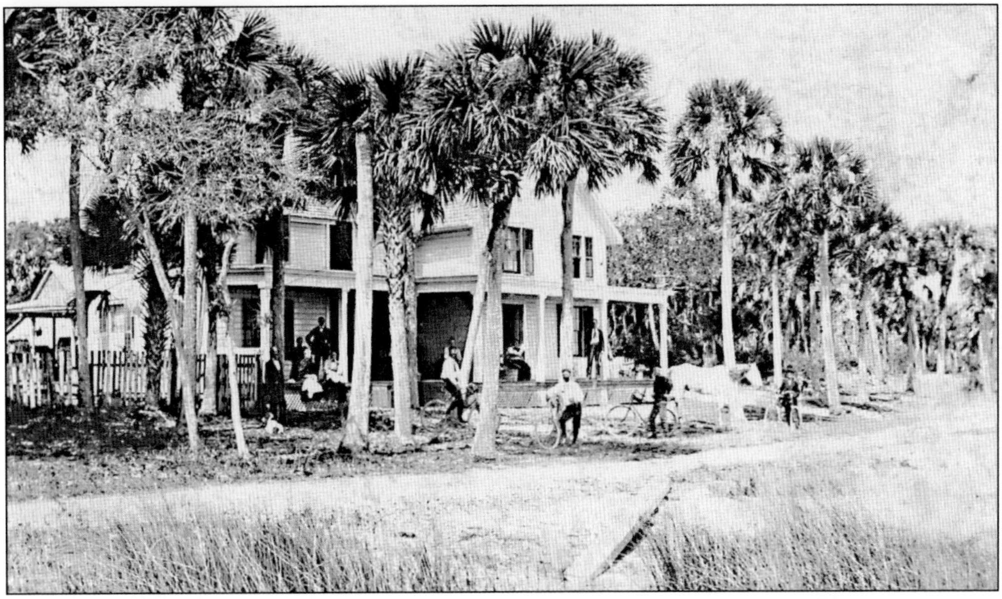

CYCLISTS, 1896. One way to keep insects off was to keep moving. These bicyclists are posing in front of the Mendell Boarding House. The four people identified on the front porch are Mamie Mendell Ruby, John E. Ruby, Rose Walters, and Alice Mendell Clinton. The woman in the doorway on the porch is Mrs. George Mendell. The man on the bicycle in the front, in a white shirt, is George E. Mendell. The man on the bicycle to the left of the horse is W. S. Hart. The others are unidentified.

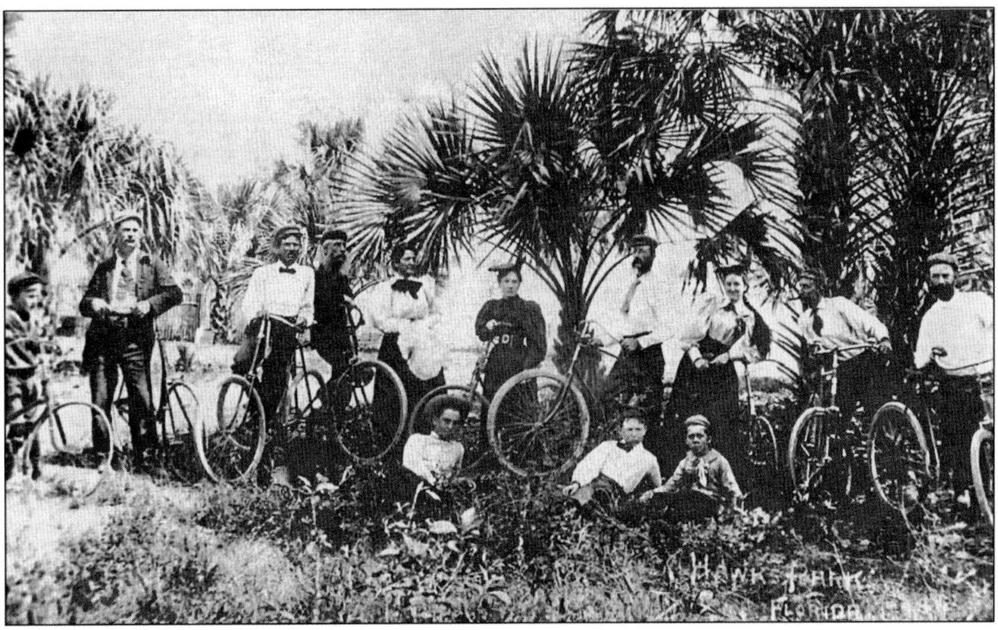

CYCLISTS, MARCH 24, 1896. Bicycling was a popular sport. Cyclists and others pictured here are, from left to right, as follows: (first row) two unidentified children and Arthur Mendell; (second row) two unidentified people, John E. Ruby, W. S. Hart, Mrs. George Mendell, Rose Walters (sister of John E. Ruby), George Mendell, Alice Mendell Clinton, and two unidentified people.

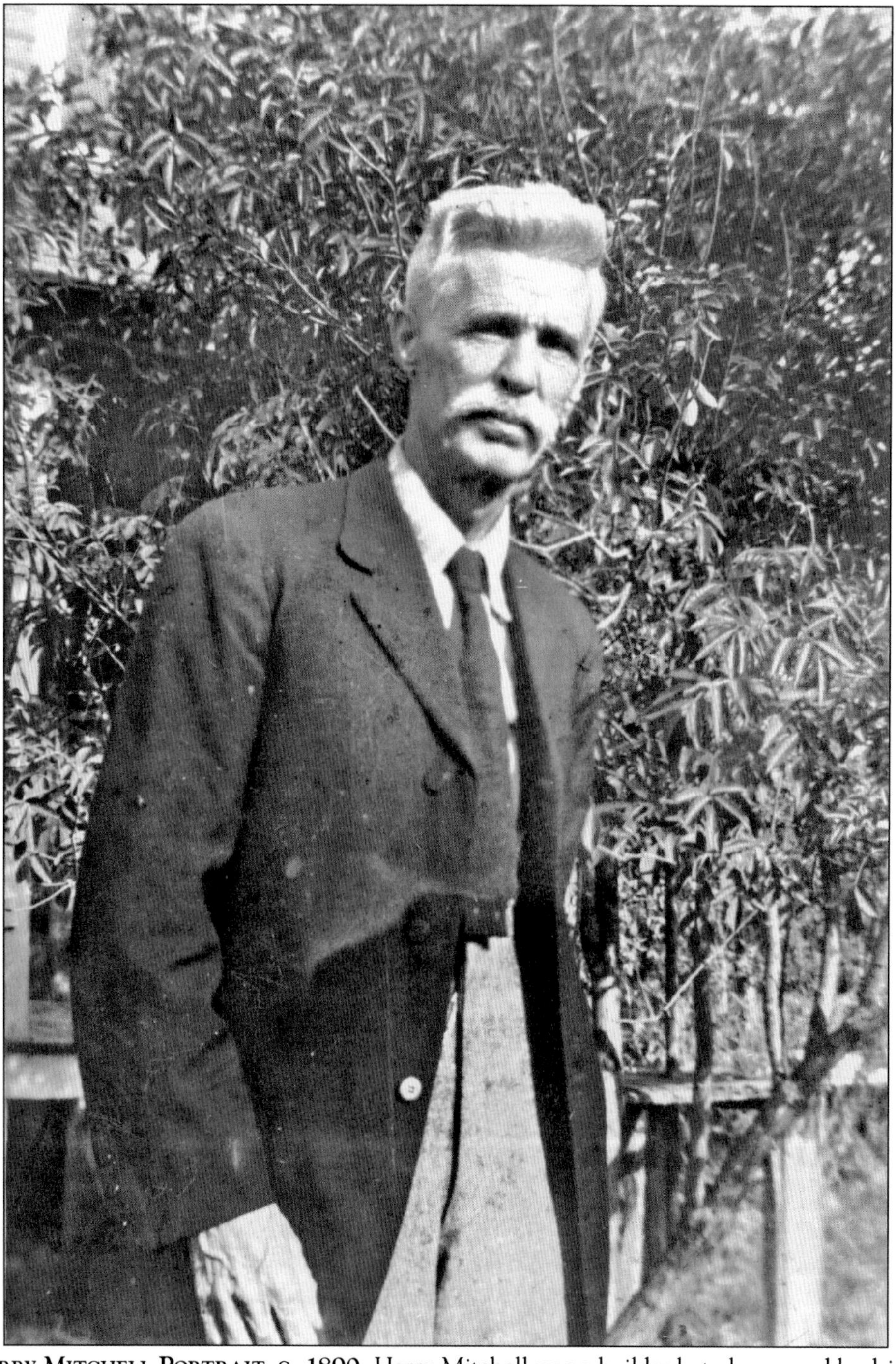

HARRY MITCHELL PORTRAIT, C. 1890. Harry Mitchell was a builder but also owned beehives, orange groves, and a plant nursery. It was helpful that many people in this frontier settlement had many talents. While overseeing the growth of his communities in Florida, Dr. Hawks also took on other jobs outside the community. At times he was notary public at-large, superintendent of Volusia County Schools, and assistant assessor of internal revenue for district No. 5; he also wrote books.

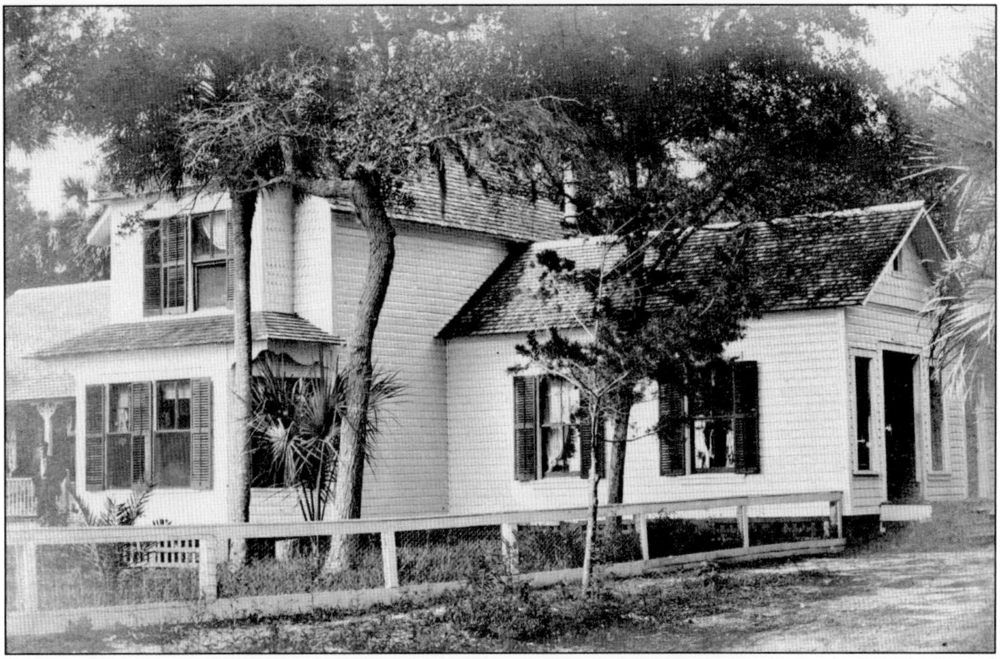

HARRY MITCHELL HOME, C. 1890. Mitchell's portrait and home were photographed by Royal Hubbell. The Mitchell home still stands along Riverside Drive, at the corner of Woodley Avenue. Harry Mitchell came from Red Wing, Minnesota, and was Royal Hubbell's brother-in-law. The house extension on the right was a small store and the post office for a time.

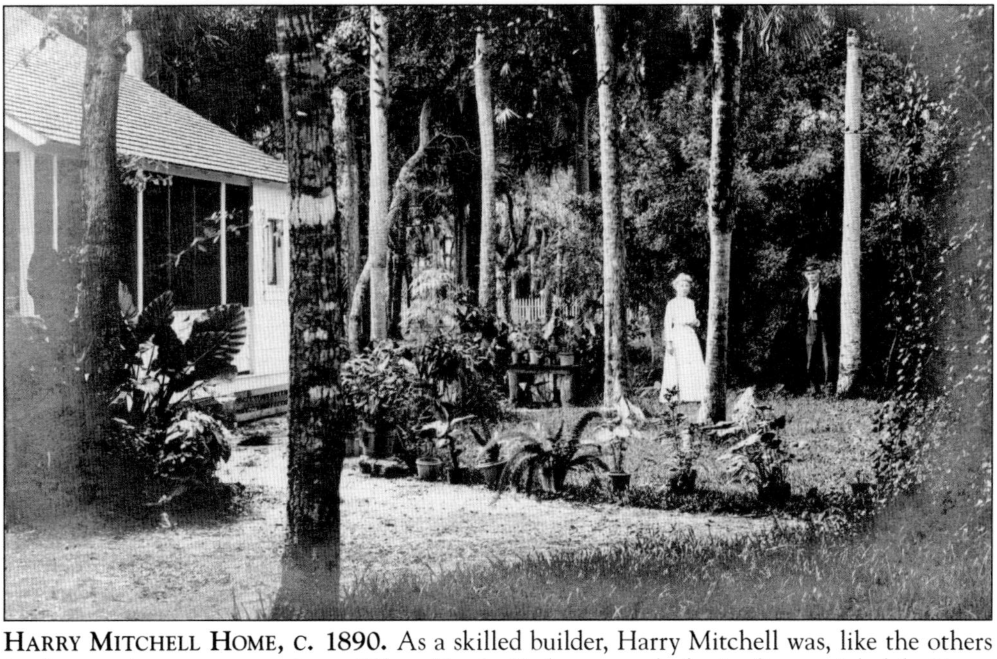

HARRY MITCHELL HOME, C. 1890. As a skilled builder, Harry Mitchell was, like the others in the growing town, very busy. When Hawks Park was ready for its first social club, Harry Mitchell and his wife donated the land for the Hawks Park Club. The women of the community raised the money, and Mitchell constructed the building. The people are unidentified. (Photo by Royal Hubbell.)

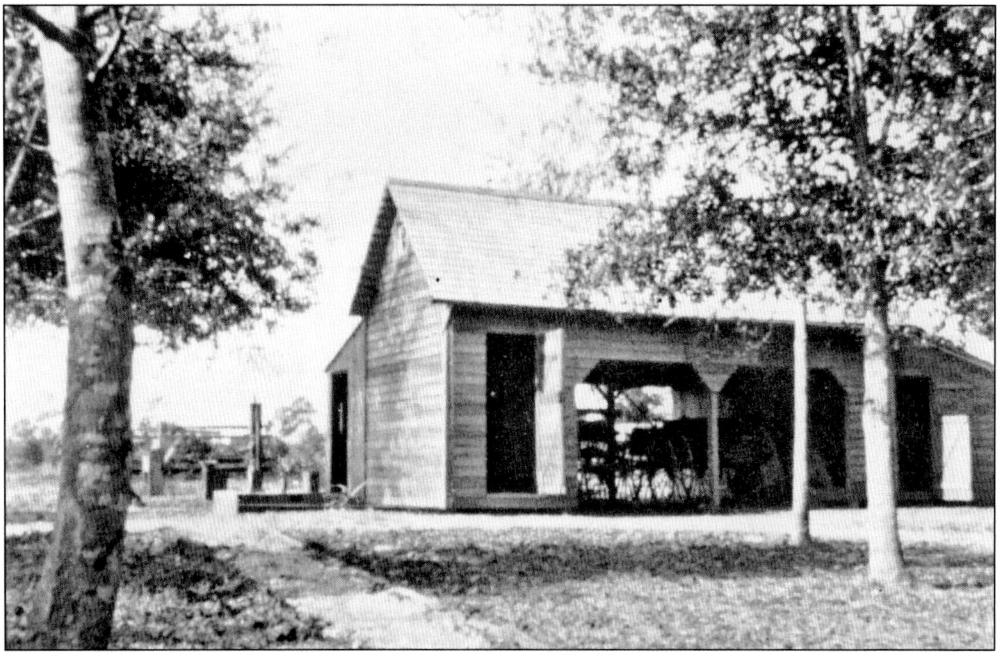

Mendell Boarding House Barn, c. 1890. Barns were important to the settlers. Most families had a horse or horse-and-buggy, so barns at that time were the garages of today. The Mendells had a "passenger express team," possibly a special horse-and-buggy that met the trains at the New Smyrna railroad station.

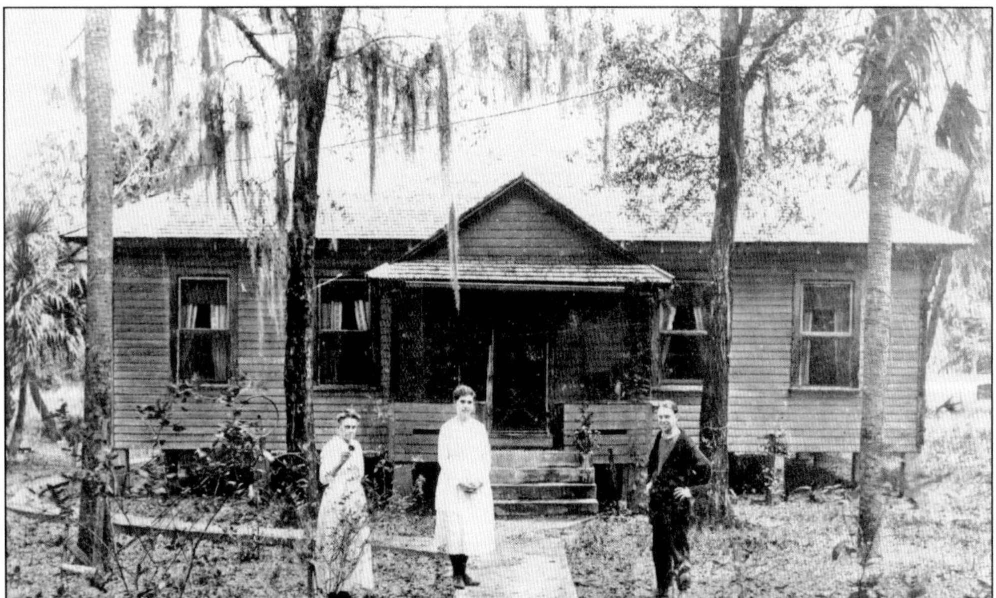

Early Home, c. 1890. The home pictured was on North Ridgewood Avenue, between Wilkinson and Lamont Streets. In the very early days of Hawks Park, Dr. Hawks wrote to the Marshalls while they were still in the North: "Neither you nor your wife would be contented (here) after she gets well. It is a frontier town, rough and rude in appearance." New settlers, however, continued to make the rough area livable. The people are unidentified.

Three

ON DEEP WATER NAVIGATION

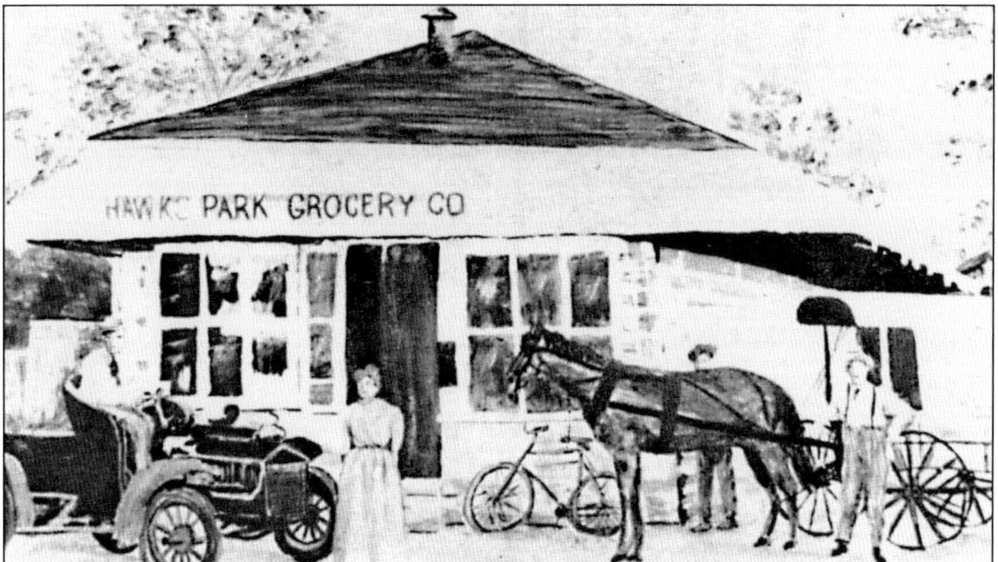

HAWKS PARK GROCERY, C. 1890. Shown here in a painting, the first grocery store was on East Ocean Avenue, near the long dock. The painting now hangs in Edgewater City Hall. Dr. Hawks said in the early days, "We go in for durable goods. I have on at this moment a pair of double solid brogans (shoes) . . . at $1.65, pants with three sorts and colors of patches and a patched blue woolen shirt." The people are unidentified.

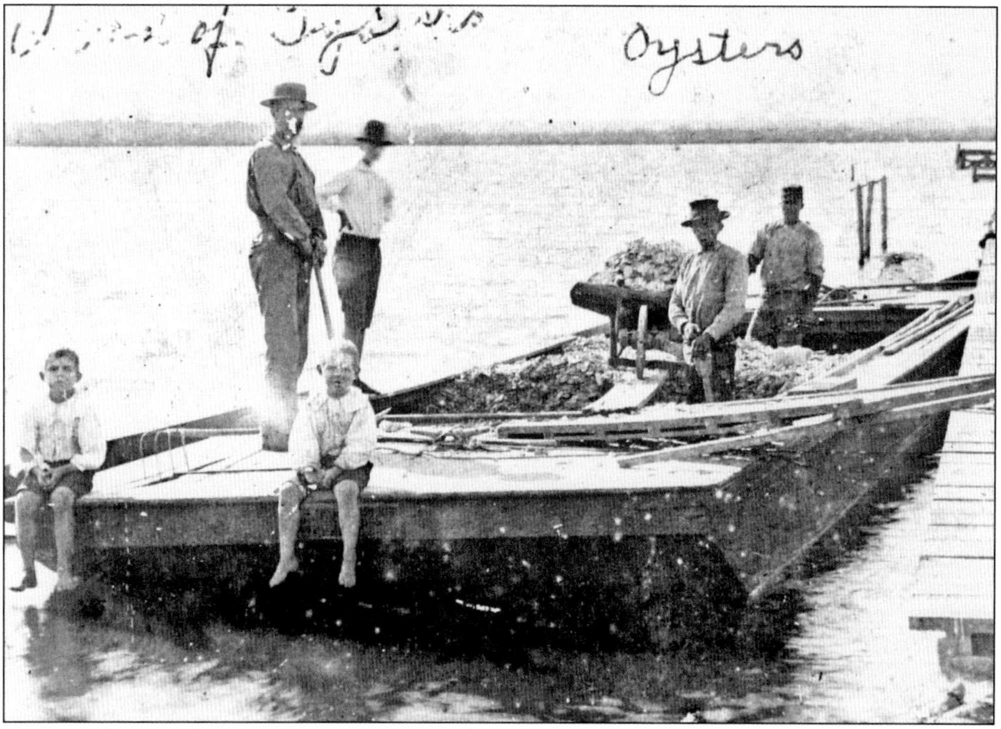

MEN ON OYSTER BARGE, C. 1895. New settlers to Hawks Park coming from the Northeastern states knew how to seed oyster beds. Dr. Hawks said, "Oysters are plenty and easily collected." The long dock can be seen to the right of the boat. The people are unidentified.

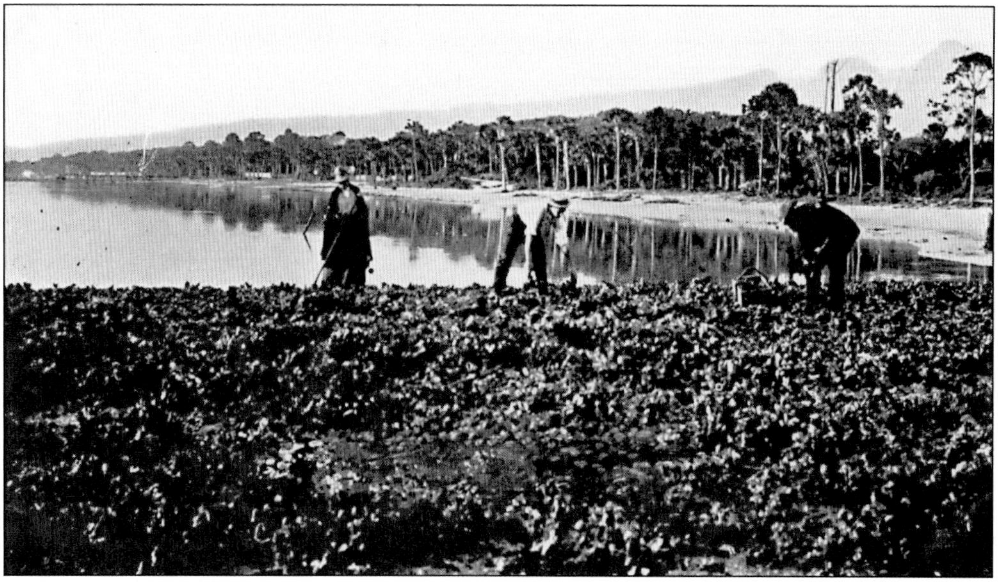

OYSTER GATHERING, C. 1900. This is a Royal Hubbell postcard. Once the large oyster beds were seeded along the river, there was an abundant supply. These oyster beds were located in the river in front of the Hawks home. According to the survey of early Hawks Park, the central park is located in the background of this photo. The people are unidentified, except it is known that A. B. Wilkinson is one of the men.

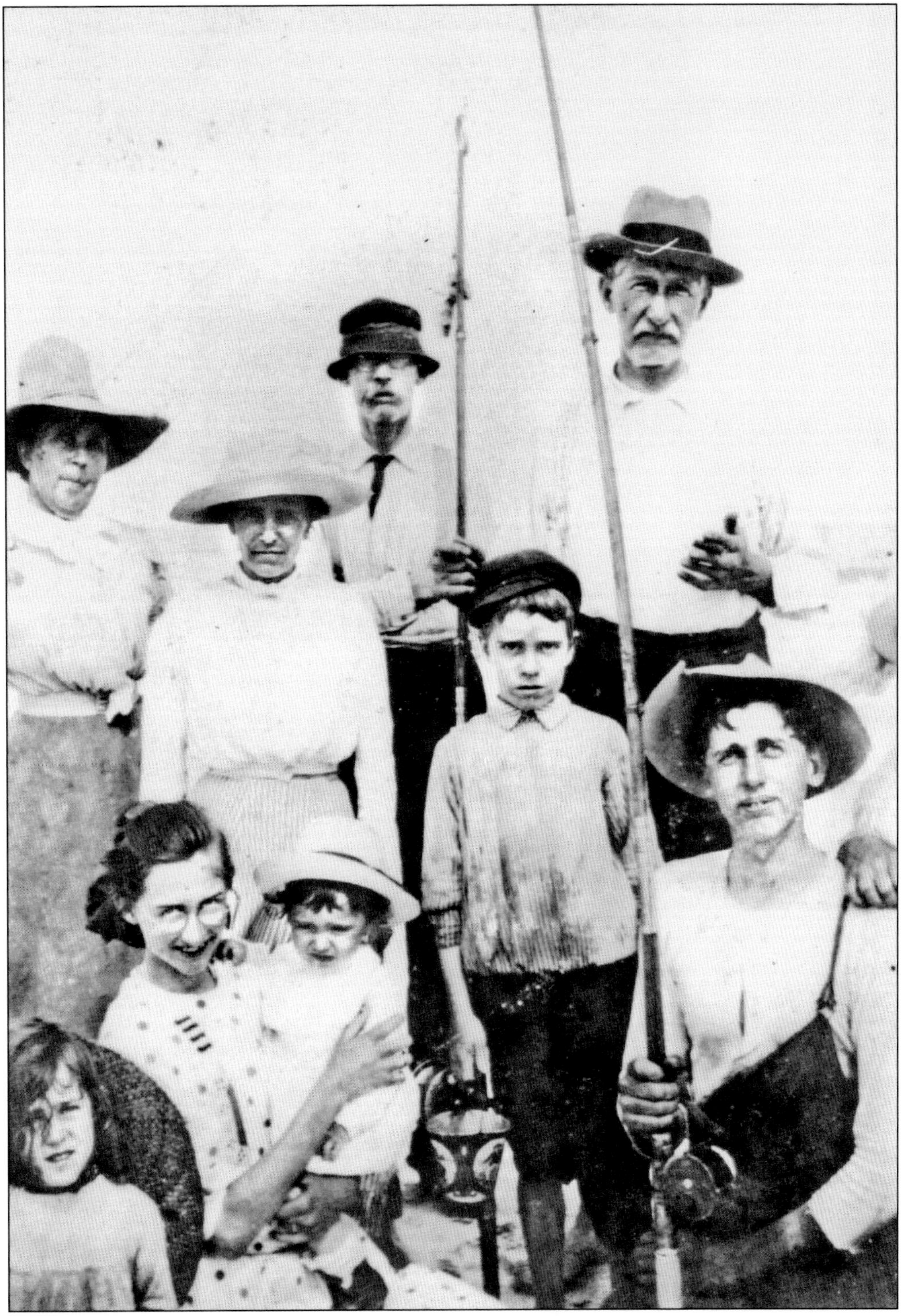

A Good Catch, c. 1910. The Lohman, Wilkinson, and Hartland families were going fishing. J. P. Wilkinson is right, in the rear, wearing a hat; the young boy in the middle is H. P. Wilkinson, but the others are unidentified.

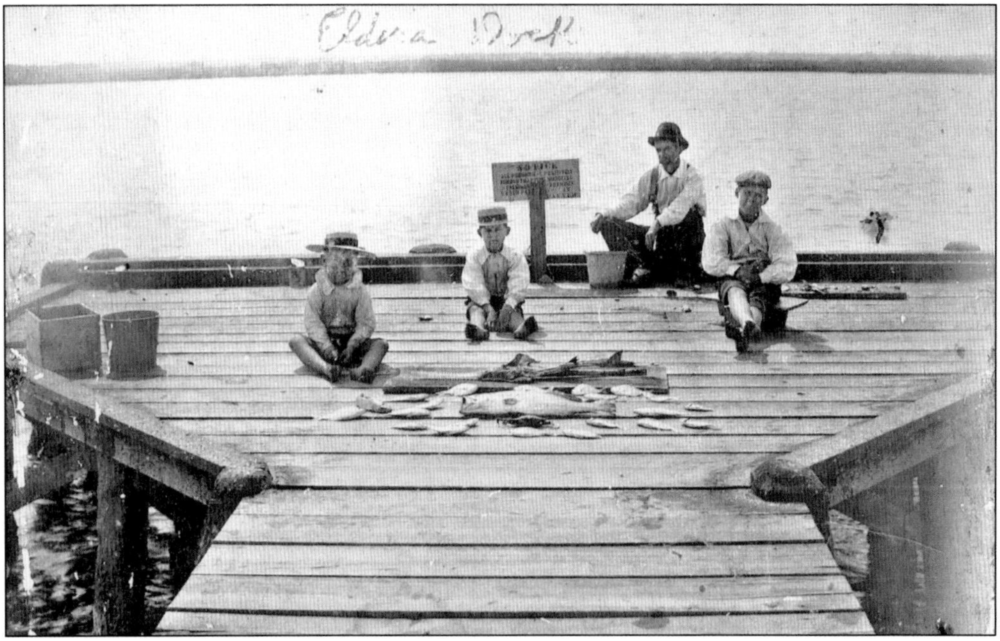

FISH FOR SUPPER, C. 1895. The fishing was good in the nearby ocean and in the river. For many people, fishing was done to put food on the table, not just for sport. The people here are unidentified.

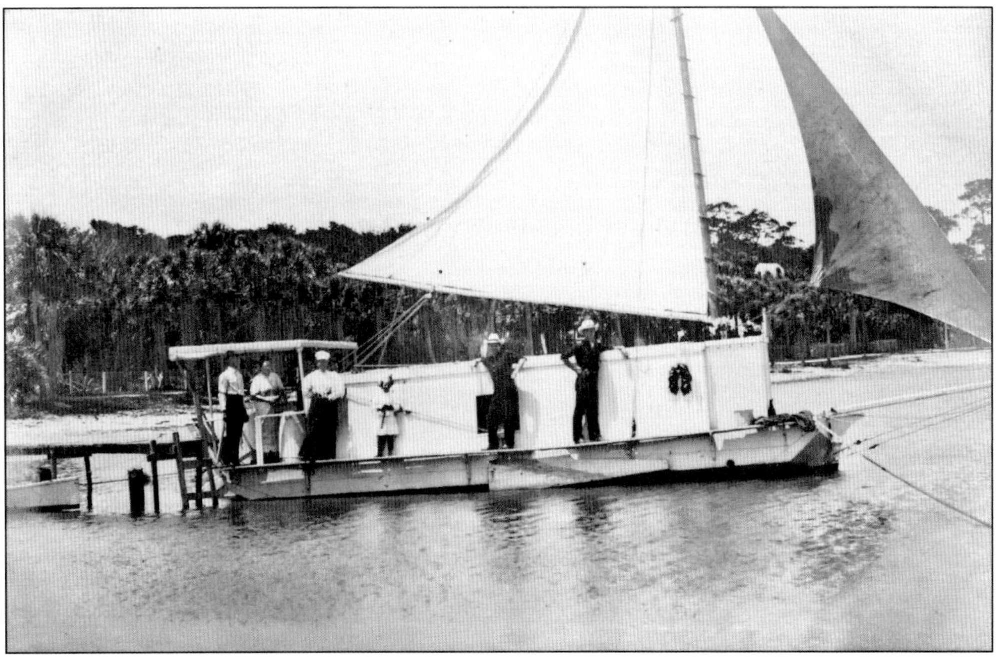

THE *HORACE H.*, C. 1910. Called "a sailing houseboat," the *Horace H.* was owned by George Mendell. The people are unidentified.

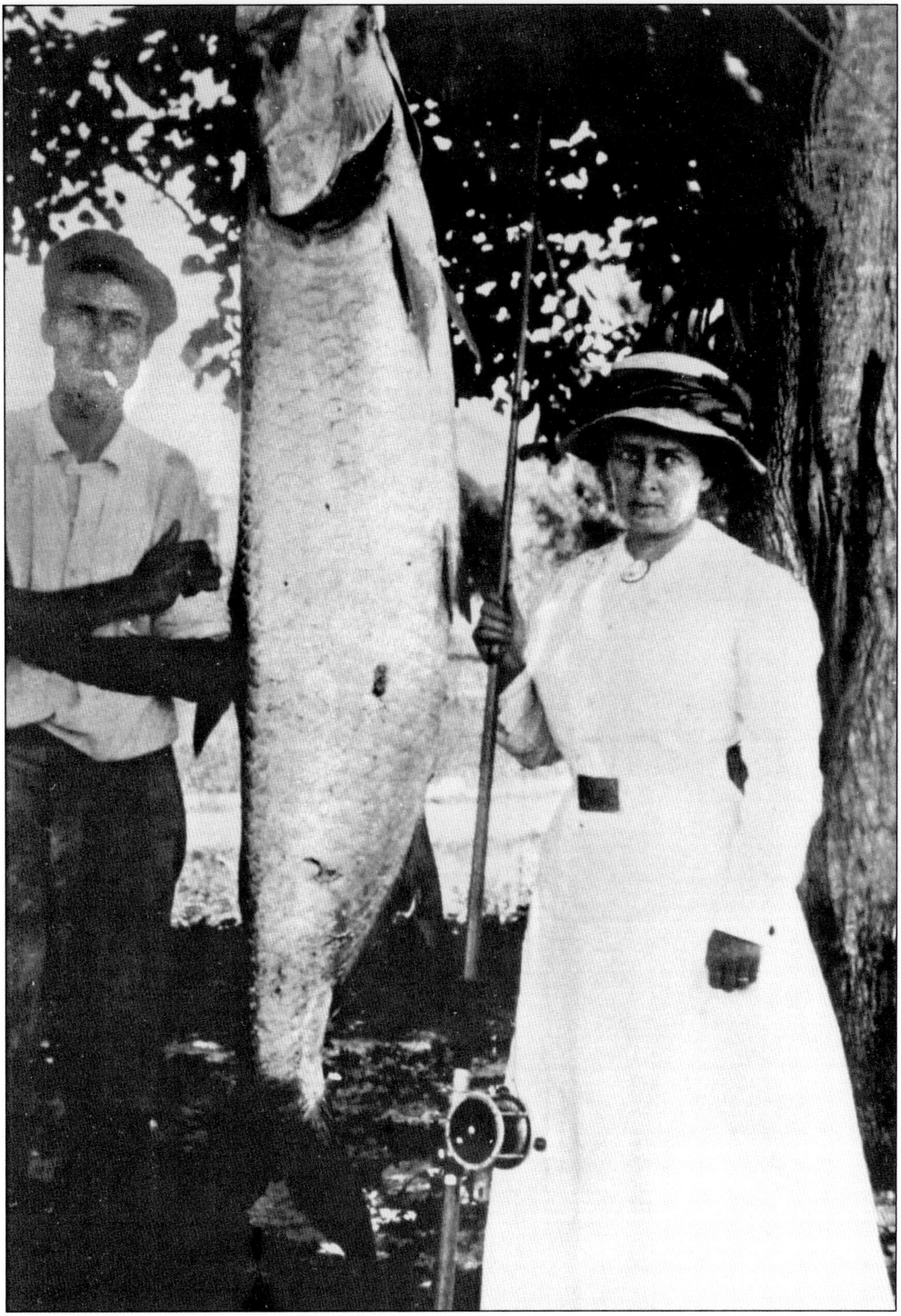

A BIG CATCH, C. 1895. An unidentified man and woman show off their large catch. The fishing was excellent. Bass might weigh in at 30 to 40 pounds, and even much larger fish were frequently caught. The fish caught here appears to be a tarpon.

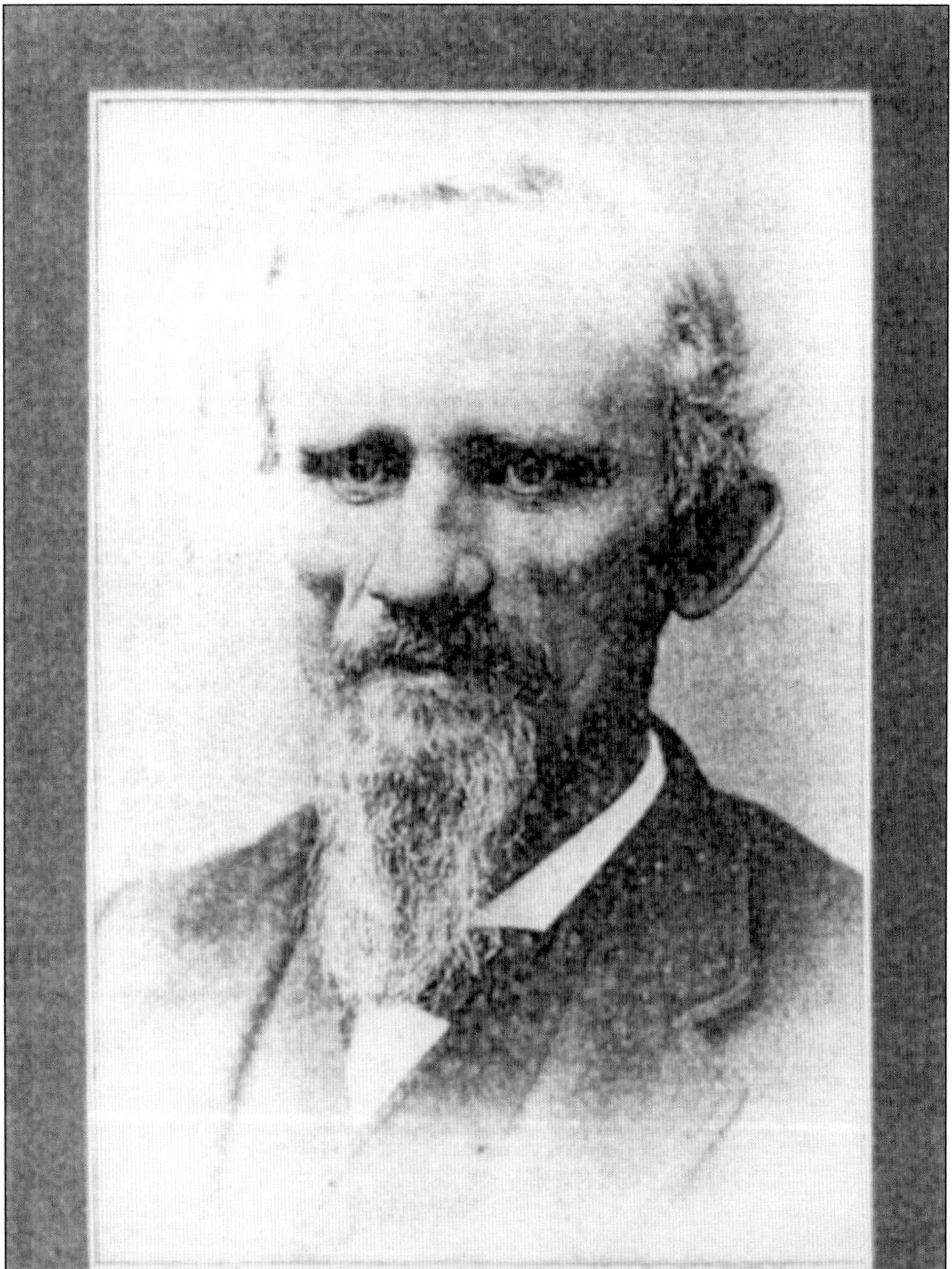

Benjamin Franklin Fox, Date Unknown. B. F. Fox came to the area from Georgia after serving in the Confederate Army in the Civil War and was probably the first physician in the area. Related to the Wilkinson family by marriage, he first lived in a log cabin southeast of Hawks Park. Being interested in plants for their possible use in medicine, he noticed that animals eating saw palmetto berries seemed to be very healthy. He sent berries to a chemist friend in Savannah for analysis and realized he had made a very valuable discovery.

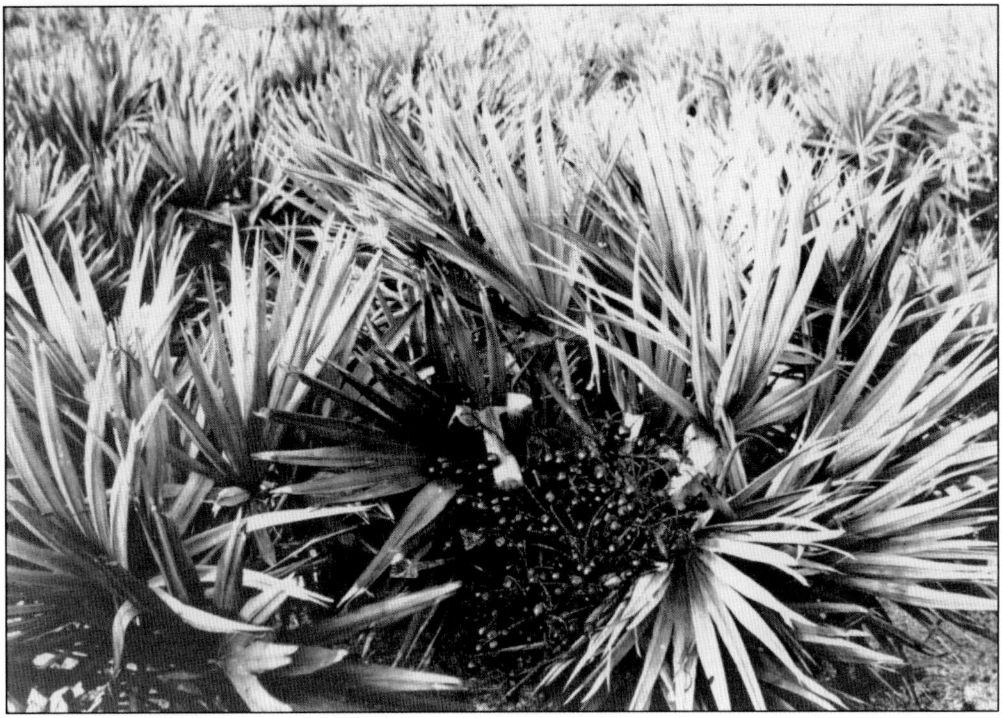

Saw Palmetto, c. 1890. In the early days, doctors were dependent upon medicines made from plants. Harvesting saw palmetto berries was to become a major industry in the Hawks Park area. The berries would be used in the manufacture of a variety of patent medicines, tonics, and elixirs.

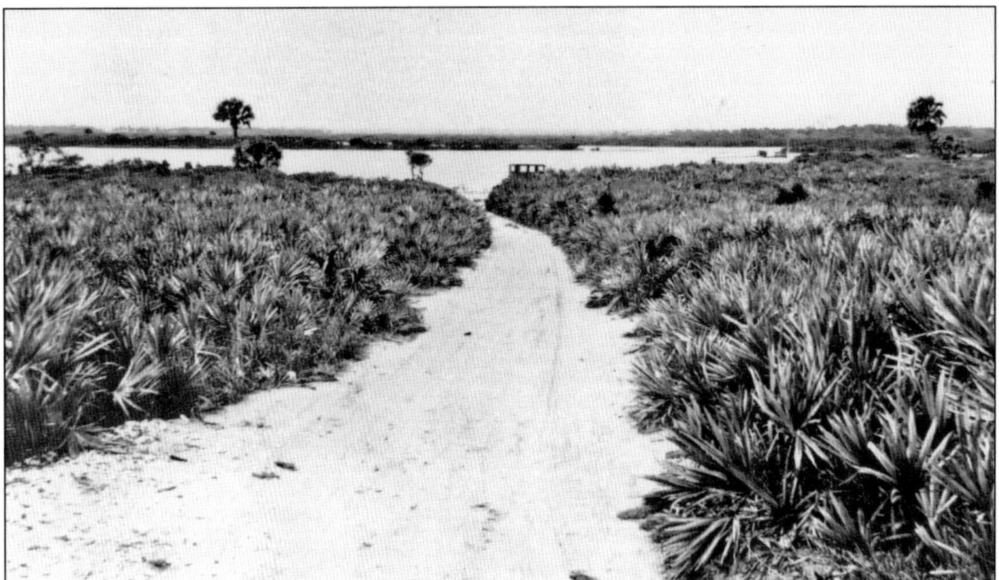

Saw Palmettos along the Beach, c. 1890. The best berries grew in profusion along the beachside, so the Wilkinson family bought three miles of beachfront, paying 25¢ an acre. The Wilkinsons then got into the business of harvesting, drying, and shipping the berries. Their business would last for several generations, and saw palmetto is still to be found in drug and health food stores today.

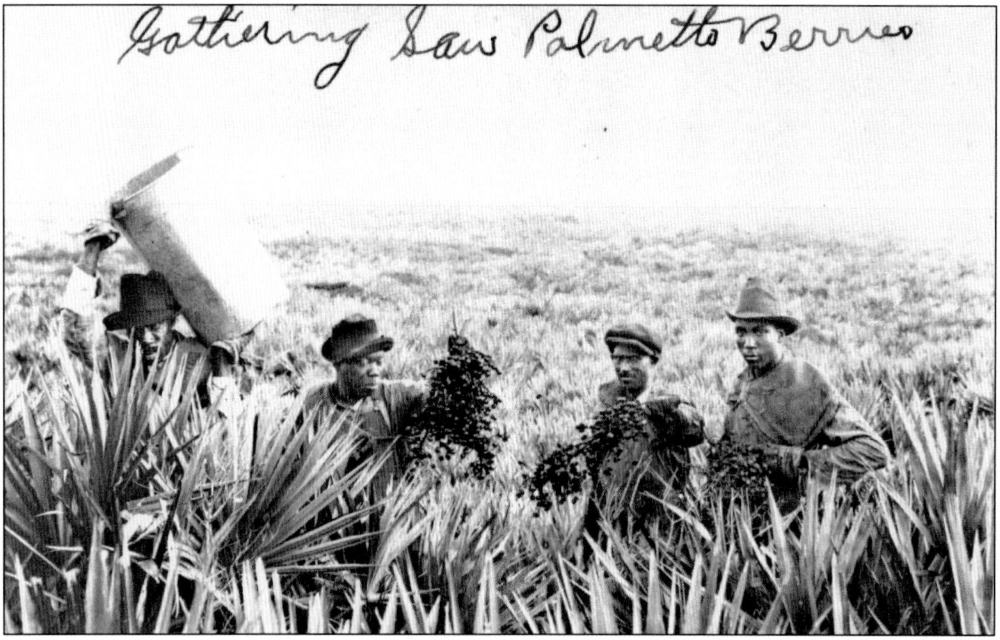

GATHERING SAW PALMETTO BERRIES, C. 1890. The saw palmetto berries grew in clusters like grapes but were the size of olives. While they were obvious on the plant, getting close enough to pick them was difficult. Saw-toothed stems tore at flesh as well as clothes. Rattlesnakes, hoping to catch a bird or other small animal making a meal of the berries, were plentiful. To prevent rattlesnake bites, the men wore heavy shoes and canvas leggings, all while working in the hot Florida sun. The men are unidentified.

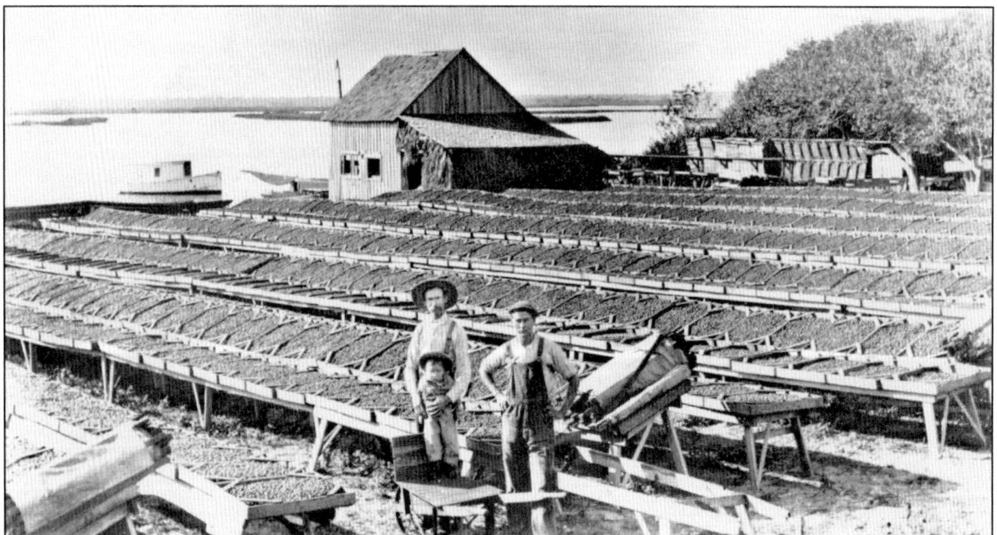

DRYING SAW PALMETTO BERRIES, C. 1905. The berries were dried in large, flat, cypress berry crates, slatted so that air could circulate, and carefully shipped across the river by barge to Hawks Park. They were checked frequently for insects and then readied for market. Medicine manufacturers had found that the berry could be prepared into a dark syrup that was beneficial to the mucus membranes of the throat to clear up hoarseness. The man in the hat is A. B. Wilkinson, the child is H. P. Wilkinson, but the worker is unidentified.

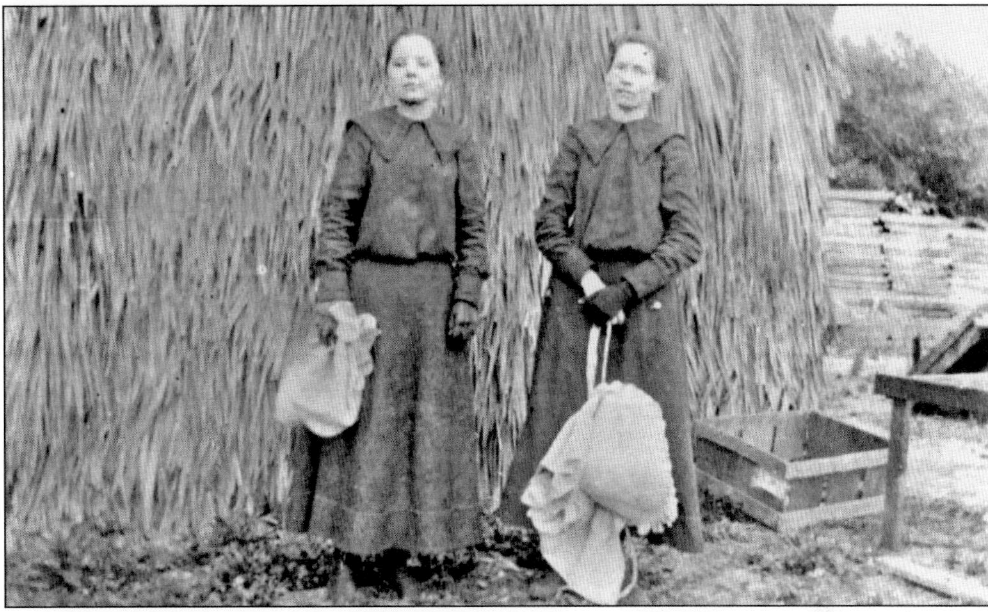

EMMARINE (EMMY) AND NELL WILKINSON BY A PALM LEAF HUT, C. 1901. Settlers used what they could. The hut shown here is made from cabbage palm branches, or fronds. The saw palmetto's root fiber was used for all kinds of brushes and the leaves were shredded and cured for use in mattresses. The stems, flexible when cut green, were used to tie up crates for shipment. The bees made honey from the saw palmetto blossoms.

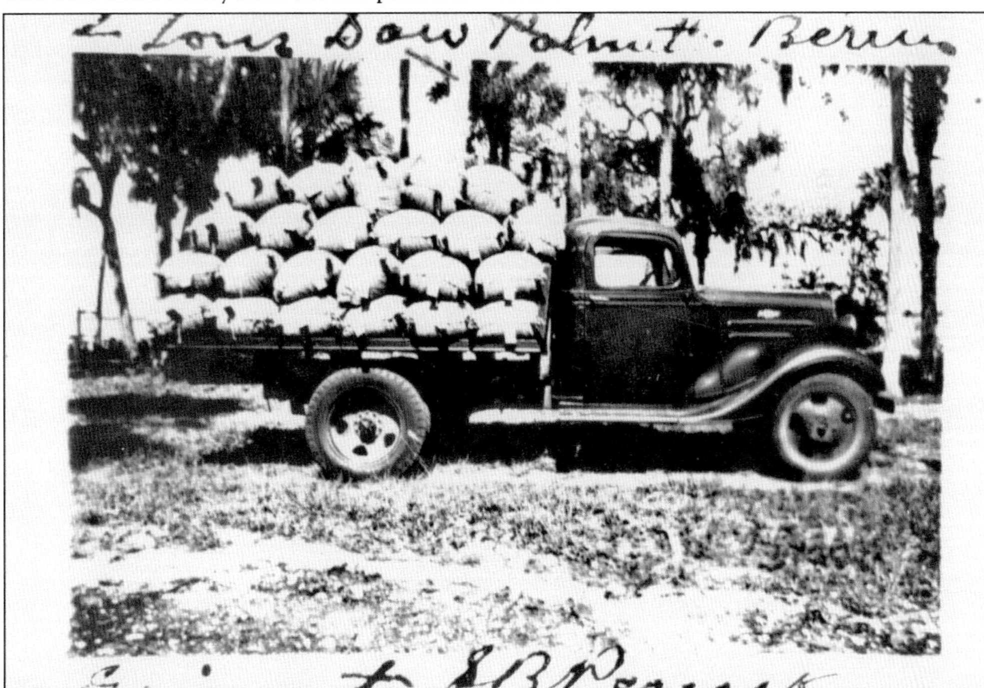

SAW PALMETTOS BERRIES IN TRUCK, C. 1936. When automobiles were available, the Wilkinsons had the berries bagged and taken by truck to the railroad depot or the steamboat. The bags were shipped to New York and St. Louis medicine manufacturers.

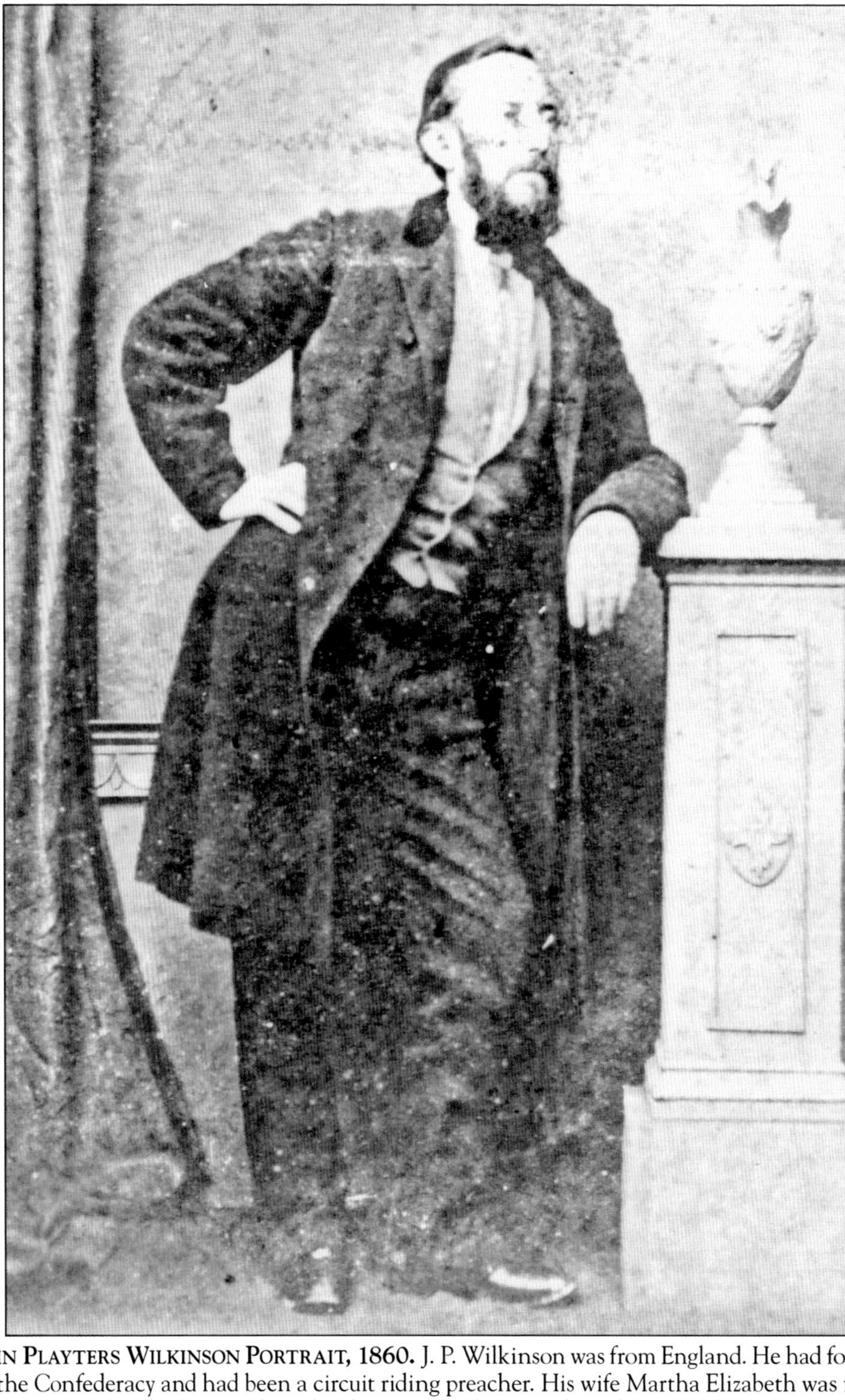

JOHN PLAYTERS WILKINSON PORTRAIT, 1860. J. P. Wilkinson was from England. He had fought for the Confederacy and had been a circuit riding preacher. His wife Martha Elizabeth was from Virginia, and they both moved to Florida, near Turtle Mound on the east side of the river. He ran the Hawks Park Grocery store for some time.

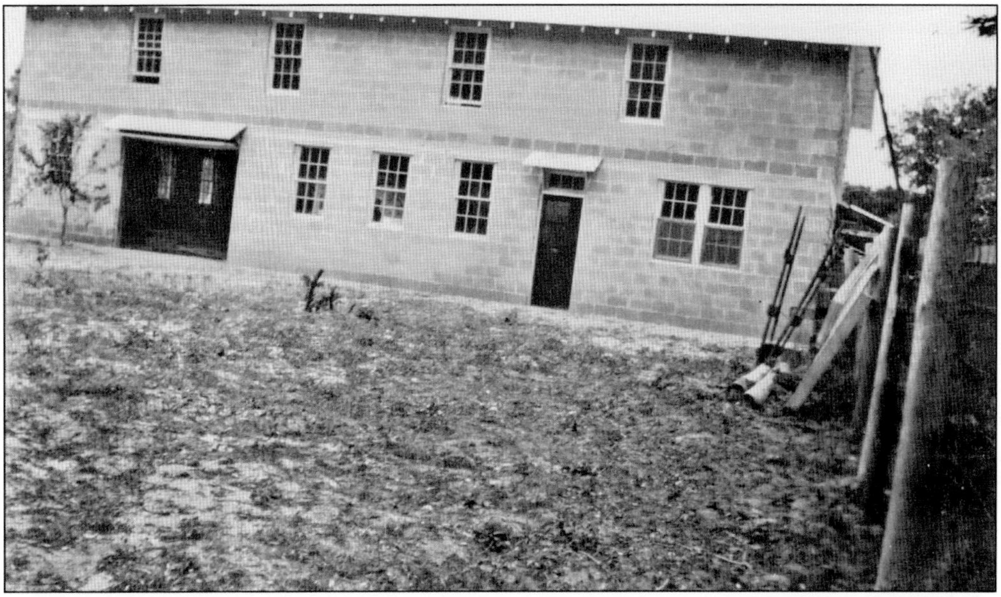

PACKING PLANT, 1910. This plant was the center of much activity. It was where cement blocks were made for some of the Hawks Park buildings, the place where lumber was prepared for use in building, and where saw palmetto berries were stored. The fresh saw palmetto berries were no longer in great demand once synthetic medicines came into use but are sometimes still recommended for prostate problems.

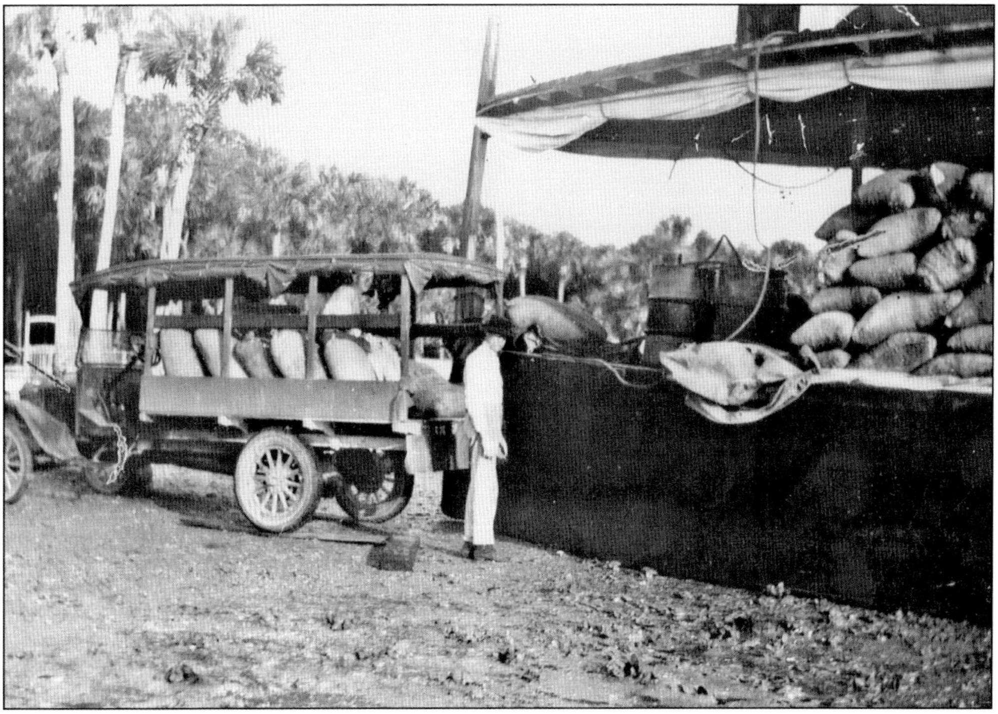

BAGS LOADED FROM TRUCK TO THE CORONA, C. 1920. Bags of saw palmetto berries were loaded onto the *Corona*, a sternwheeler and flat-bottomed steamboat. The men are unidentified. The Model T shown was owned by the Wilkinson family and later used as a school bus.

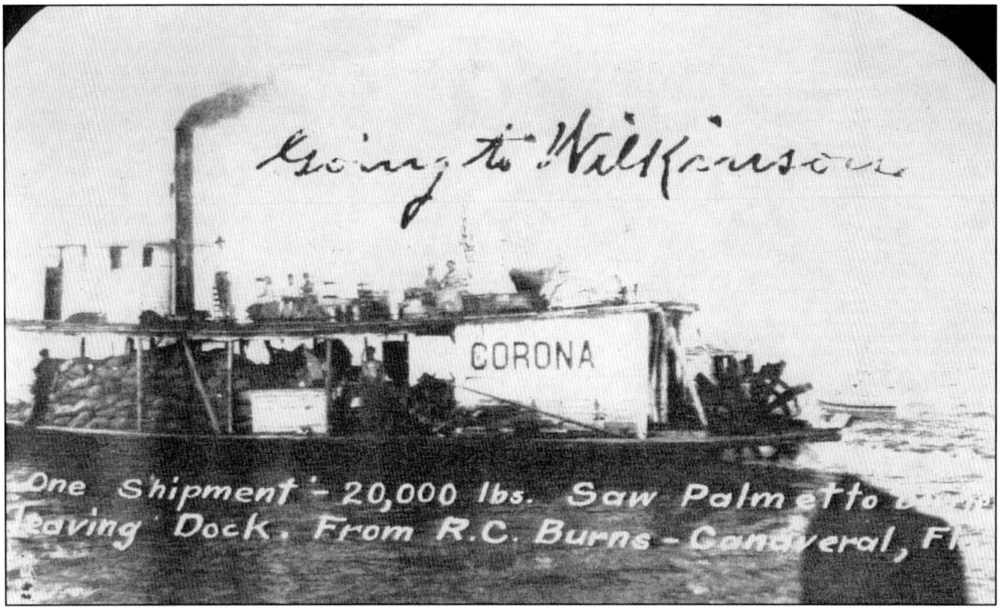

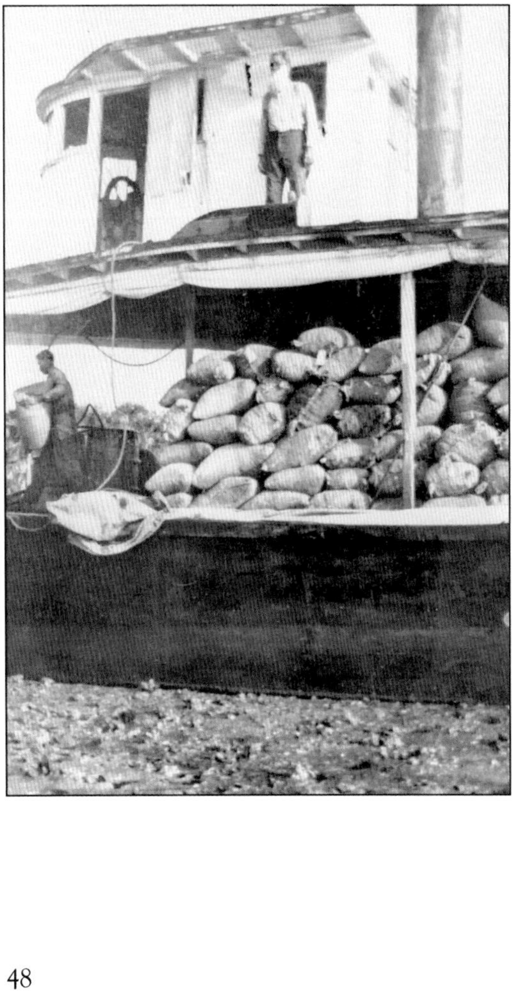

THE CORONA, C. 1920. Captain Cone, the owner of the *Corona*, lived in Canaveral, south of Hawks Park. The Wilkinsons' bags of saw palmetto berries were picked up at Hawks Park, at the east end of New Hampshire Avenue, on Captain Cone's trip up the river. Captain Cone is on the upper level of the boat; the other people are unidentified.

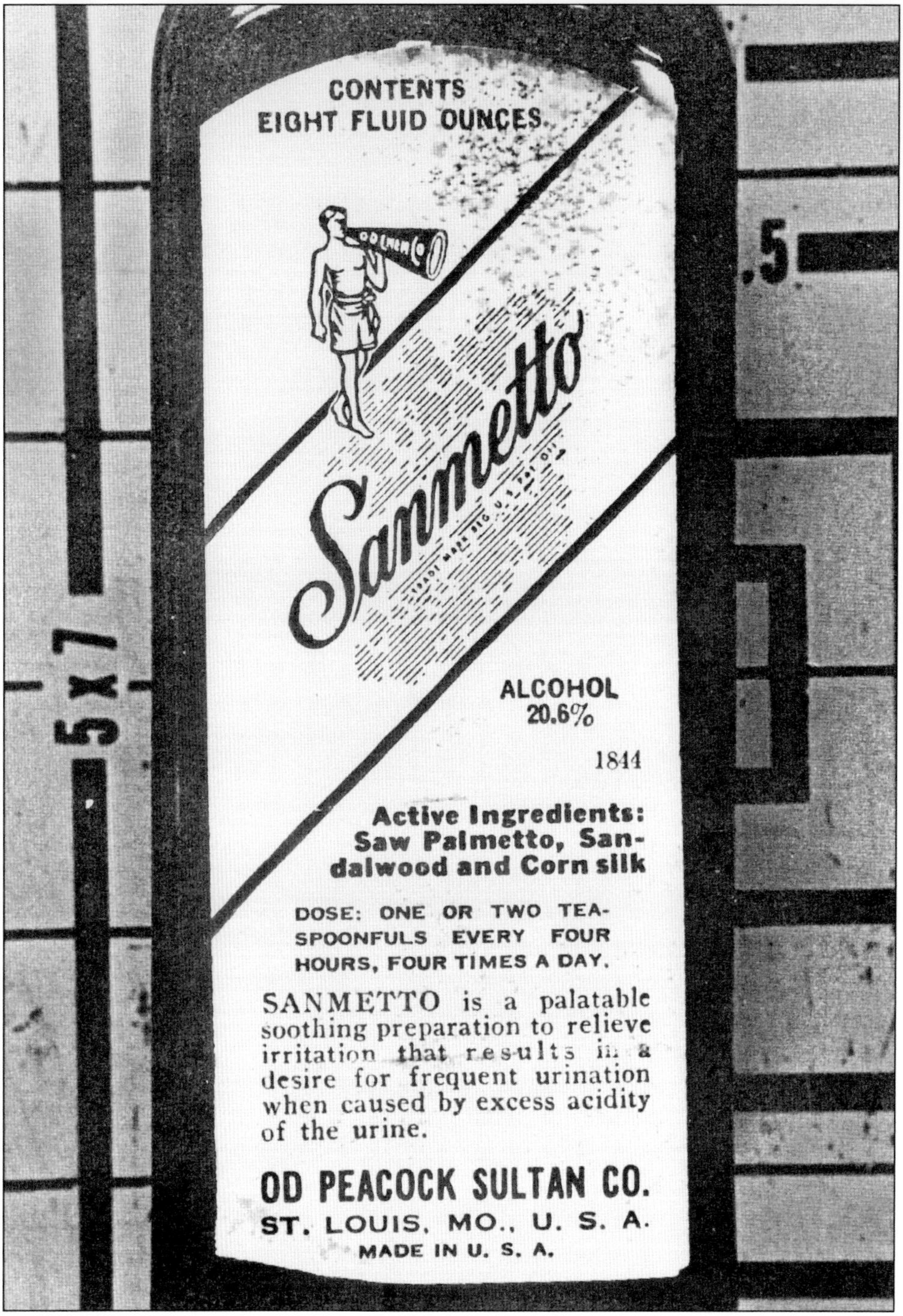

SANMETTO BOTTLE, C. 1920. Notice the alcohol content in this remedy. Patent medicines were popular in the mid-1800s. Even Dr. Hawks had made his own when he was a young doctor. In *The East Coast of Florida,* Hawks advertised another cure-all: "A great blood remedy from the North! Dr. R. W. Loubee's Vitalizing Compound! For the radical cure of scrofula, cancerous tumors, diphtheritic or Mineral Blood Poisoning, Rheumatism, Dyspepsia, Dropsy, and Liver Complaint."

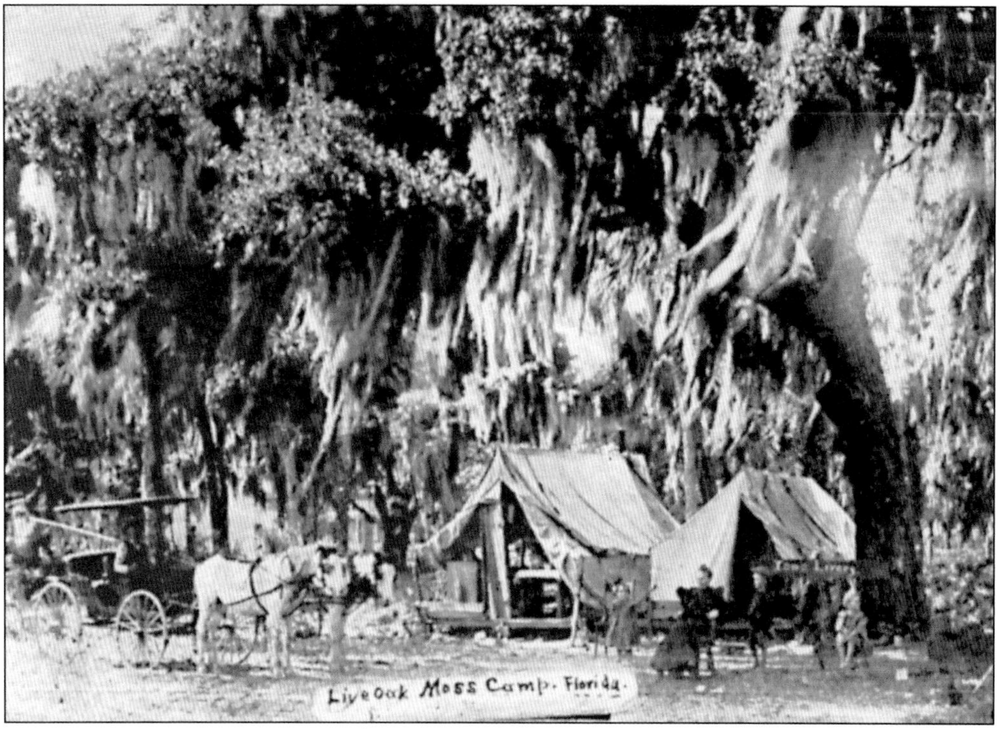

LIVE OAK MOSS CAMP, C. 1890. This is a Royal Hubbell postcard. The men are shown collecting Spanish moss hanging from the trees. A large bamboo pole, with a wire attached to the top, was used to reach into the trees, twist, and pull down the moss. Dried Spanish moss was used even into the 1950s for car seats and other furniture. The people are unidentified.

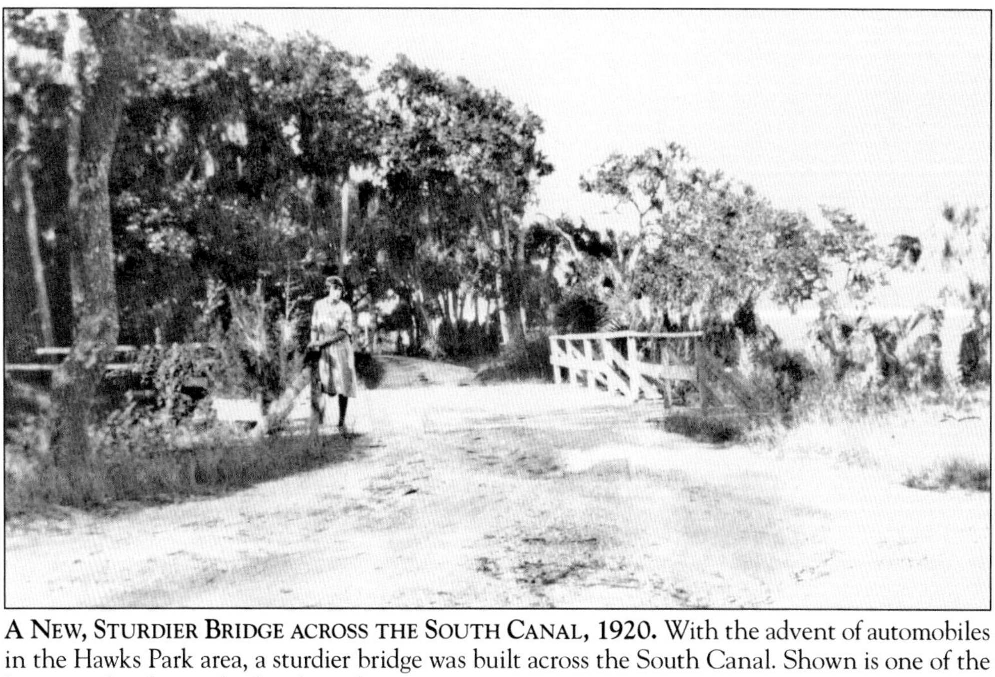

A NEW, STURDIER BRIDGE ACROSS THE SOUTH CANAL, 1920. With the advent of automobiles in the Hawks Park area, a sturdier bridge was built across the South Canal. Shown is one of the Leeming daughters who lived nearby.

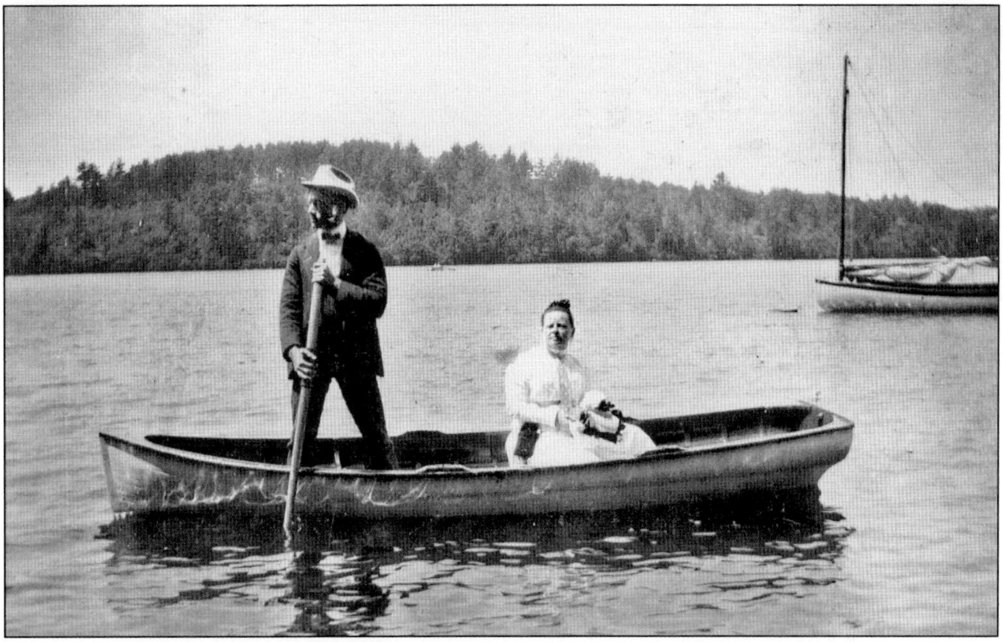

POLING A BOAT TO SHORE, C. 1910. Turtle Mound, one of the large Native American shell mounds, is in the background. Turtle Mound still stands today, a protected area of the beach, part of the Canaveral National Seashore. In the very shallow water close to shore, it was easier to pole the boat than to row it. George Wilkinson and his wife, Mary, are in the boat.

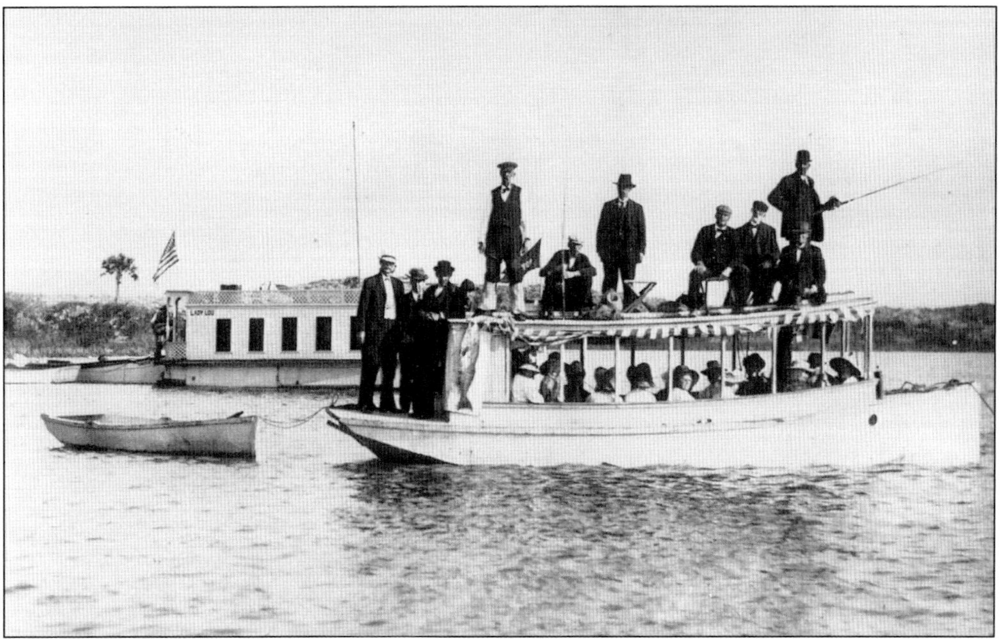

PARTY TIME ABOARD THE *WANTAH*, C. 1920. Locals and party folks seem to be on the river for a day of fun. The *Wantah* was a touring boat owned by the Wilkinson family, taking locals and visitors out to see the manatees, dolphins, pelicans, egrets, herons, and more on the beautiful river. They went for picnics, for fishing, or just for an enjoyable time. The large fish would indicate this was probably a fishing trip. The people are unidentified.

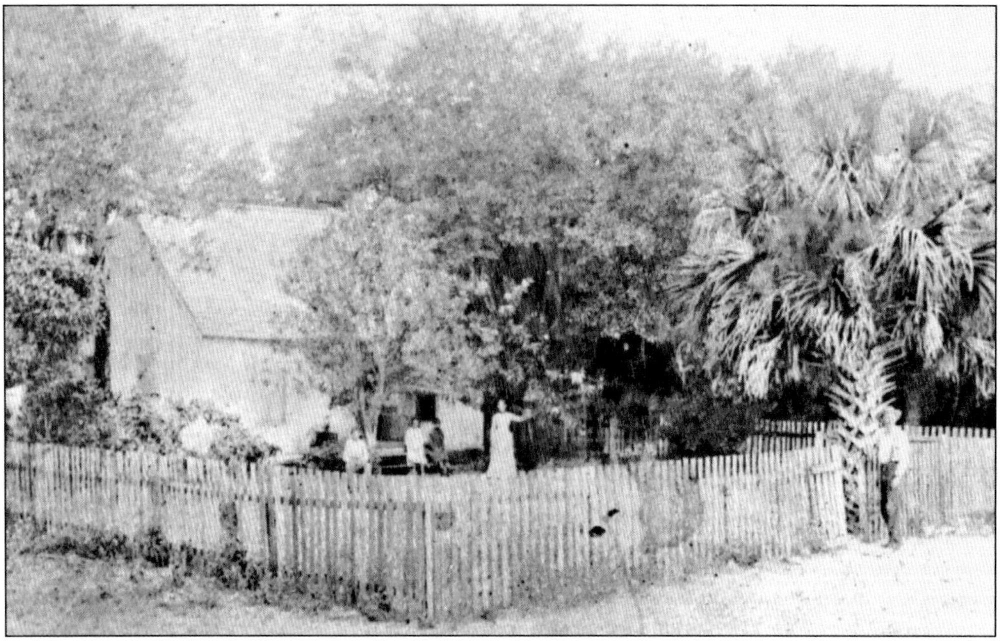

EARLY HAWKS PARK HOME, C. 1900. As the community grew, new houses still needed the fence surrounding the yard to keep out wild animals. The people are unidentified.

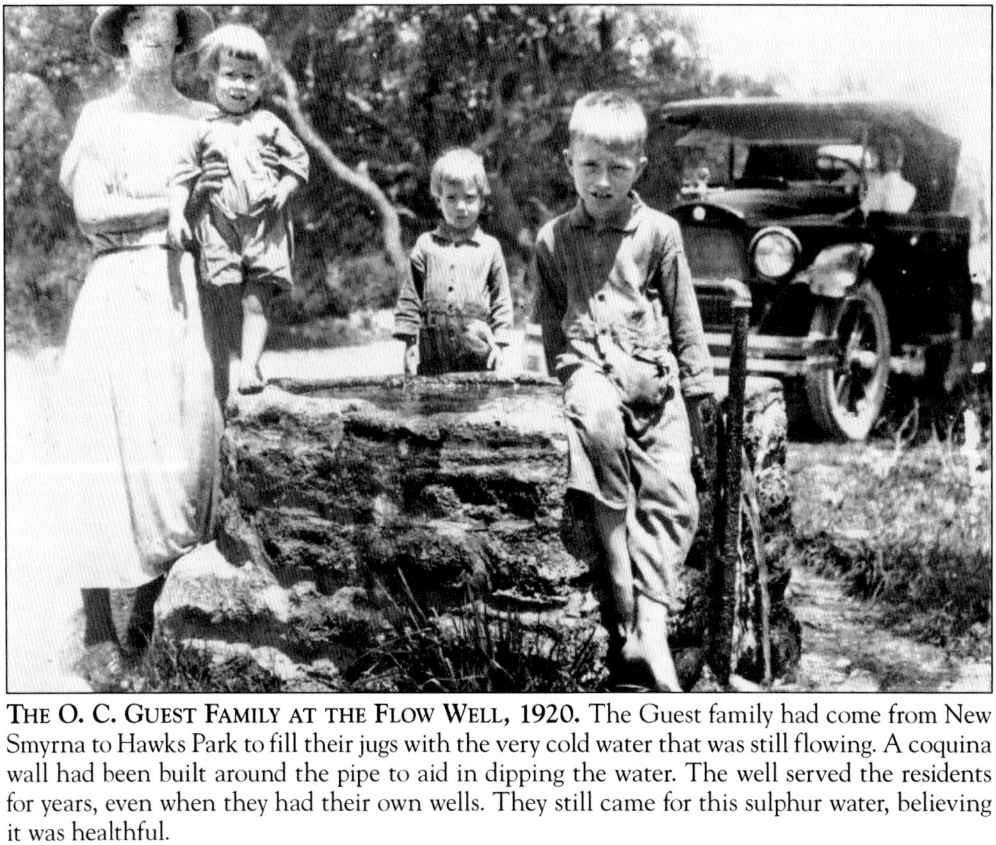

THE O. C. GUEST FAMILY AT THE FLOW WELL, 1920. The Guest family had come from New Smyrna to Hawks Park to fill their jugs with the very cold water that was still flowing. A coquina wall had been built around the pipe to aid in dipping the water. The well served the residents for years, even when they had their own wells. They still came for this sulphur water, believing it was healthful.

Four

LAND HIGH AND DRY

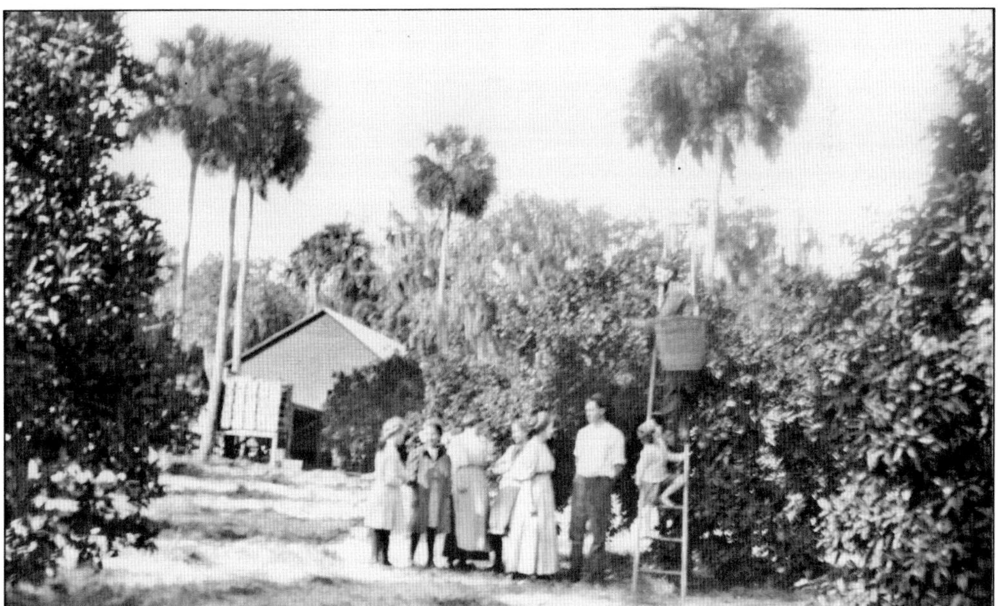

FAMILY IN ORANGE GROVE, 1910. The whole family would help at harvest time. This photo shows a packing house conveniently nearby. The people are unidentified. (Photograph by Royal Hubbell.)

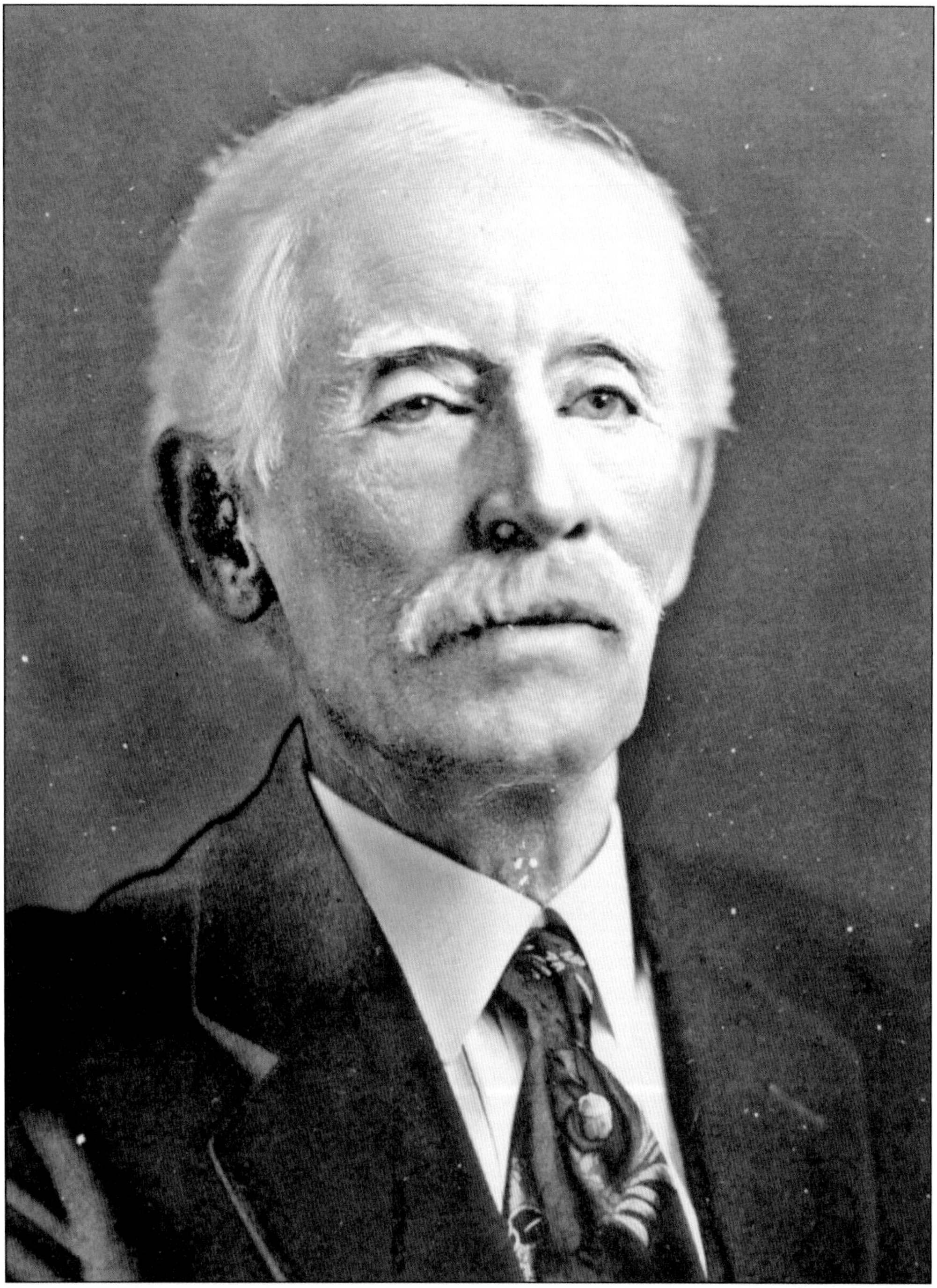

WILLIAM S. HART, C. 1910. W. S. Hart was a member of the Hawks Park Company and an early entrepreneur in Hawks Park. An orange grove manager and honey producer, he was also the first teacher in the first school. Dr. Hawks, who had been learning about citrus production ever since he first set foot in Florida, worked with Hart and others who put in groves, until citrus was a large business in Hawks Park. The number of acres planted in groves swelled from 13 to well over 100 acres.

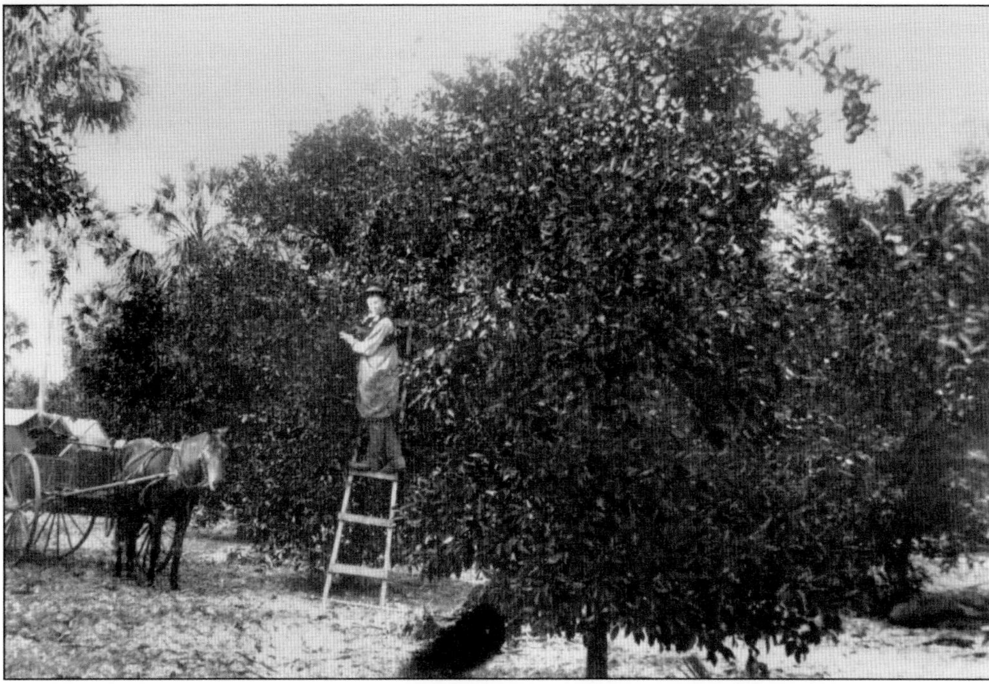

Worker Picking Oranges, c. 1910. W. S. Hart bought 200 acres of the Sanchez Grant to the north of Hawks's Geronimo-Alvarez Grant. The northern boundary of the Hart property was the South Canal. This acreage was described in these words by Dr. Hawks: "A body of hard wood land covered with a variety of oaks, hickory, bay, cedar, pine and palm. A ride or walk through it among the orange groves is a delightful treat." The worker is unidentified.

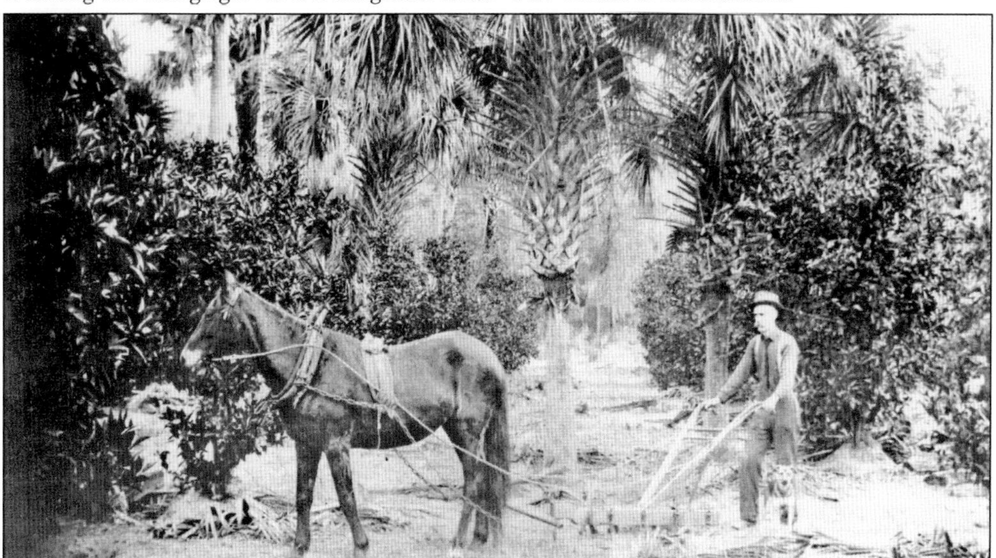

W. S. Hart in Grove, c. 1910. Beehives are not seen among the orange trees in this photo, but Hart also kept honeybees. He and Dr. Hawks were always testing their Yankee ingenuity, and one idea that worked well was to move the bees to where the flowers were. After the orange blossoms were gone, bees and beehives were placed on large flat-bottomed barges and moved across the river to blooming mangrove and saw palmetto flowers.

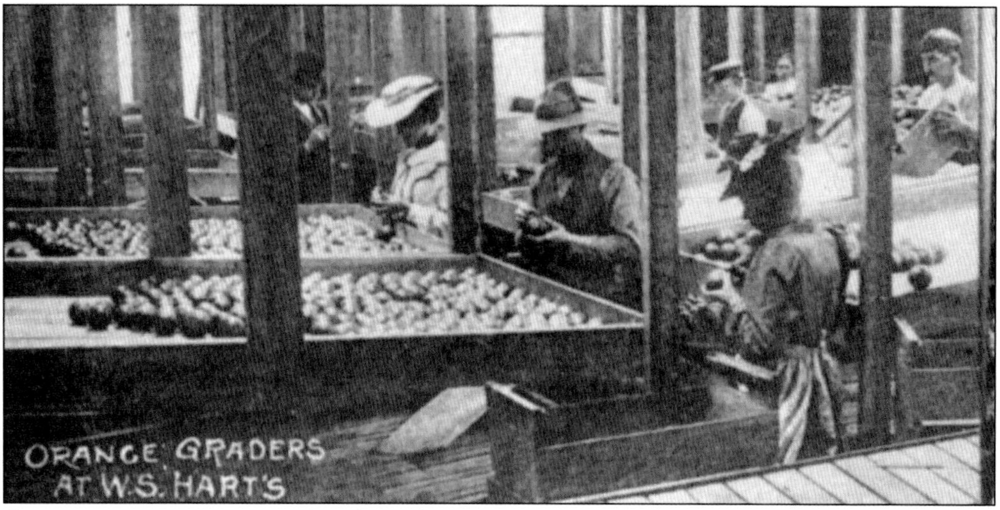

ORANGE GRADERS, C. 1910. Hawks Park citrus was shipped all over the eastern United States. When the name of the river was changed from the Hillsboro to the Indian River, the name of the fruit would become famous as Indian River citrus. The three flavors of honey—orange, mangrove, and saw palmetto—were also produced in abundance and shipped to market from the long dock at Ocean Avenue in Hawks Park. In 1888, W. S. Hart shipped 11 tons of honey. The people are unidentified.

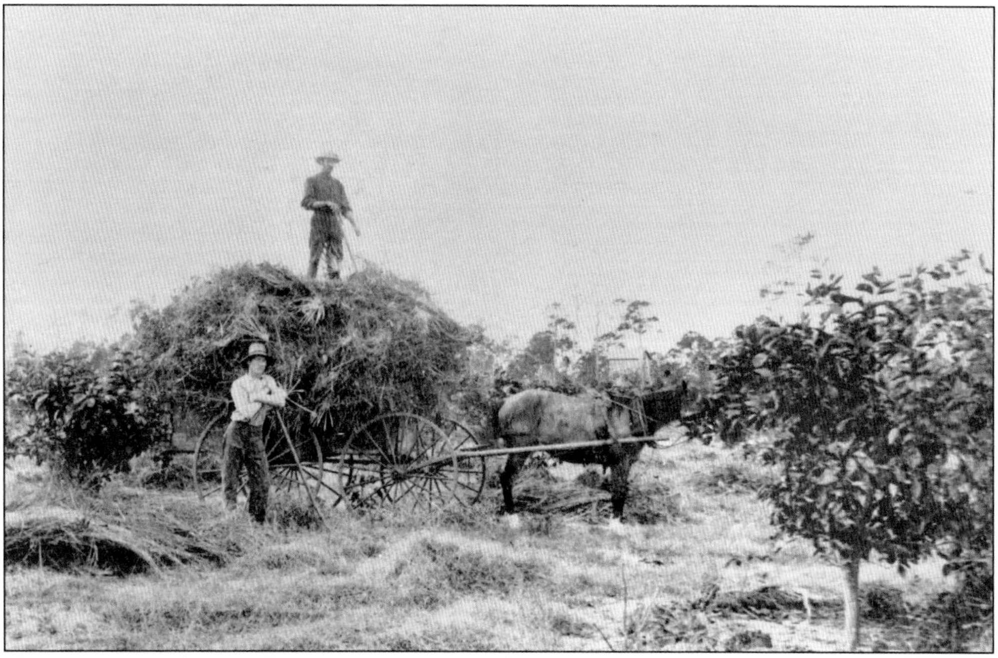

HAYING IN THE CITRUS GROVES, C. 1910. Weeds constantly needed to be cut in the groves, but even that harvest could be used. The dried hay would be kept for the winter months when there was danger of a freeze. Citrus harvest time is during the winter, and if a freeze was predicted, the hay would be piled at the base of the trees, to protect the tree trunks and roots from the cold temperatures. If the freeze was prolonged, however, the fruit and the trees could be lost. The men are unidentified.

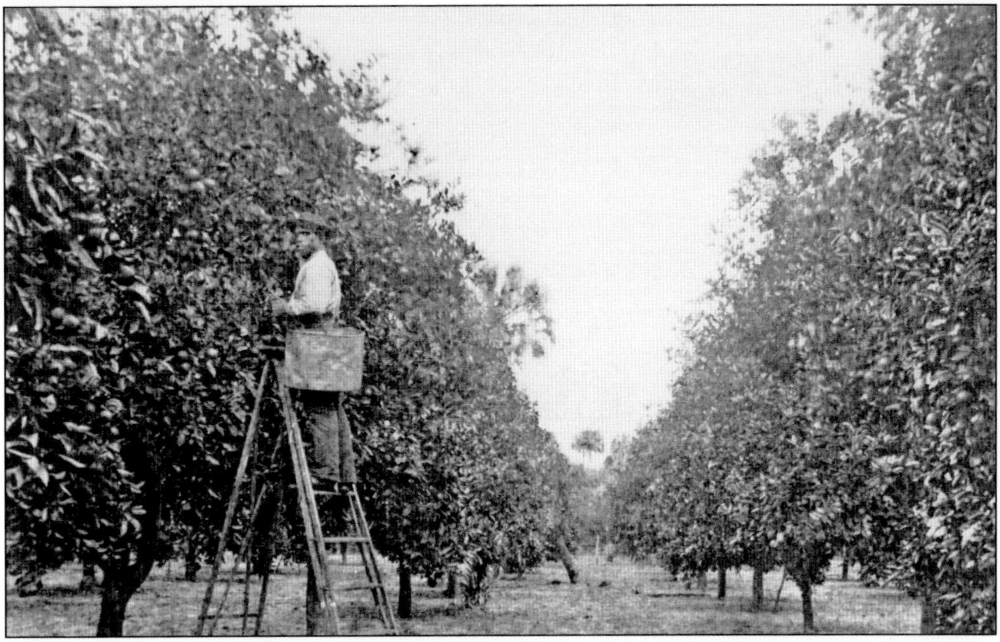

CITRUS HARVEST, C. 1910. Dr. Hawks said about his community: "This is the neighborhood where the celebrated East Coast or Indian River oranges were first known in Florida, and where they continue to grow to the greatest perfection. Lemons, figs, and all semi-tropical fruits, do well; also, garden vegetables of every sort." The person is unidentified.

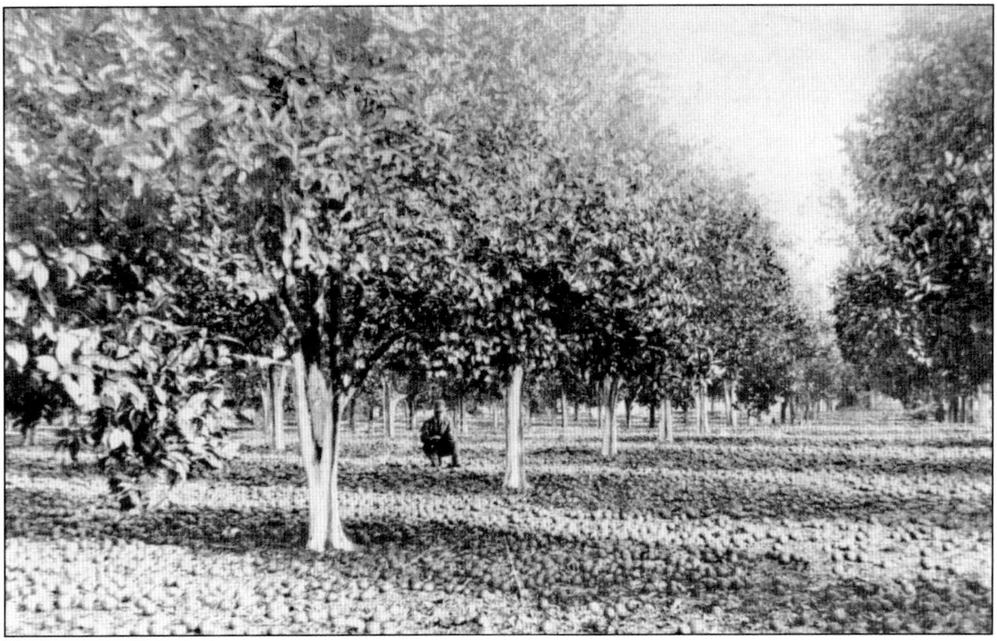

AFTER A FREEZE, 1894. The temperature on December 29, 1894, was the lowest ever recorded to that time in Hawks Park. All the citrus was frozen solid. Another freeze in February 1895 was devastating to the citrus industry throughout Volusia County. Tender new growth had just sprouted, and the second freeze killed the trees themselves. They had to send to California for bud-wood to graft the damaged fruit trees. The man is unidentified.

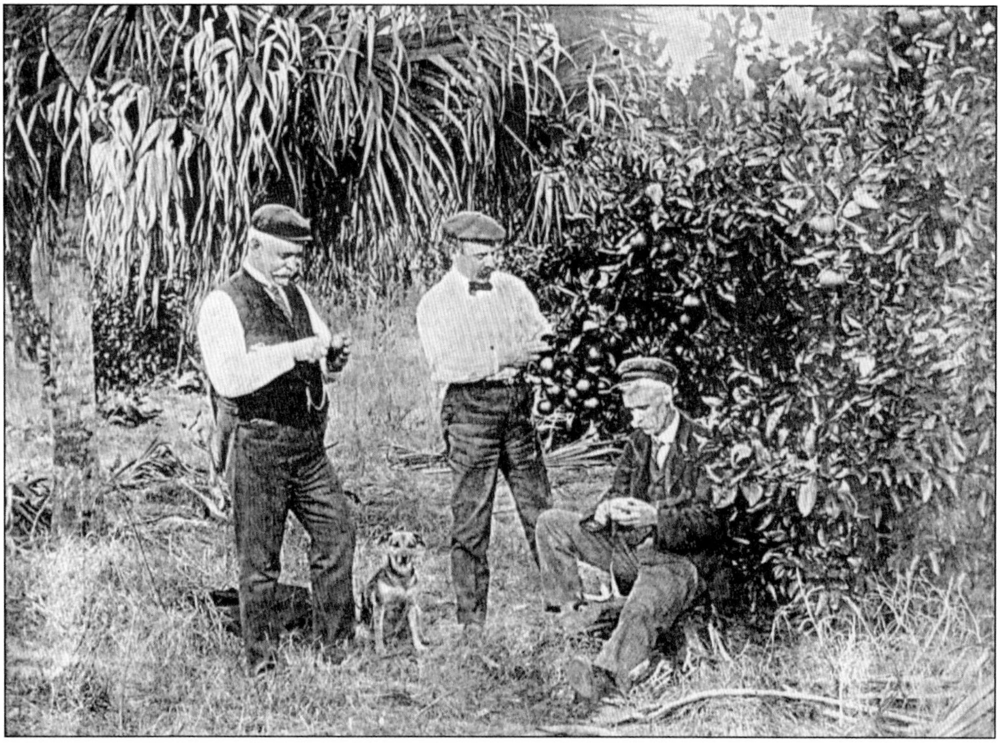

HARRY MITCHELL IN ORANGE GROVE, C. 1890. The owner of the Manoma Groves, Harry Mitchell, is at right. The other men are not identified, but they appear to be peeling oranges to check the quality or perhaps to eat.

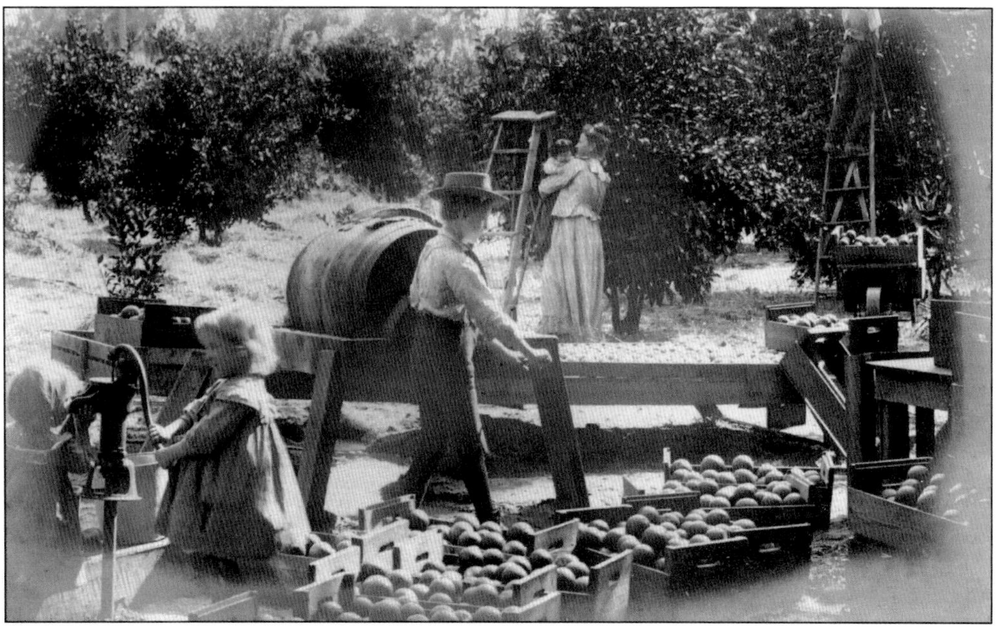

MANOMA GROVES, C. 1890. Many of the Hawks Park settlers planted citrus trees. Some planted just a few, while some entrepreneurs like Harry Mitchell planted groves. The people are unidentified. (Photograph by Royal Hubbell.)

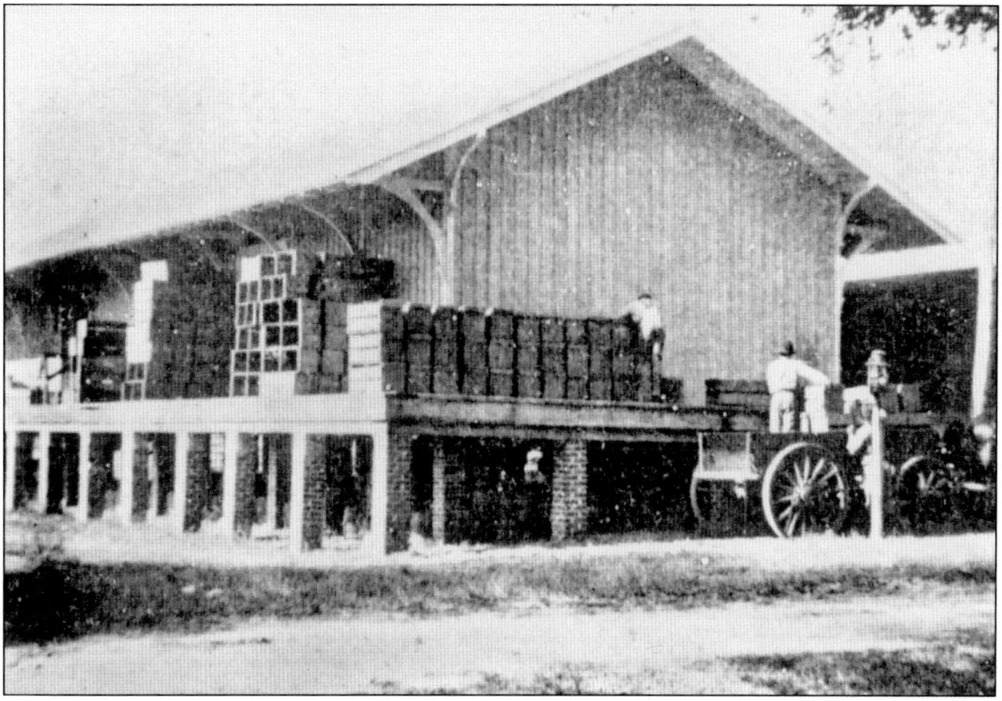

CITRUS AT A RAILWAY STATION, C. 1890. W. S. Hart had a citrus packing house between Riverview Street and Rio Vista. Dr. Hawks said, "The chief industries are orange and lemon growing, bee keeping, poultry keeping, planting and caring for groves of non-residents." The people are unidentified.

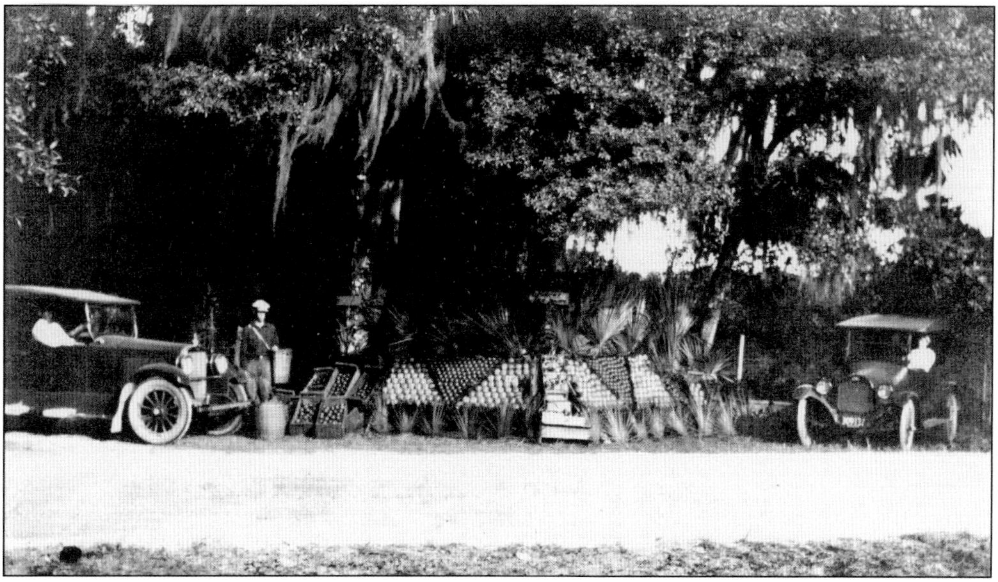

SELLING CITRUS ALONG RIDGEWOOD AVENUE, C. 1930. Members of Hubbell's family remember working at a stand on Ridgewood Avenue (U.S. 1) selling citrus and juice to tourists during the Depression years. John Milton Hawks, in describing the town, said, "Oranges and grapefruit fresh from the trees and large luscious strawberries, tomatoes and other vegetables as well as fresh eggs are abundant." The people are unidentified. (Photograph by Royal Hubbell.)

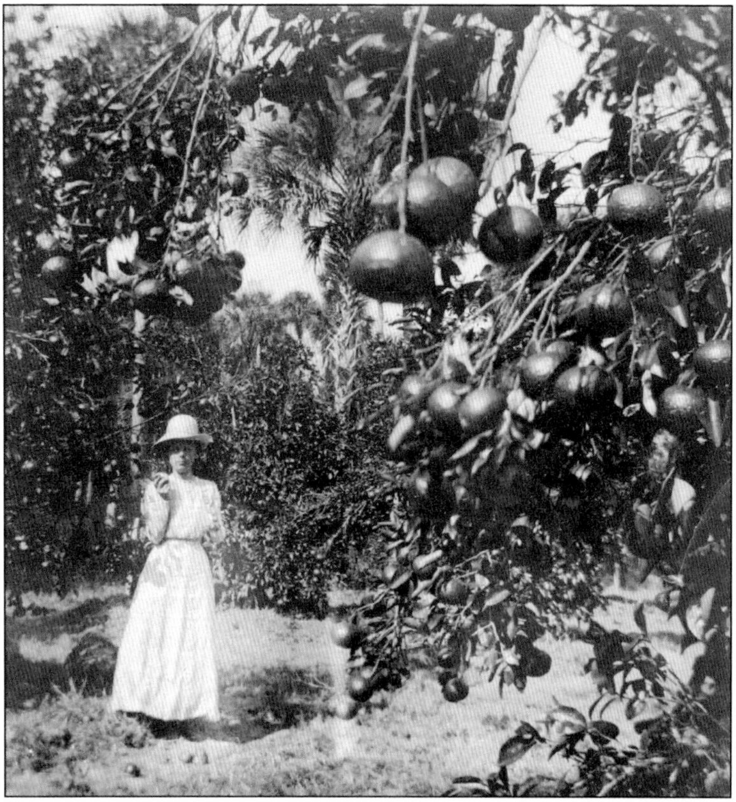

WOMAN IN CITRUS GROVE, 1910. The woman is identified as "Aunt Lo," or Louiza Haughton. To settlers and visitors alike, being able to pick an orange off a tree was a thrill. Many groves encouraged this with signs stating: "Pick an orange." Over 180 acres were in citrus groves by 1900.

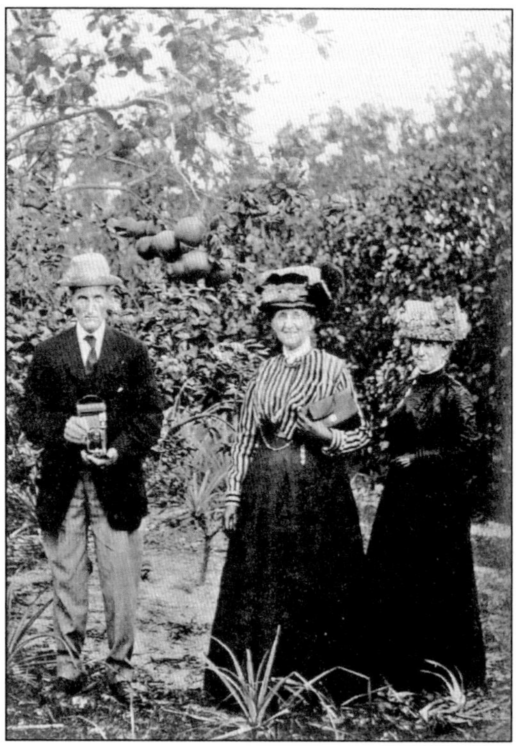

VISITORS IN A CITRUS GROVE, C. 1900. The scent of orange blossoms and the chance to pick an orange off a tree was "true Florida" to visitors. The people pictured here are unidentified, but the story is told that they actually put up a tent in a grove and stayed there on vacation.

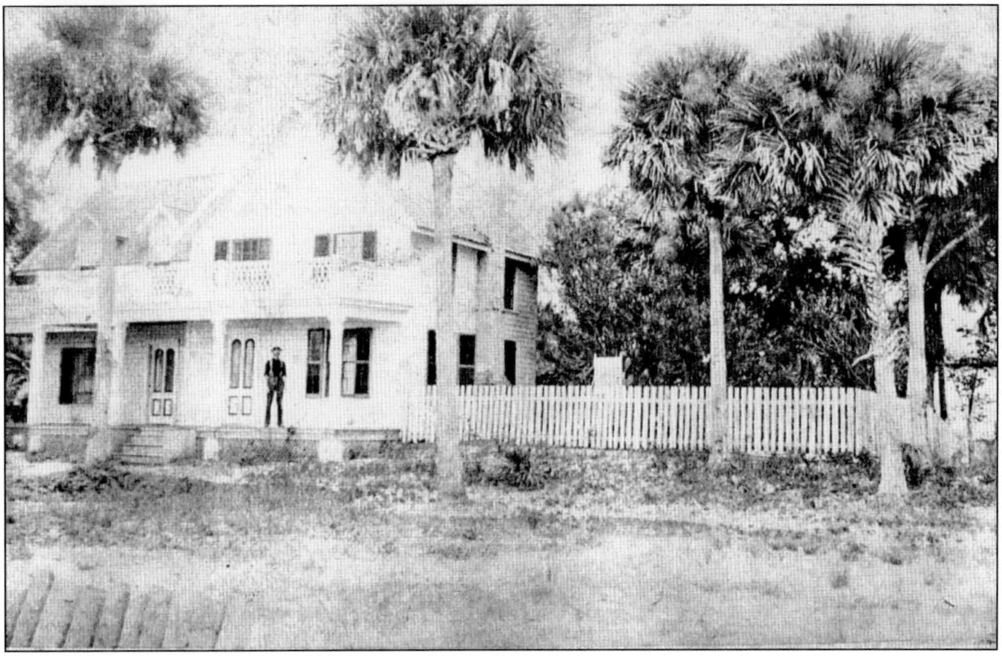

OLD HOUSE, C. 1890. We do not know the owners of this house or if they kept bees, but records tell us that the bee keepers in the early days were W. S. Hart, Ezra Hatch, Harry Mitchell, O. O. Poppleton, and J. M. Smith. Some of the people made bee houses or shacks in which to house the hives, to outwit bears trying to get to the honey. The tale is told of one family who, after cleaning out the shack, lived in it for a short time. The person here is unidentified.

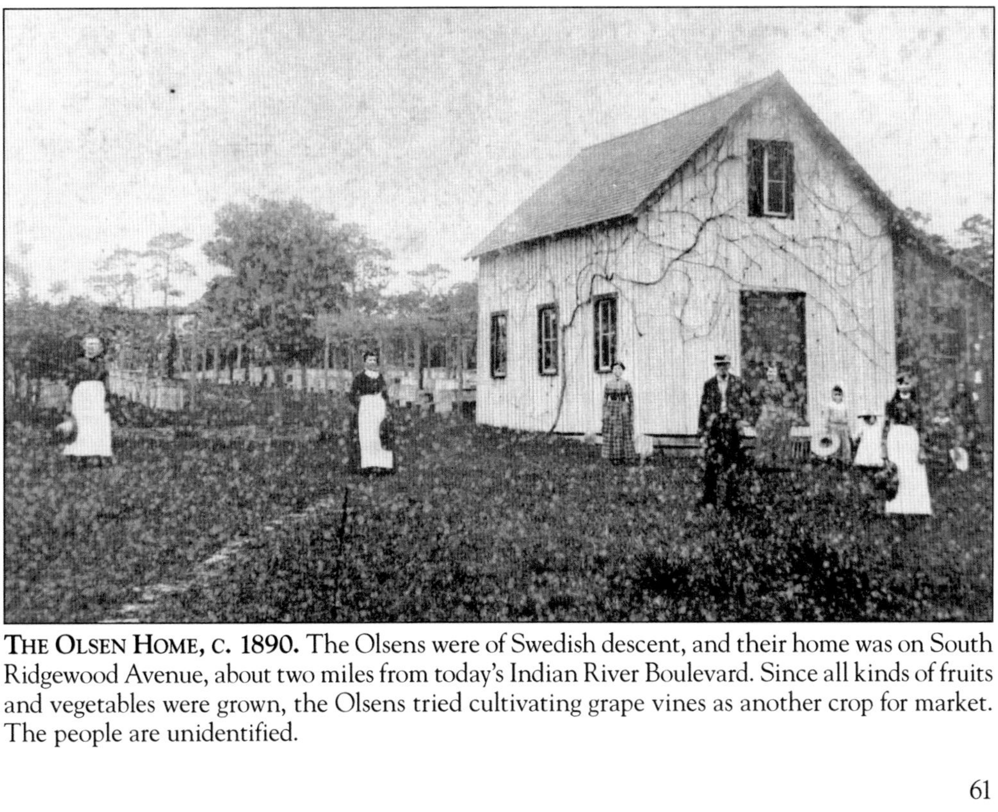

THE OLSEN HOME, C. 1890. The Olsens were of Swedish descent, and their home was on South Ridgewood Avenue, about two miles from today's Indian River Boulevard. Since all kinds of fruits and vegetables were grown, the Olsens tried cultivating grape vines as another crop for market. The people are unidentified.

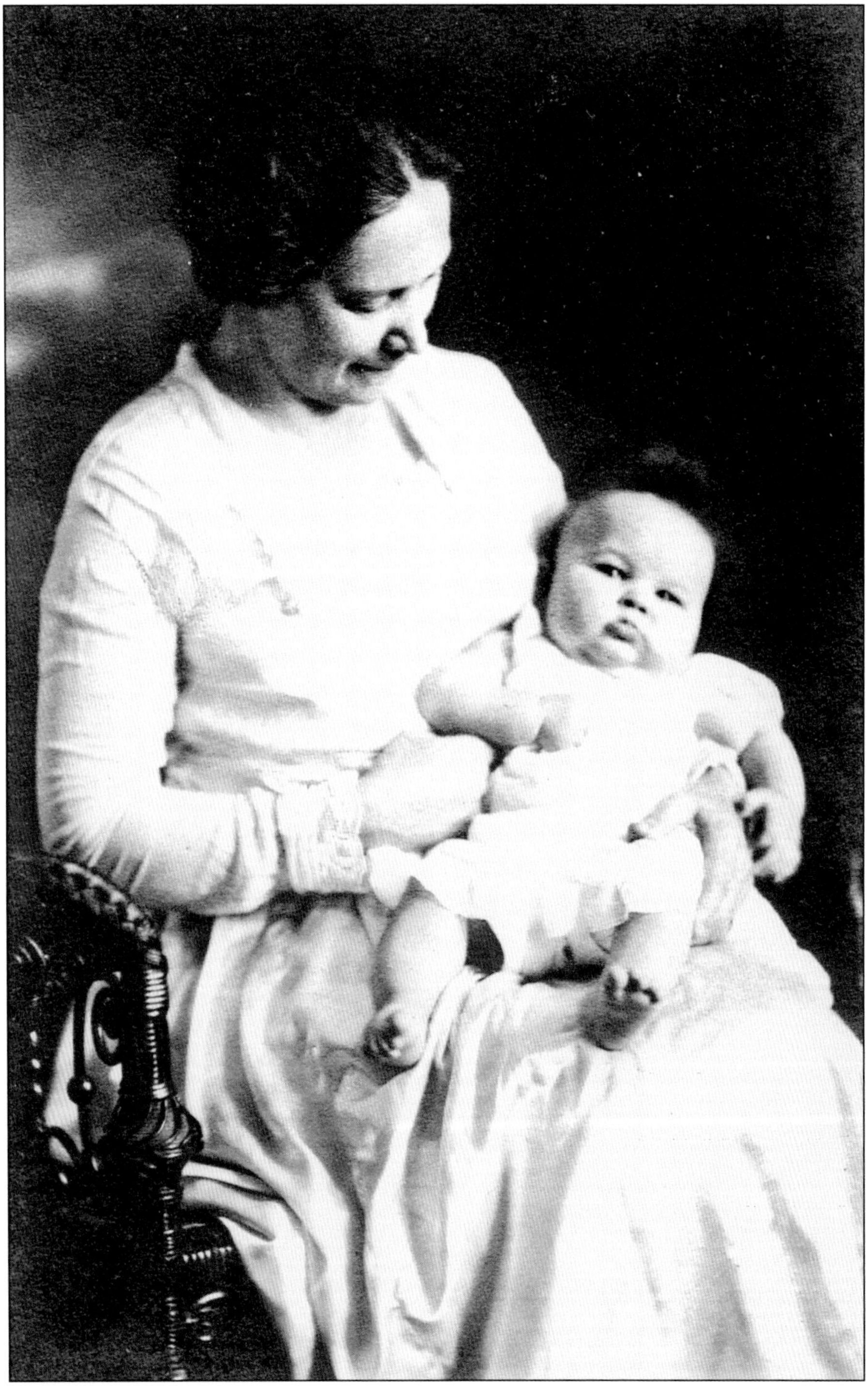

"AUNT NELL" HOLDING BABY, C. 1884. Believed to be Nell Wilkinson, daughter of John Playters Wilkinson, this woman is simply identified as "Aunt Nell." The baby is unidentified. The whole community was interested in the education of the young, and Dr. John Milton Hawks had earlier been Volusia County's first post–Civil War superintendent of schools.

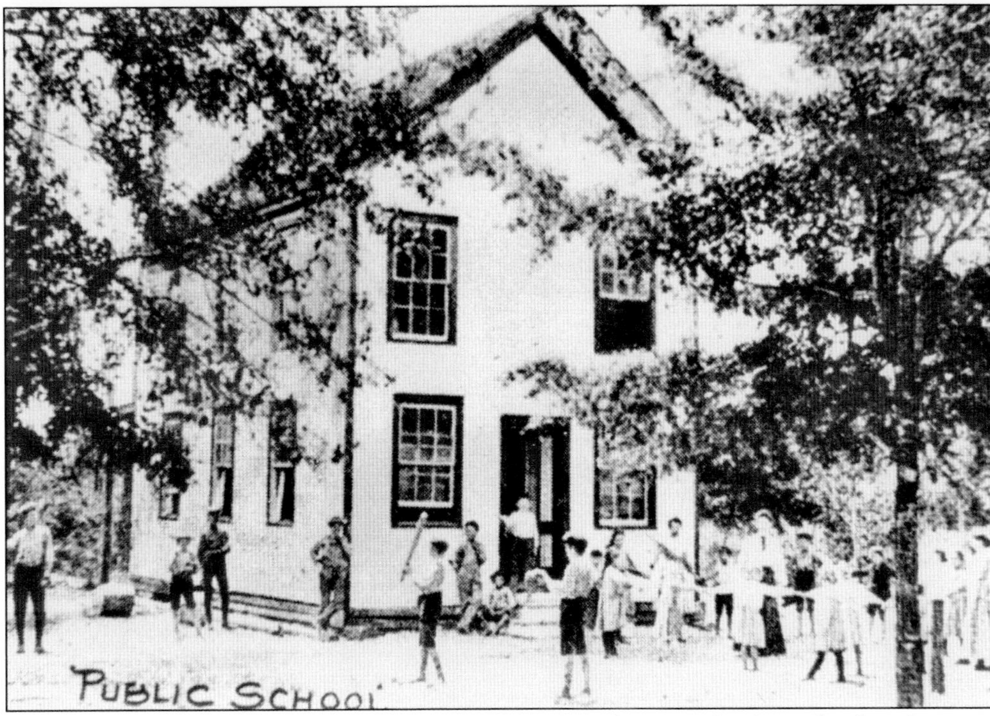

WOODEN SCHOOLHOUSE, C. 1900. In 1879, W. S. Hart became the first schoolteacher, in a cottage owned by Dr. Hawks. The first school building was later erected at the southwest corner of Ridgewood and Park Avenues on one acre donated by Dr. Hawks, which he deeded to the Volusia County Board of Instruction. Two stories tall, the upper story was used for "lectures and other public entertainments and for religious services," while the first floor was one large room for grades 1–12, with one teacher in charge. The people are unidentified.

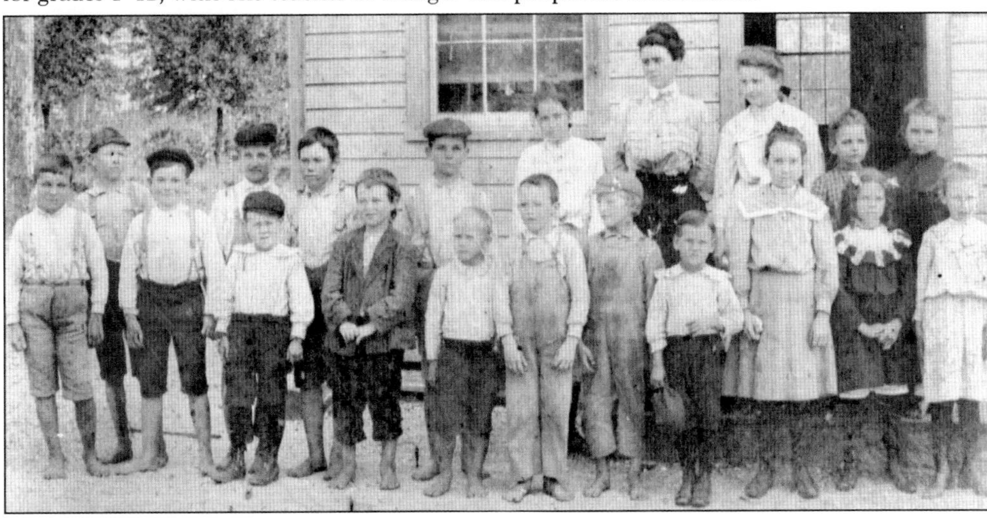

WOODEN SCHOOLHOUSE, C. 1905. On a very cold day in 1910, Raymond Clifton, the teacher, decided to put more fuel in the furnace while the students were out to lunch. The furnace exploded and demolished the building. Fortunately no one was hurt, and the children were delighted when they thought there would be no school. Classes went on, in W. S. Hart's fruit packing house, and no school was missed. The people are unidentified, but notice the bare feet.

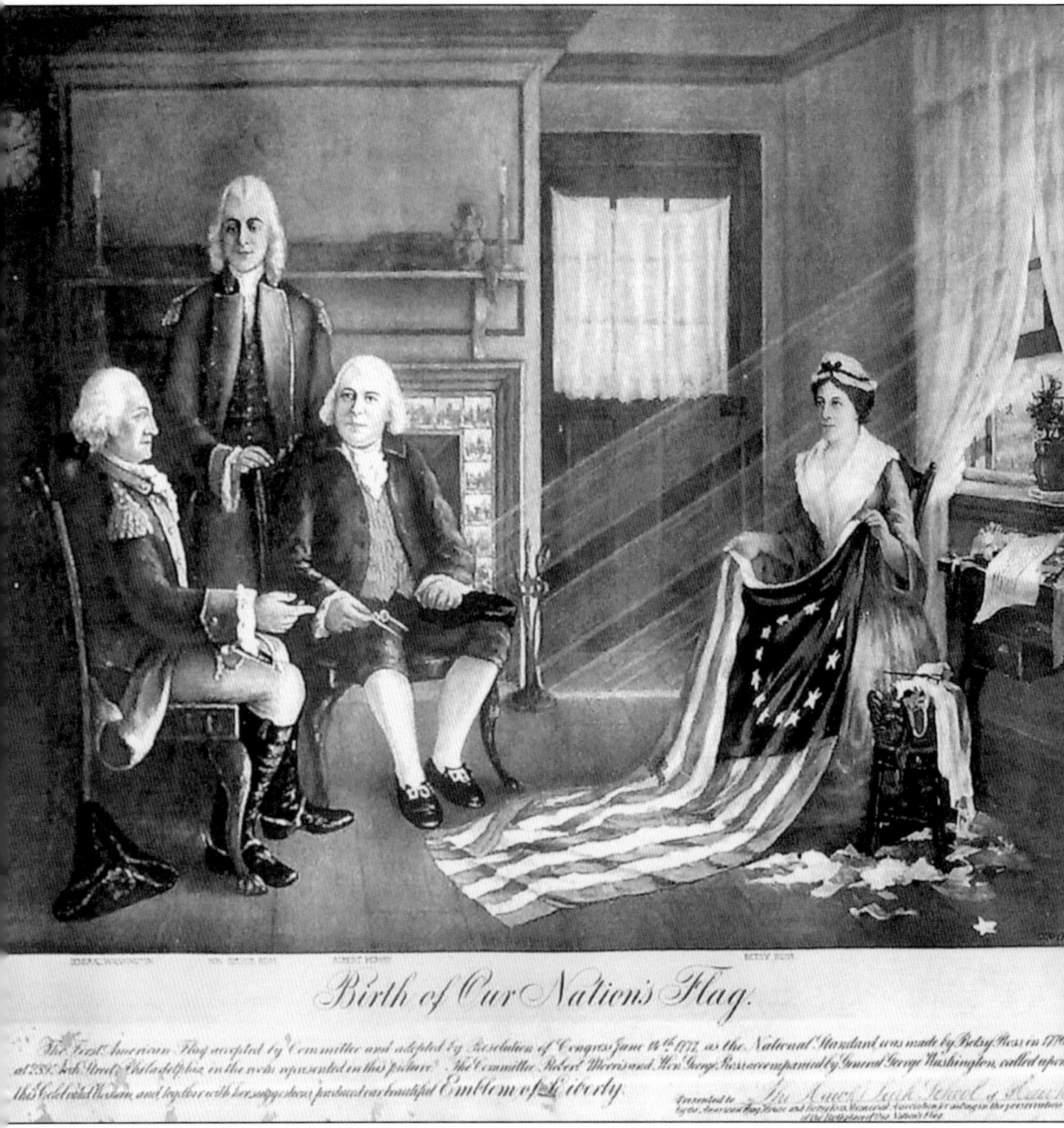

BETSY ROSS PICTURE, C. 1912. This print, which now hangs in the Edgewater Historical Museum, depicts Robert Morris and Hon. George Ross, accompanied by Gen. George Washington, visiting with Betsy Ross. The print is of a painting by artist C. H. Weisgerber, who developed the project to fund preservation of the house where Betsy Ross made the first American flag in 1776. Any child who sent 10¢ to the American Flag House received a small certificate of recognition. The print was probably presented to the Hawks Park school sometime between 1911 and 1917. The inscription reads, "Presented to The Hawks Park School of Hawks Park, Florida by the American Flag House and Betsy Ross Memorial Association for aiding in the preservation of the Birthplace of Our Nation's Flag." The new school was therefore named the Betsy Ross School.

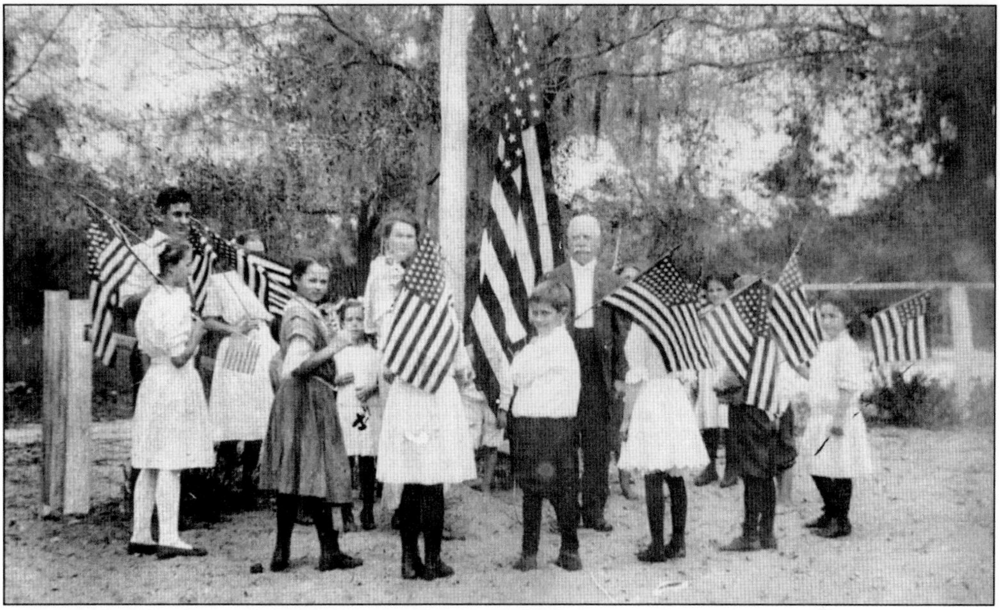

BETSY ROSS SCHOOL DEDICATION, 1912. The children are unidentified, the older man is W. S. Hart, and the man on left is probably Raymond Clifton, the teacher. Mr. Green from the Betsy Ross Memorial Association in Washington, D.C., presented flags to each of the children and one for the school. The school was completed in 1912, and 30 students participated in its dedication ceremony. The school proudly displayed the flag on a new flagpole.

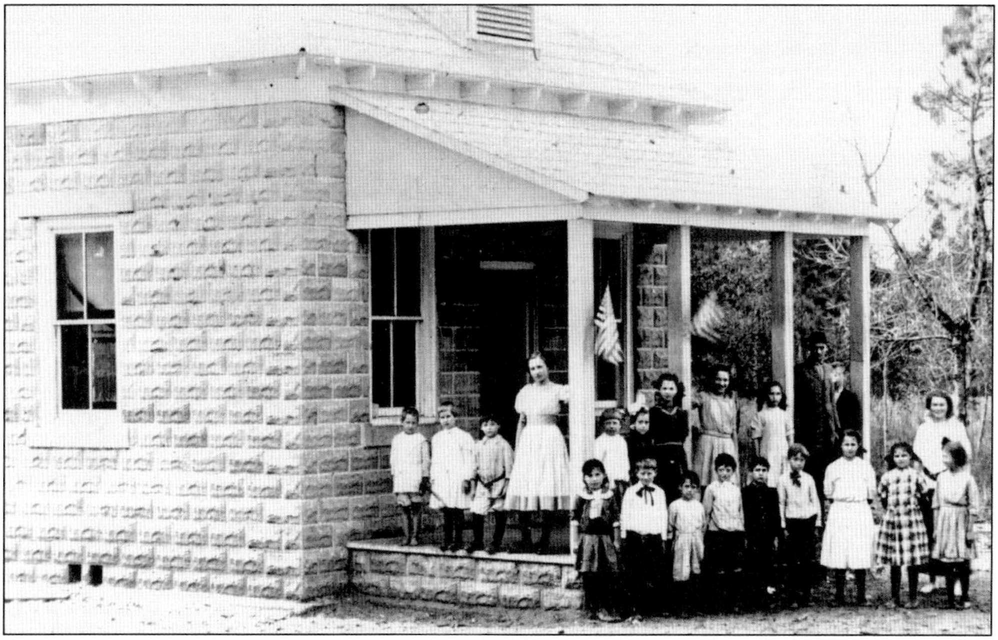

BETSY ROSS SCHOOL, C. 1912. Constructed on the same site as the wooden schoolhouse, this school would be the same dimensions, 20 by 30 feet. This time, however, it was built of hand-molded blocks of river shell and cement. The blocks were solid, and six inches thick—no one wanted this schoolhouse to burn down! The people are unidentified, but Raymond Clifton may be the man on the right side of the porch.

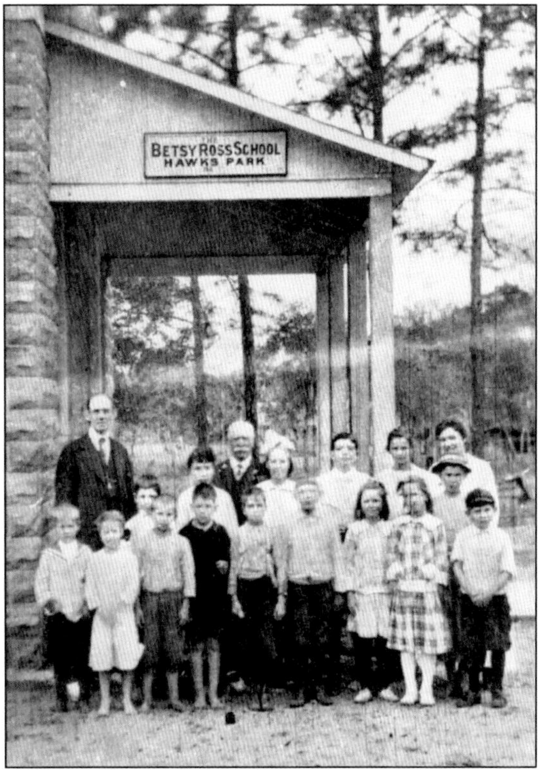

BETSY ROSS SCHOOL, 1912. Children sometimes attended school in bare feet. The thick, stiff brogans worn by the men and boys had to be worn a long time before they no longer constantly hurt the feet. W. S. Hart is pictured here, but the others are not identified.

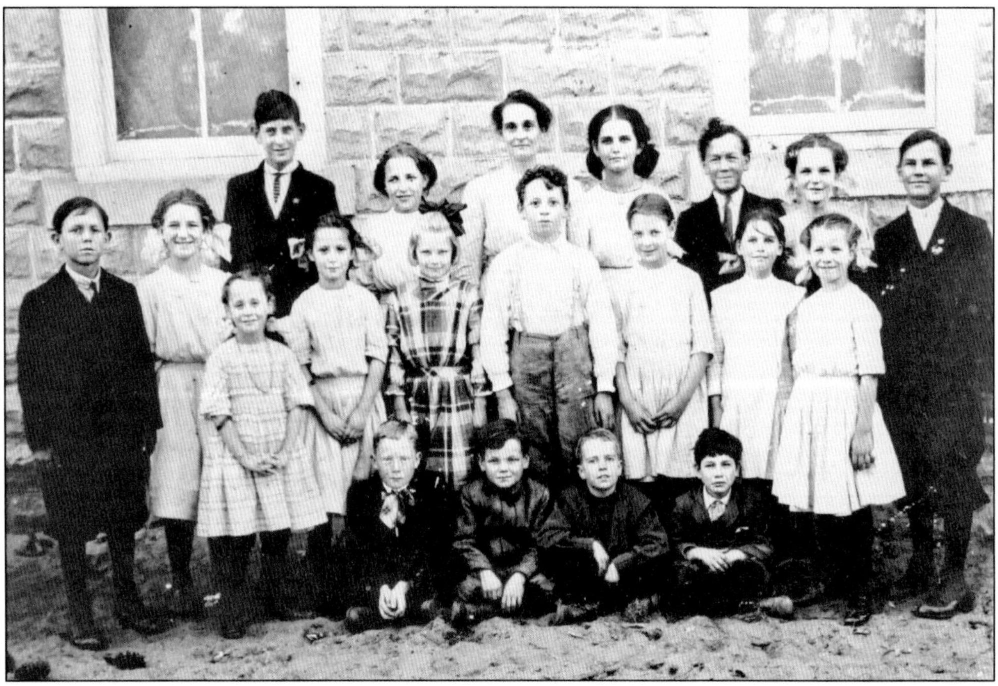

BETSY ROSS SCHOOL, C. 1915. The Betsy Ross School was only used for five years before a decision was made to bus the Hawks Park students to a larger New Smyrna school. The children here are unidentified.

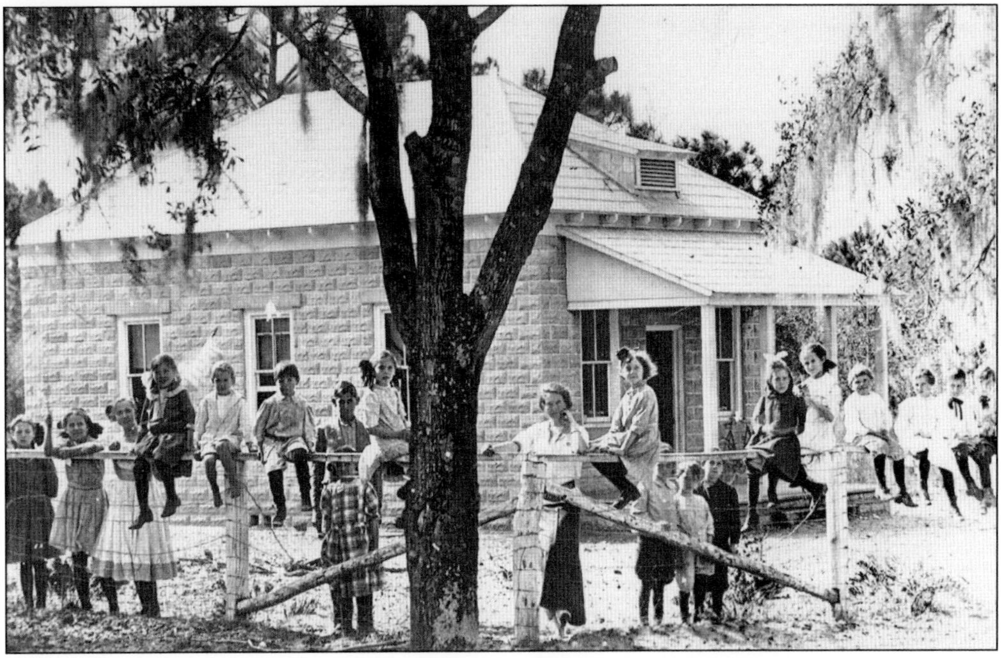

BETSY ROSS SCHOOL, C. 1912. In 1917, this school closed and students were taken to the Faulkner Street School in New Smyrna, just a few miles north. The roof of this school still can be seen in Edgewater today as part of the American Hardware store, on U.S. 1 and Park Avenue. The people are unidentified.

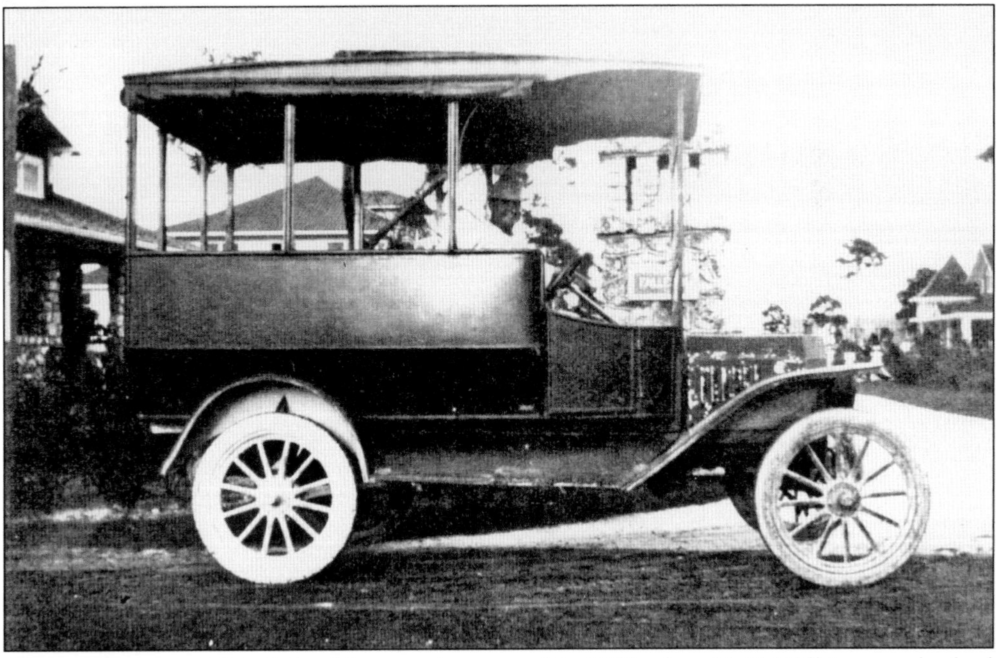

SCHOOL BUS, C. 1920. School bus service started in 1920 when H. P. Wilkinson, who had bicycled to New Smyrna to attend sixth grade, became the first bus driver. His bus was a converted Model T truck, and the students sat along the sides and in the back. He supplied the truck and gas and was paid $60 a month for this work.

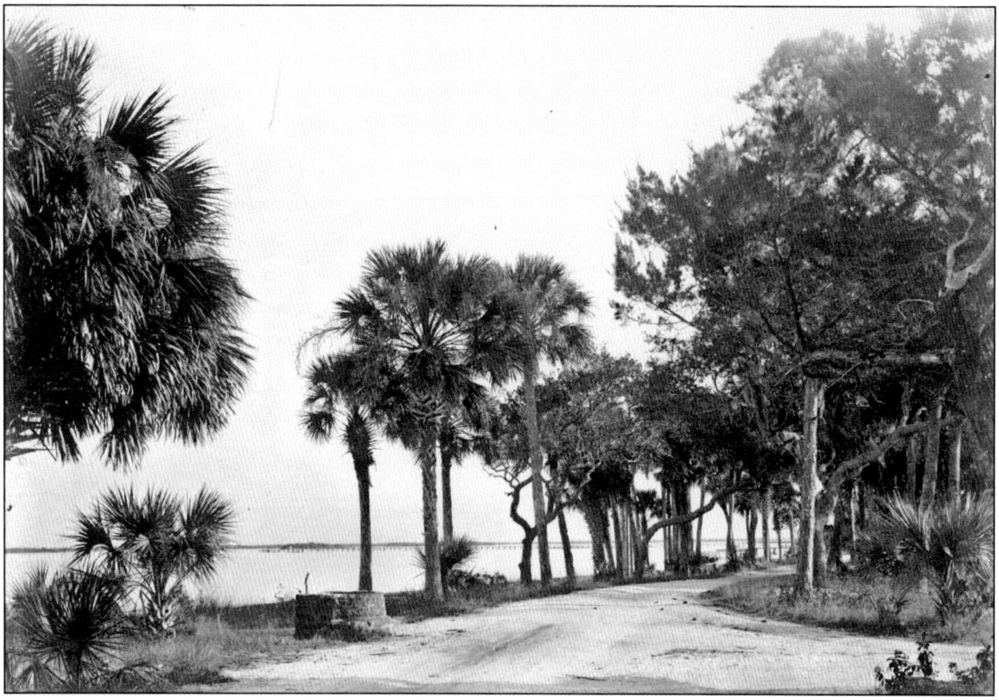

OLD FLOW WELL, 1910. Water was used from the well until the 1950s. It was then turned into a picturesque wishing well.

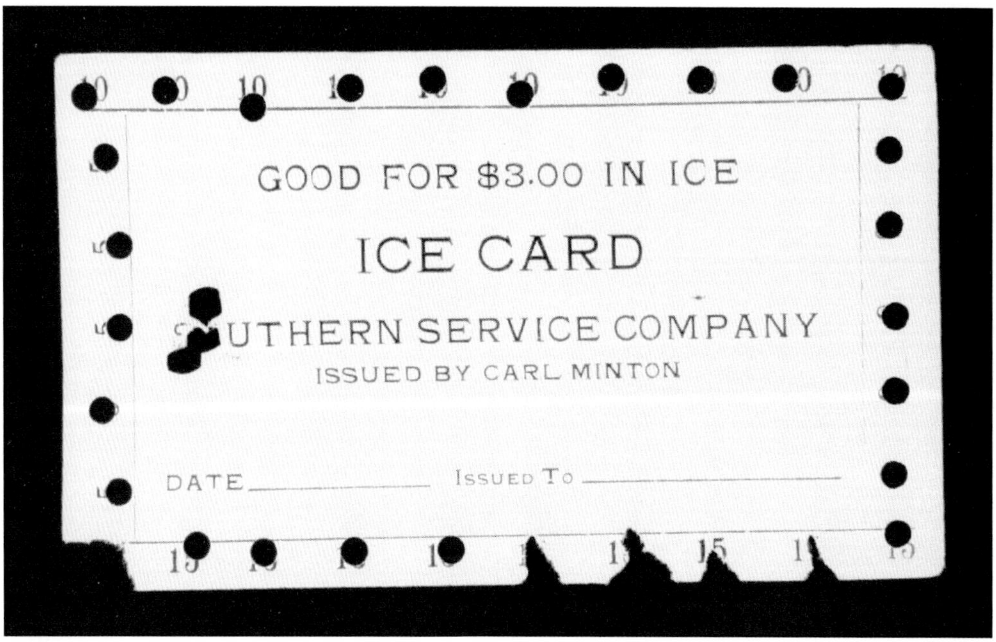

ICE CARD, C. 1912. Before electricity was available in the area after World War I, ice boxes were used to keep food cold, and an ice card was punched when delivery was made. Home delivery was available daily from the Southern Ice Plant, which was located near the railroad tracks in New Smyrna. The ice plant's main business was to furnish large chunks of ice for refrigerated railway cars.

Five

LOCATION HEALTHY

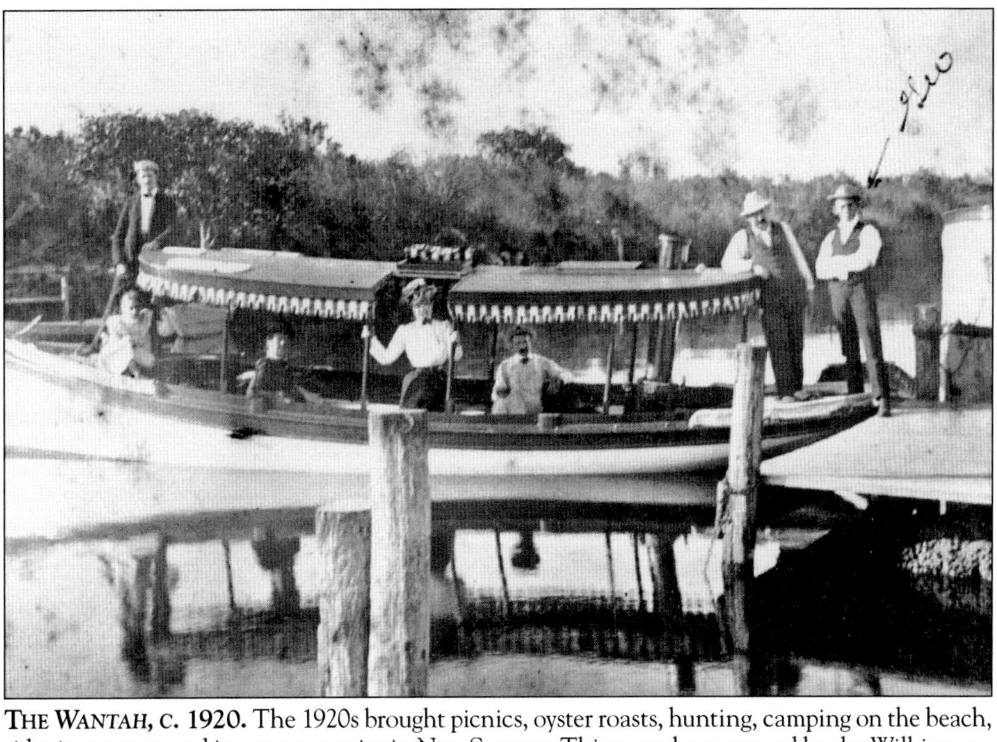

THE *WANTAH*, C. 1920. The 1920s brought picnics, oyster roasts, hunting, camping on the beach, rides in a surrey, and ice cream parties in New Smyrna. This party boat, owned by the Wilkinsons, would take you anywhere you "wantah" go. Automobile and boat trips were made to Daytona and Miami. George Wilkinson is on the far right, and the others are unidentified.

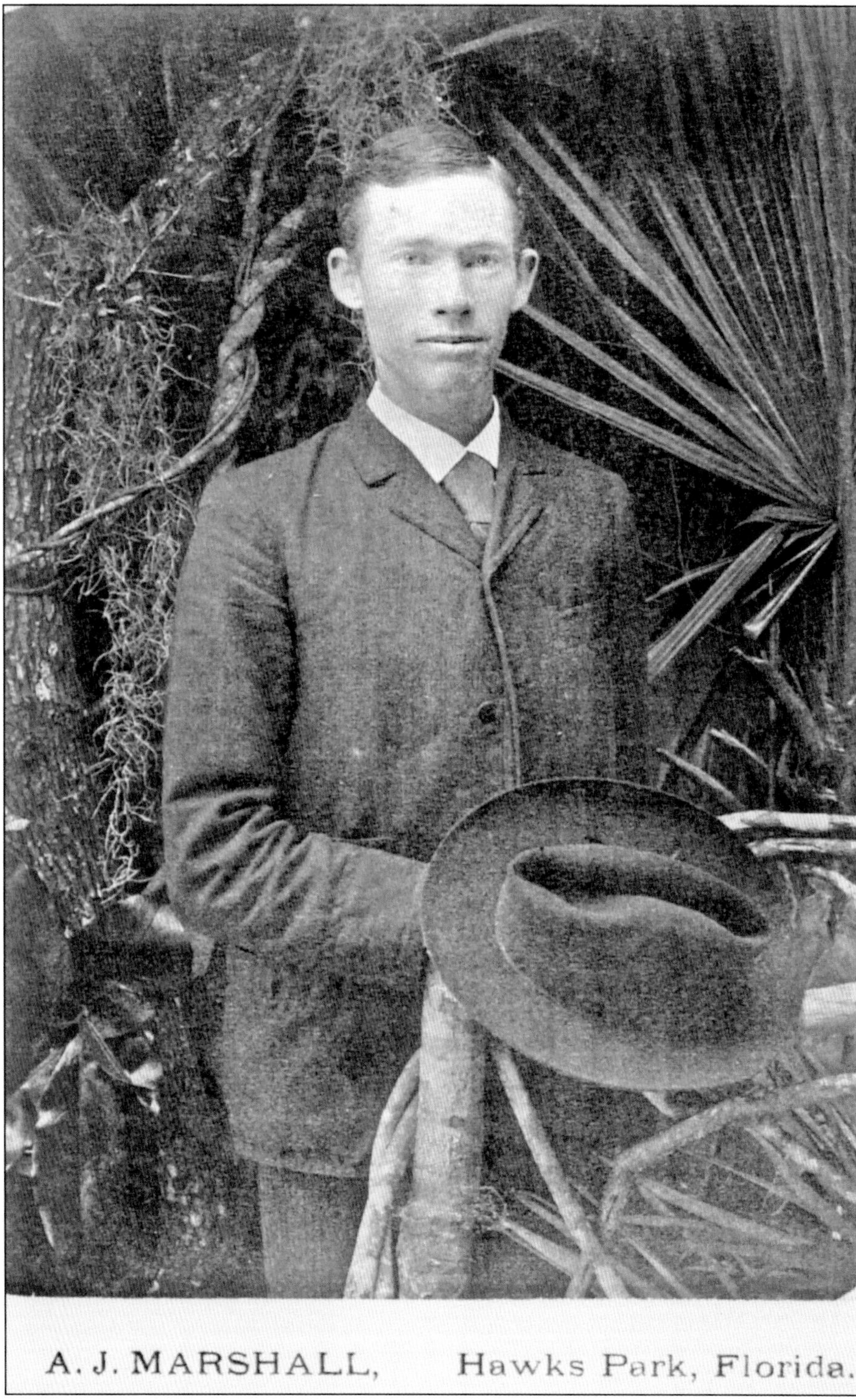

A VISITOR TO HAWKS PARK, C. 1900. Early visitors loved to have their formal photographs taken by A. J. Marshall or one of the other Hawks Park photographers. The photos would then be made into postcards that would be sent back home. The man here is unidentified.

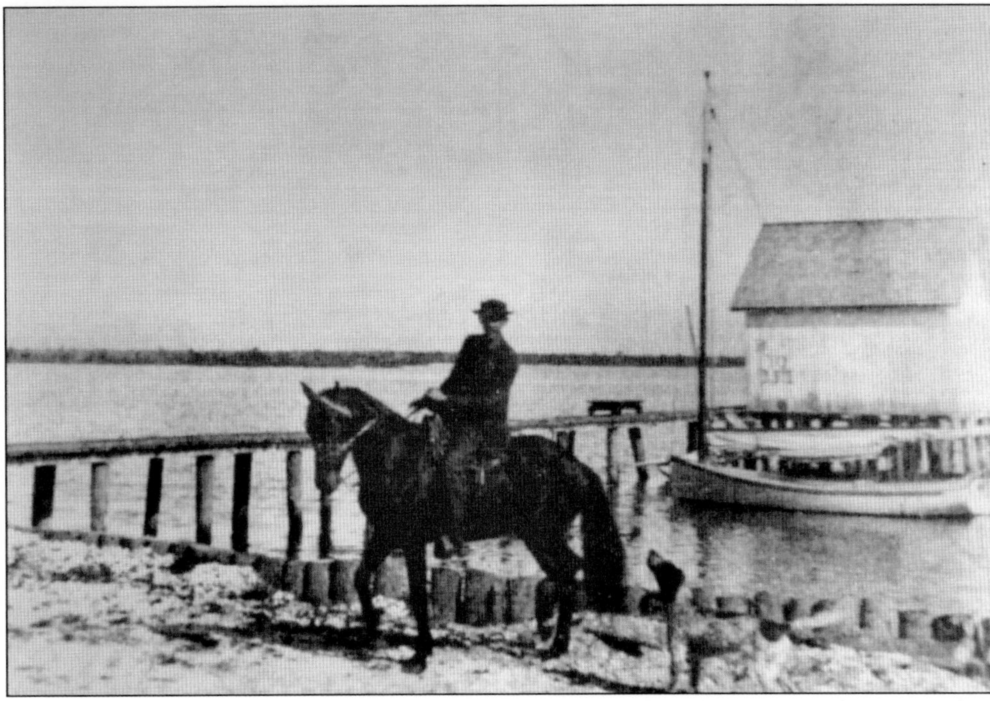

A. J. MARSHALL, PHOTOGRAPHER, C. 1900. A. J. Marshall set his camera then jumped on his horse to take his own photo. The horse shifted his weight to allow for the sudden motion on his back. This photo was later used in a mural depicting Hawks Park's history in one of Edgewater's parks.

CASH STORE!

A. J. MARSHALL,

Hawk's Park, Florida,

DEALER IN

GENERAL MERCHANDISE.

AGENTS FOR Maynard & Noyes' Inks: Harwood's Chair Bottoms; Parker & Wood's (Boston) Garden and Flower Seeds; Dr. Lougee's Vitalizing Compound, the Great Blood Purifier; Pinkham's Sachet Powders; Gilman Bros.' Arnold's Balsam.

AD FOR CASH STORE, C. 1887. The Marshall family had come from Bradford, New Hampshire, and started the "cash only" store. In letters written to the Marshalls, Hawks said to "Bring blankets, nearly as many as you use up North, also barrels of potatoes, onions, beets, turnips, oatmeal (if you like it), carpenter's tools, and nails. Anything like this will sell in your store."

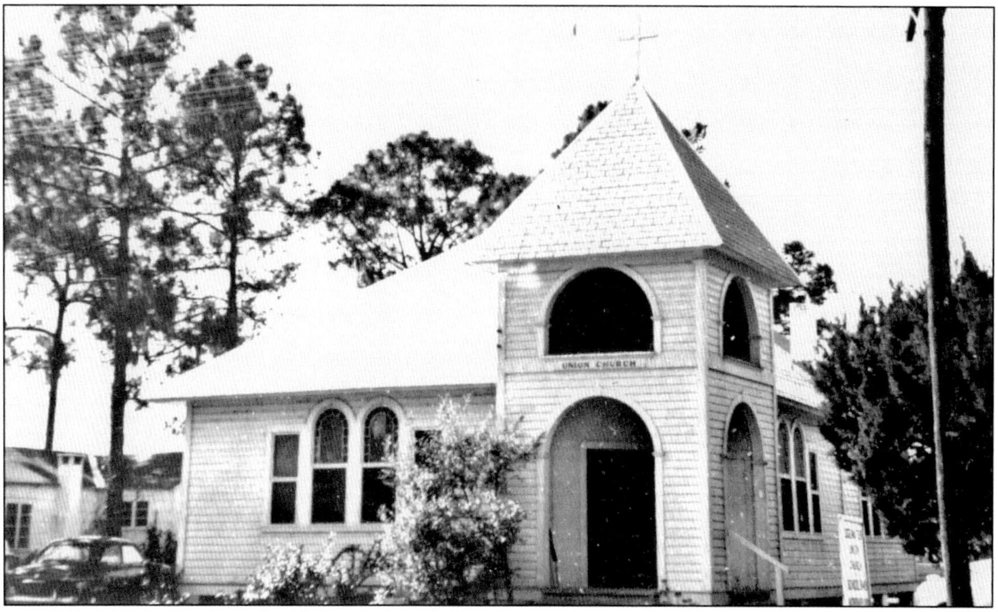

UNION CHURCH, C. 1940. Finished in 1912, the church had no electricity, no plumbing, no wire screens, and a tin roof. Unfortunately, when it rained on the tin roof, the parishioners couldn't hear the sermon! The bell became very important to the community. Single tolls called the people to worship. When it tolled over and over, folks dropped what they were doing to run to the fire or other emergency. It rang to warn of a freeze and sometimes to announce that ice cream was being delivered!

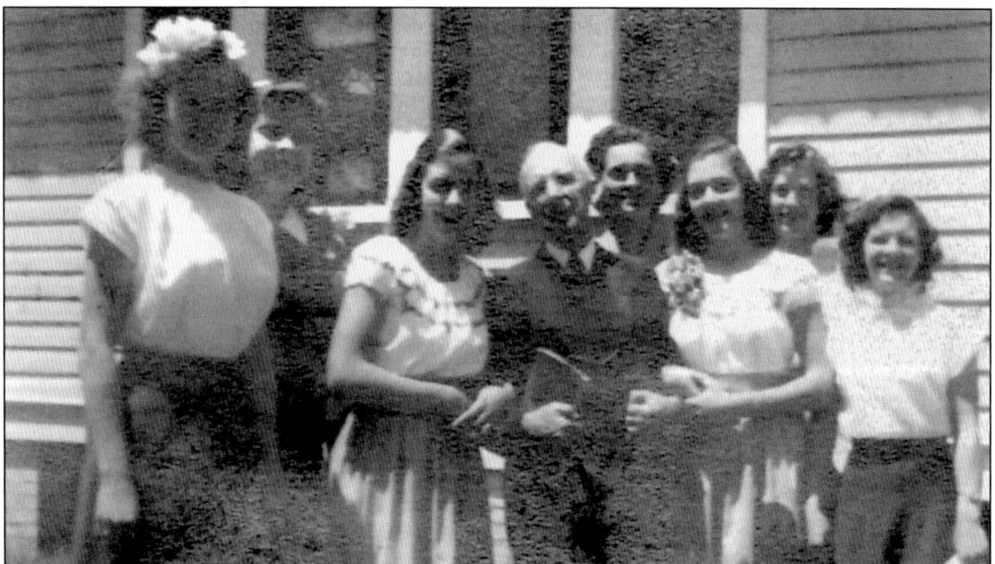

UNION CHURCH WITH MINISTER, C. 1946. Church services in early Hawks Park were held in people's homes, and later, services were held on Sunday afternoons in the wooden schoolhouse. Mrs. Fuller wrote, "We heard ALL flavors of doctrines preached. Baptist, Methodist . . . and even a priest or two, as ministers came from just about anywhere." In this photograph, from left to right, are Karlene Eckhardt, Barbara Elderton, Judy Mattison, Rev. William Richards, Helen Sweeney, Jean Mattison, Mary Ann Miller, and Barbara White.

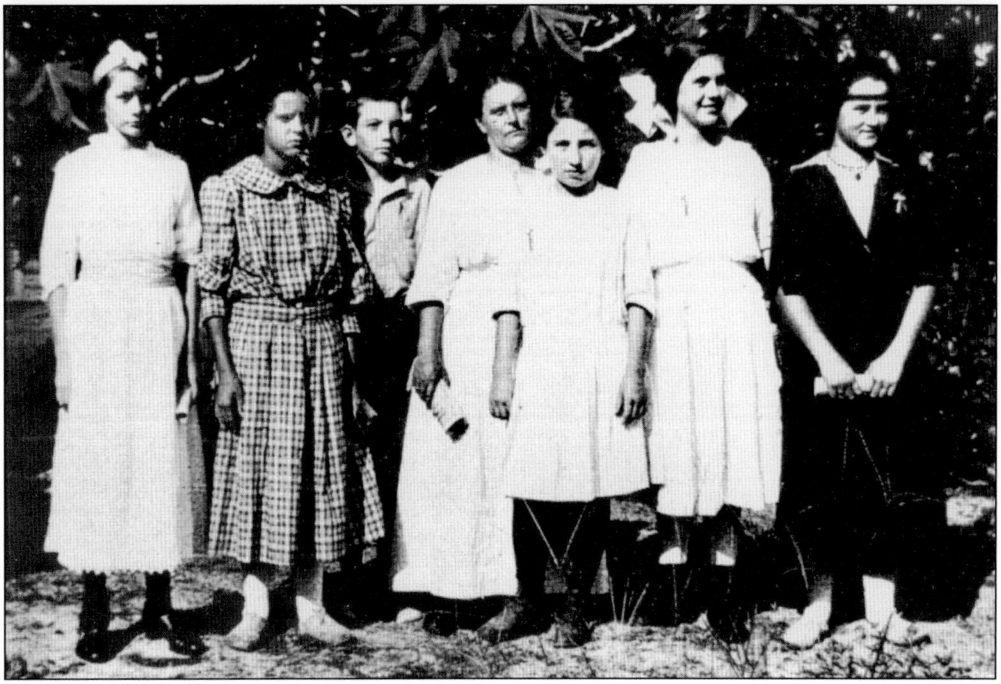

SUNDAY SCHOOL CLASS, 1917. Mrs. E. P. Fuller and her mother-in-law, Mrs. E. Fuller, organized a Sunday school. The story is told that the two ladies went out to the islands in the river to invite the children of moonshiners to church. When the ladies realized that the children needed clothing to wear to Sunday school, they started making clothes for them. The people are unidentified.

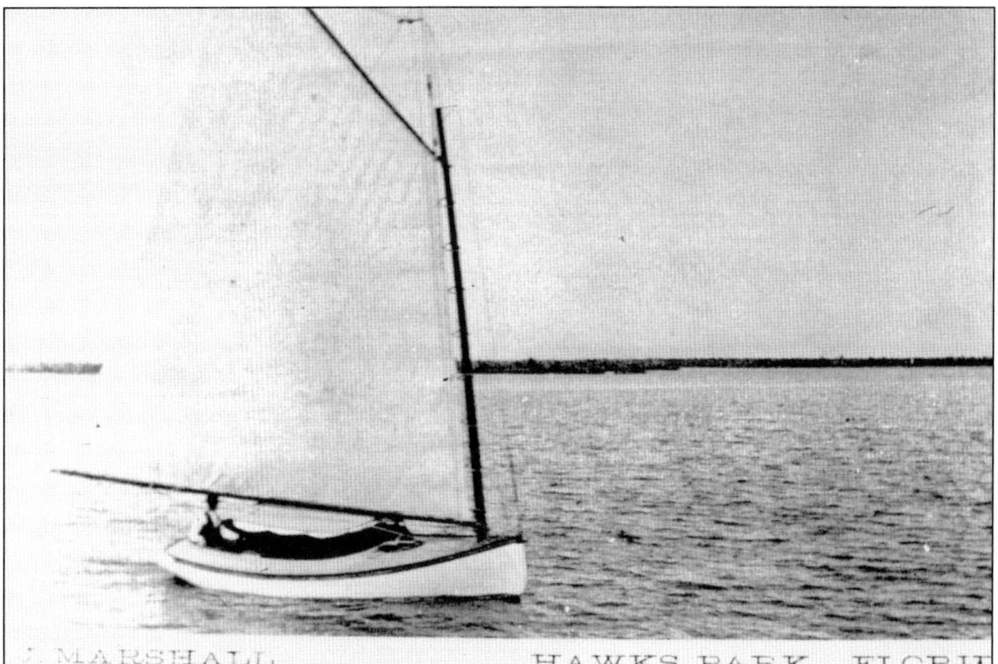

THE NAUTILUS, C. 1890. *The Nautilus* was a one-mast schooner owned by the Marshall family and was a typical small boat of the day.

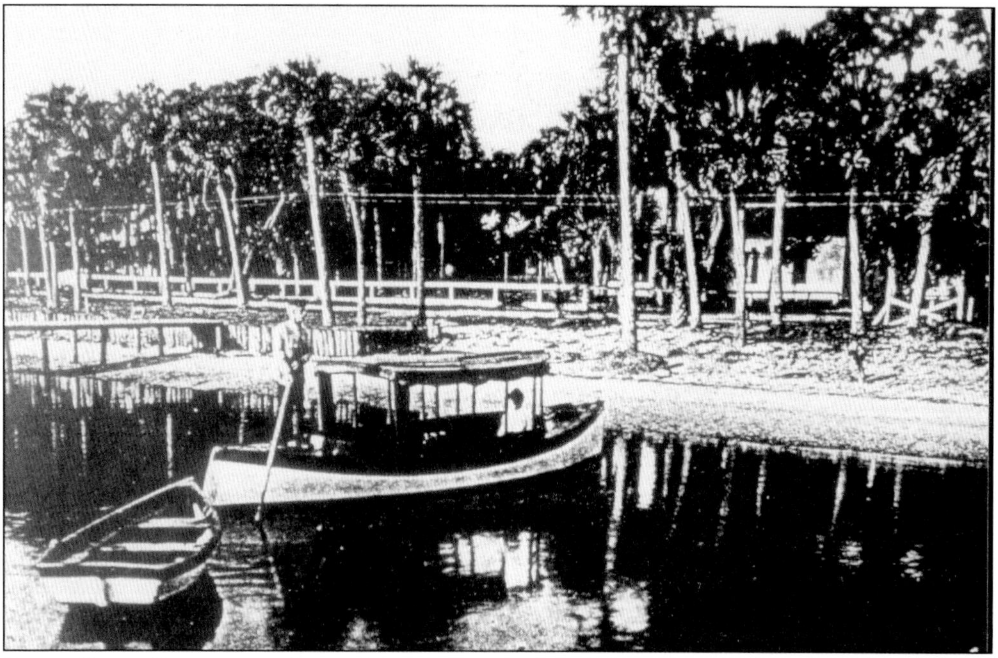

PARTY BOAT OWNED BY HARRY MITCHELL, C. 1910. There was usually a boat available for parties or other purposes. The people here are unidentified. Ice cream would have tasted good on those hot days, but that was a treat and a rarity. Hawks Park residents would gather at the dock to take a boat to New Smyrna. They met at Ritzey's Store on Canal Street where they enjoyed their delightful treat.

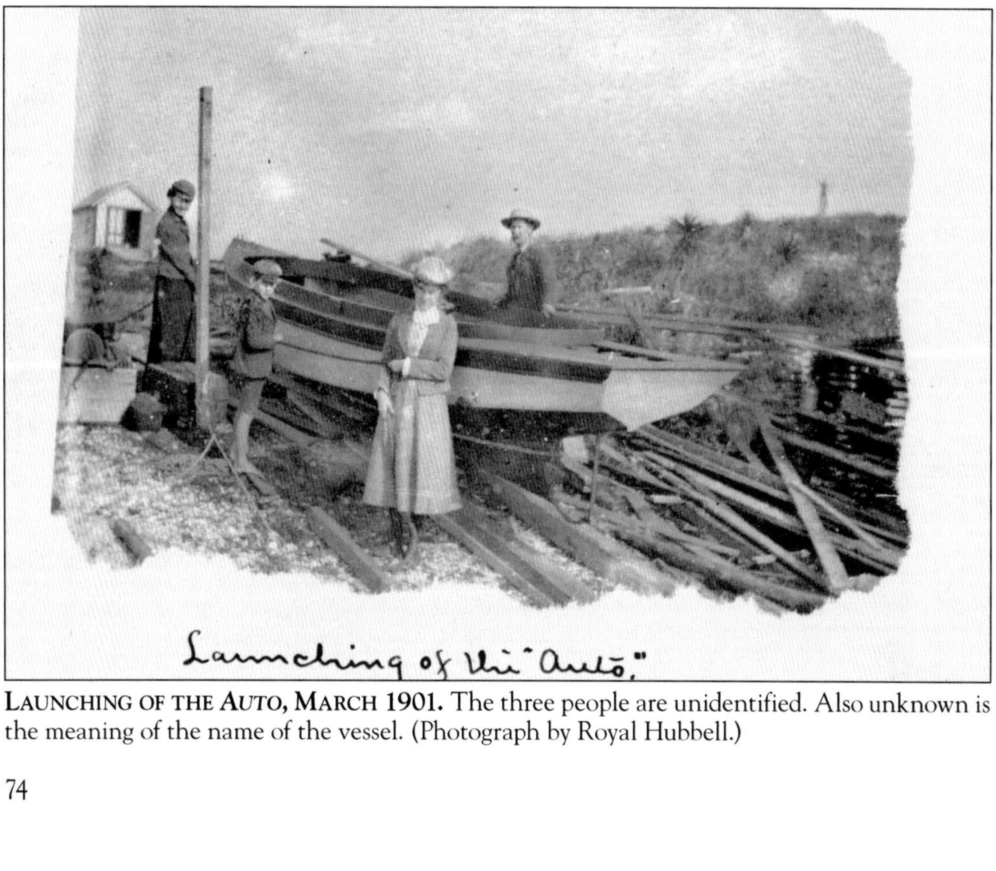

LAUNCHING OF THE *AUTO*, MARCH 1901. The three people are unidentified. Also unknown is the meaning of the name of the vessel. (Photograph by Royal Hubbell.)

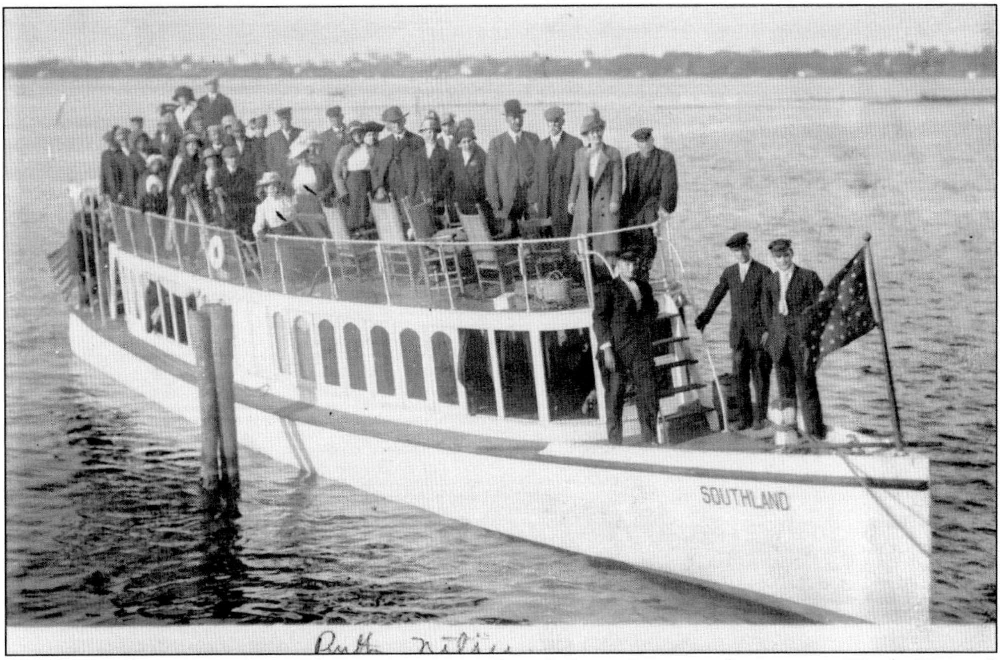

THE *SOUTHLAND*, c. 1920. This was a postcard, and the only names known are "Ruth, Nettie." "Ruth" might be Ruth Hubbell, to whom the postcard was addressed. "Nettie" sent the postcard. (Photograph by Royal Hubbell.)

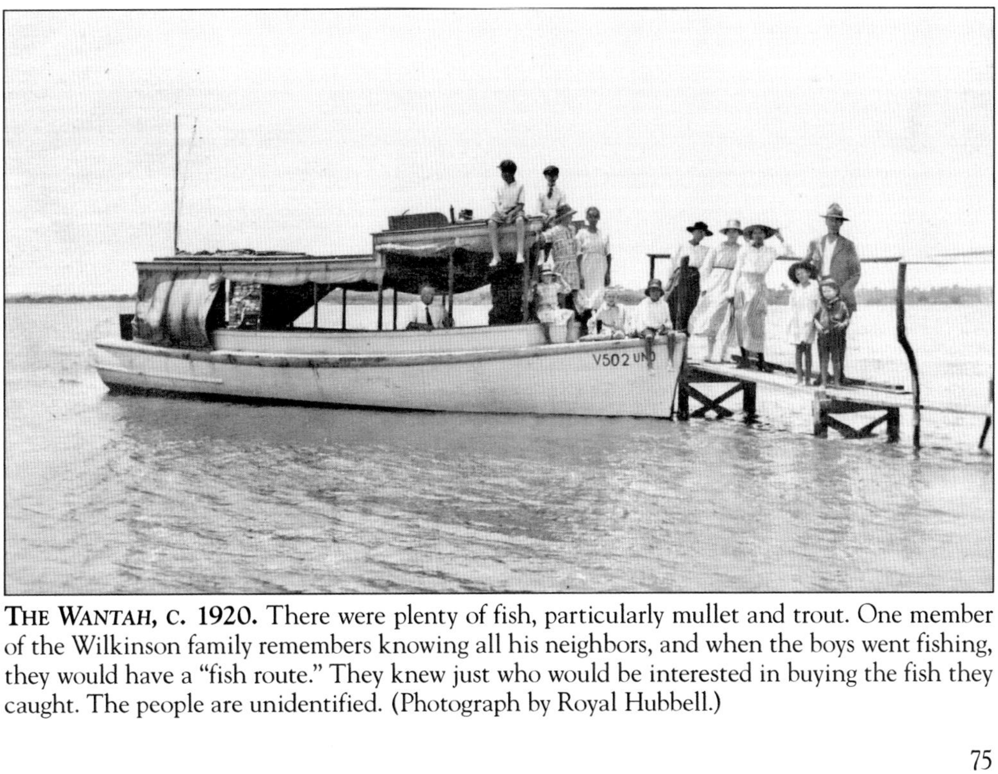

THE *WANTAH*, c. 1920. There were plenty of fish, particularly mullet and trout. One member of the Wilkinson family remembers knowing all his neighbors, and when the boys went fishing, they would have a "fish route." They knew just who would be interested in buying the fish they caught. The people are unidentified. (Photograph by Royal Hubbell.)

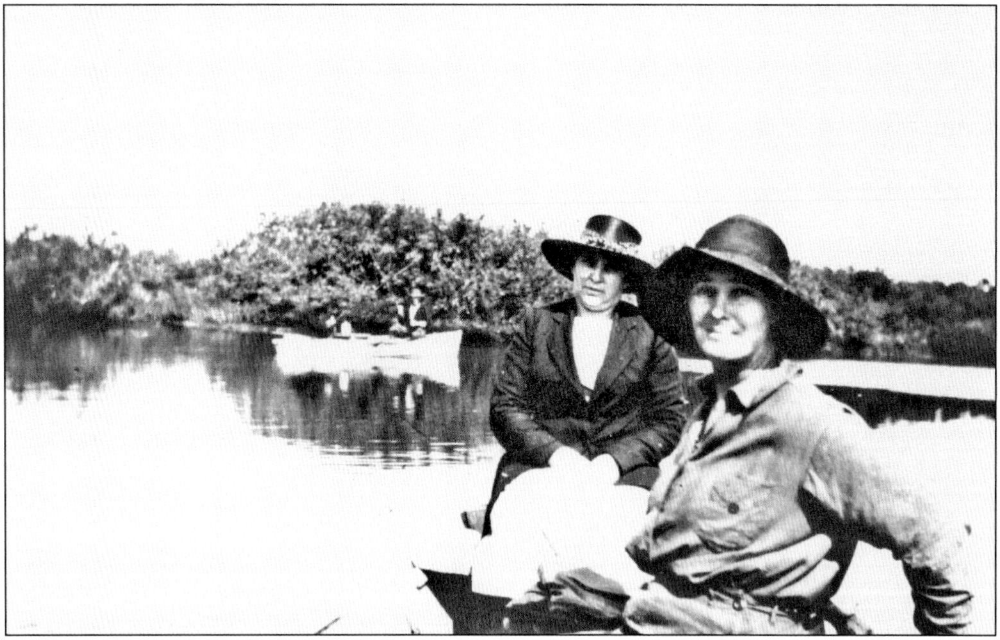

LUCY HAWK AND LOTTIE BITTINGER, C. 1915. Lucy Hawk was not related to John Milton Hawks. Lottie Bittinger and her husband came to Hawks Park in two separate automobiles all the way from Ohio. The back seats of the Bittinger car had been removed so they could transport their goats to Florida. The Bittinger family's home still stands on East Palm Way and has been remodeled through the years.

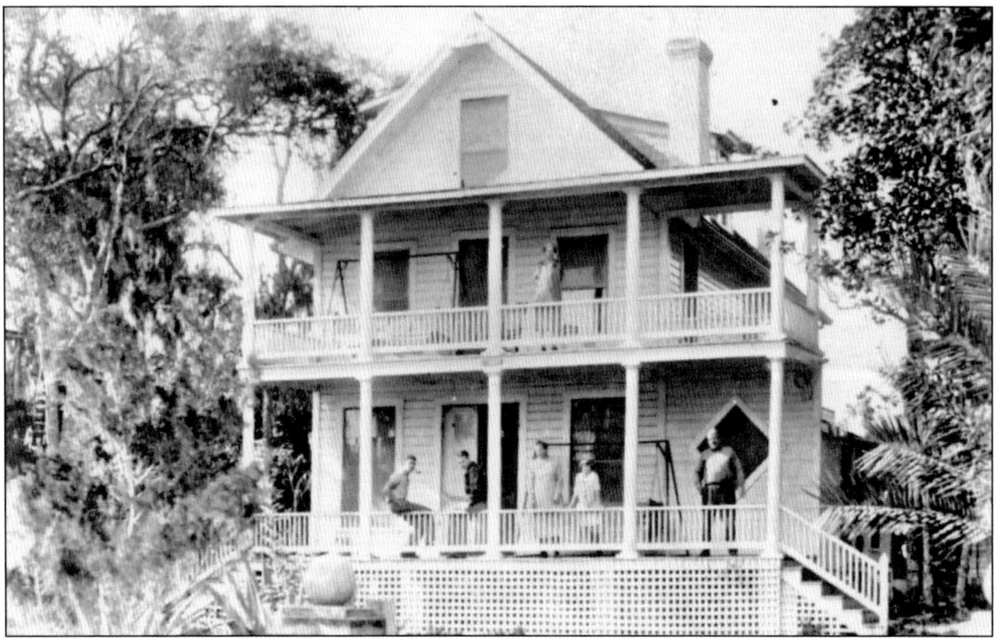

ARTHUR MORSE RESIDENCE, C. 1920. The owners of this home rented out rooms. A photographer, possibly F. W. Hill, rented the room with the diamond-shaped window. One of the rooms was rented for use as a finishing school, where some of the children were taught etiquette and manners. The people are unidentified.

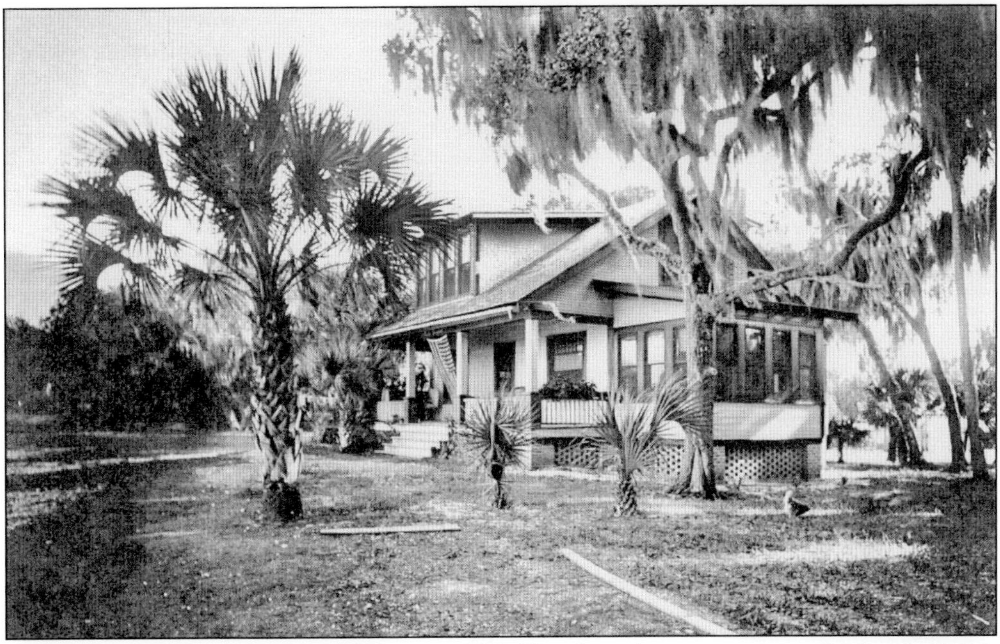

HARRY AND ROSE HAMILTON HOME, C. 1900. Hamilton Avenue was near the South Canal, the dividing line between New Smyrna and Hawks Park. This is the home of Harry and Rose Hamilton, on Hamilton Avenue, photographed by F. C. van de Sande of New Smyrna. Harry Hamilton was a builder. Note the lattice between the house and the ground. No large animals would be able to get under this house.

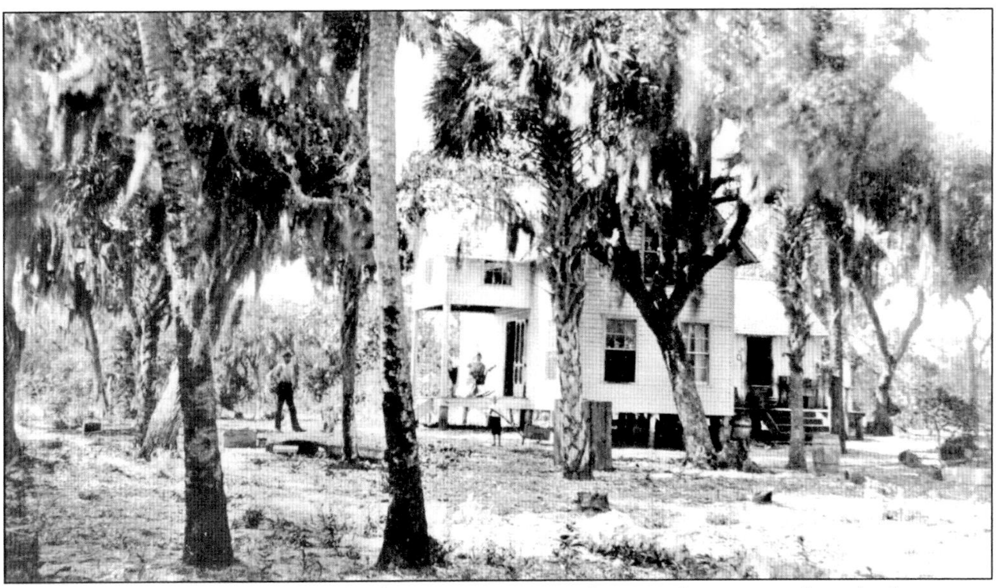

HAWKS PARK HOME, C. 1900. This home, too, seems to have no fence around it, which was rare in early Hawks Park days. The people are unidentified.

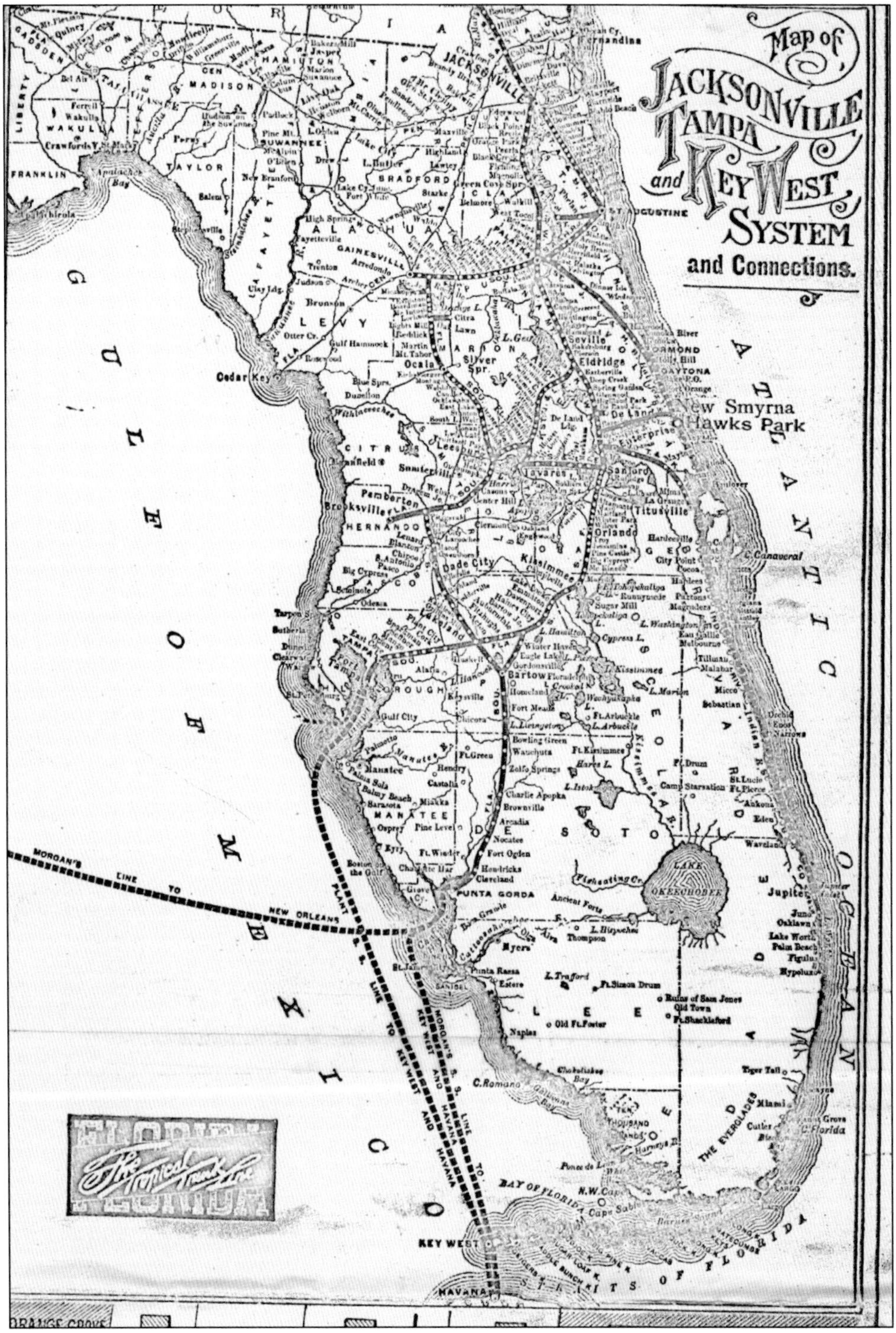

Map of Railroad Showing Hawks Park, c. 1890. Another of Dr. John Milton Hawks's dreams came true when mail service came by train to his community. Because of increasing need for railroad service in southern Florida, Henry Flagler decided to extend his Florida East Coast Railway, reaching Key West in 1912.

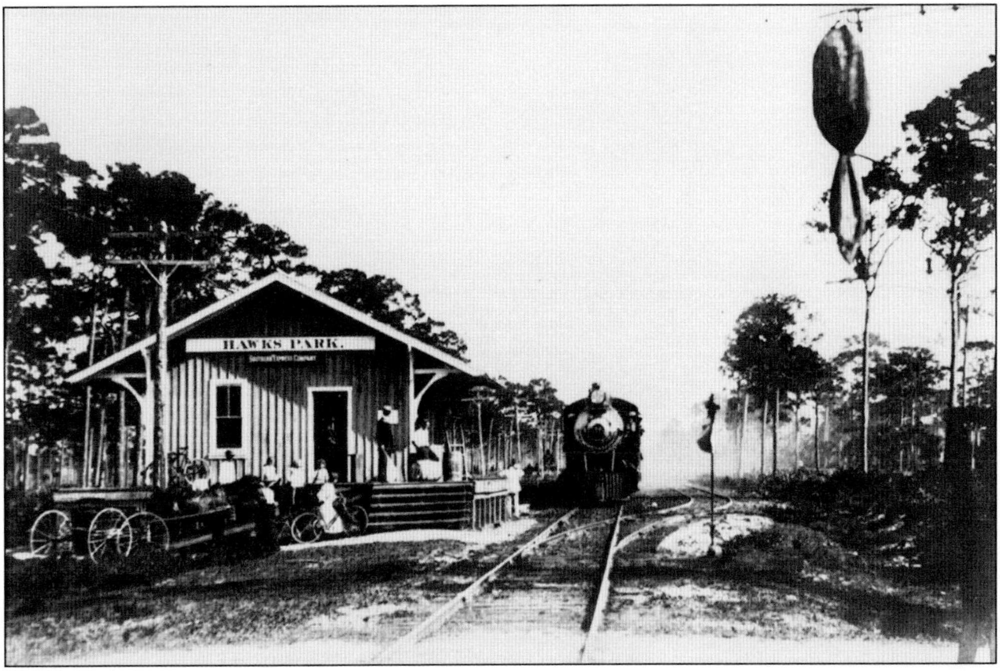

HAWKS PARK RAILROAD STATION, C. 1906. The railroad depot at Hawks Park was located on West Park Avenue, actually on the southeast side of the tracks. A mail arm would hold a sack of mail, which could be picked up as the train slowed down at the station. One of the Wilkinson boys remembers using a white handkerchief to flag down the train for a ride to New Smyrna. It worked! The people are unidentified. (Transposed photograph by Royal Hubbell.)

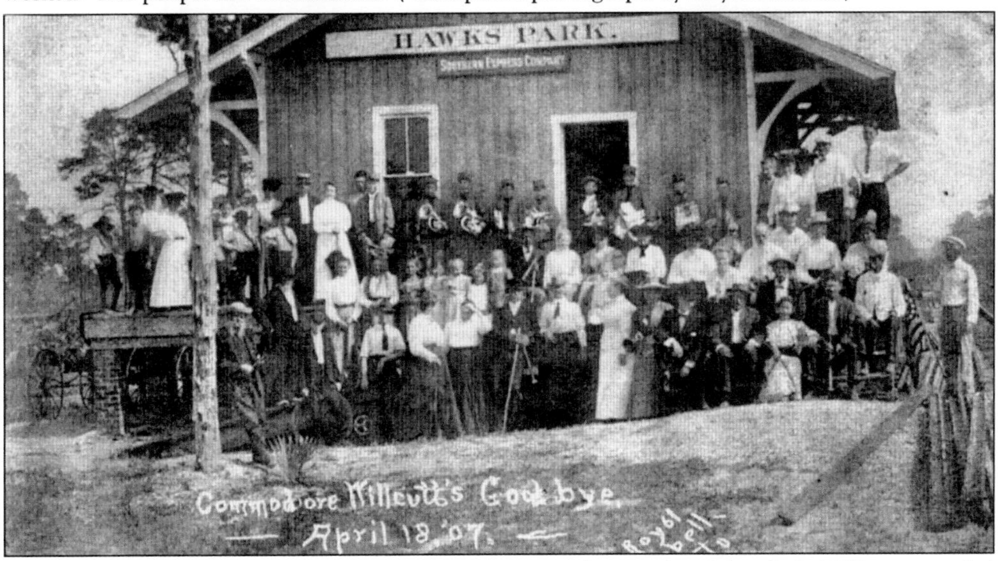

COMMODORE WILLCUTT'S GOOD-BYE, 1907. A postcard scene dated April 18, 1907, was entitled "Commodore Willcutt's Good-bye." Over 60 people pictured were bidding goodbye to a good friend. The people are unidentified, but some of the band members in uniform are part of the Boys Band of Faulkner Street School. The railroad helped the town grow, but by 1989, the city council discussed a ban on blowing the train whistles in the middle of the night as they went through Edgewater.

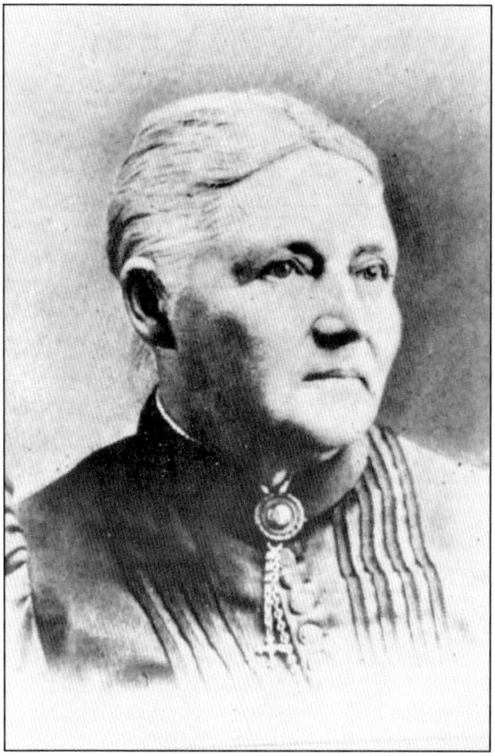

ESTHER HILL HAWKS, C. 1900. Esther Hill Hawks's death on May 6, 1906, would mark the end of a 52-year marriage with her devoted husband. She lived until 72 years of age and was childless. She had worked with her husband during the Civil War and had lived with him in Port Orange during the time Hawks tried to create a haven for freedmen there. She then went north to create her own very successful career as woman medical doctor, teacher, and community leader in Lynn, Massachusetts.

ESTHER HILL HAWKS'S GRAVE, 2004. Since she died in the North, Esther was buried in Manchester, New Hampshire, and not beside her husband in Hawks Park Cemetery. Humanitarian to the end, she left $1,000 to build a Hawks Park library and town hall, and money to many charities, for scholarships, and to endow an on-going prize for students who wrote the best essay on the subject of "peace." She chose the words to go on her gravestone: "On the proper training of the children, rests the hope of the world."

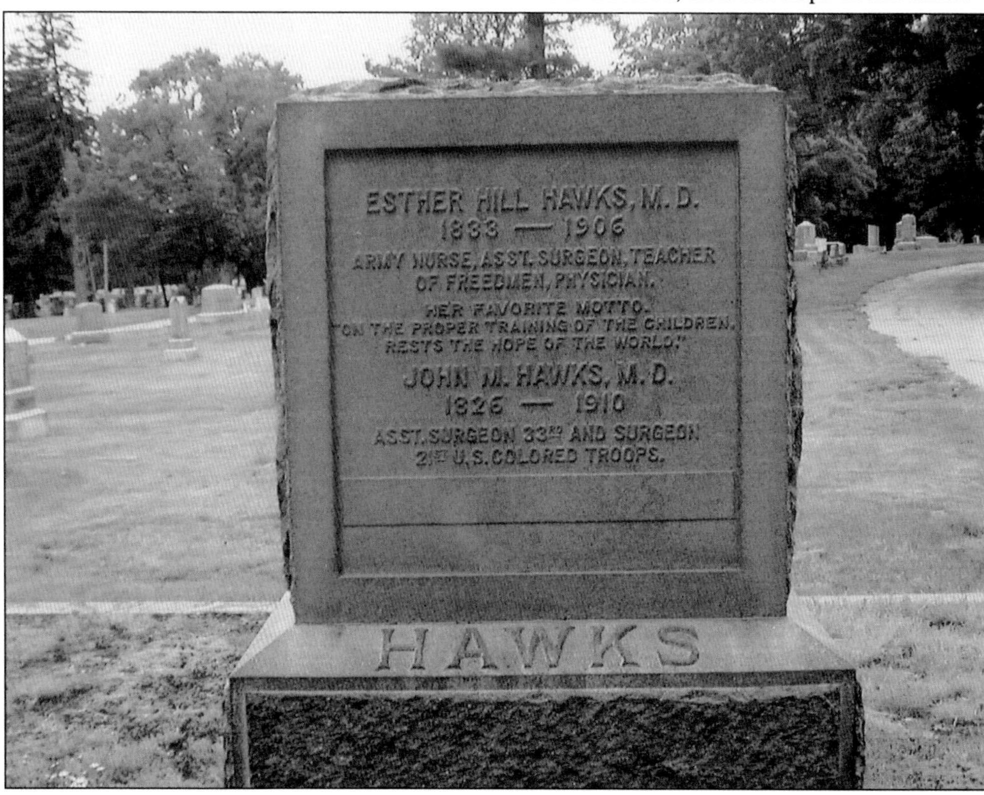

JOHN MILTON HAWKS, C. 1900. At 84 years of age, knowing he was dying, Dr. John Milton Hawks calmly gathered his friends and advisors to his bedside to ensure that his beloved community would go on. He left land ("just west of the alligator pond") on which to build the new library and town hall. He died peacefully on April 2, 1910, and was buried in Hawks Park's cemetery. That same day, Mary Jane Marshall wrote to her children, "You will be shocked to learn that Dr. Hawks has left us."

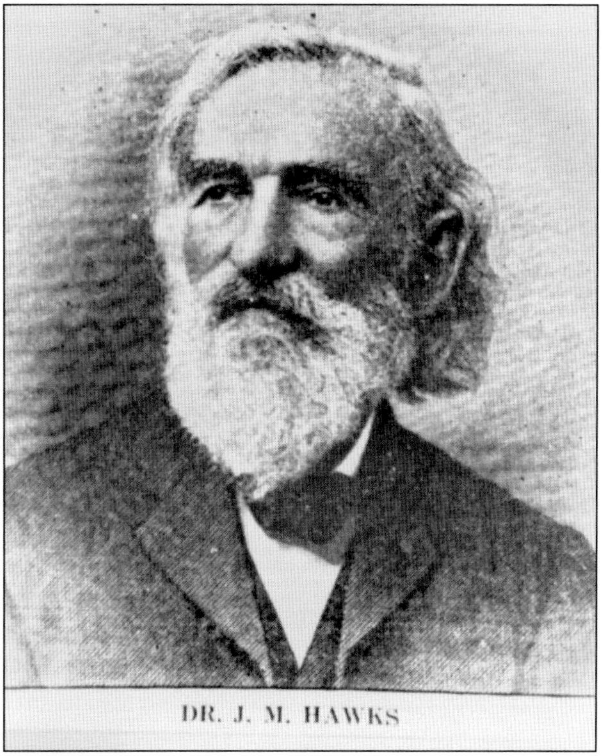

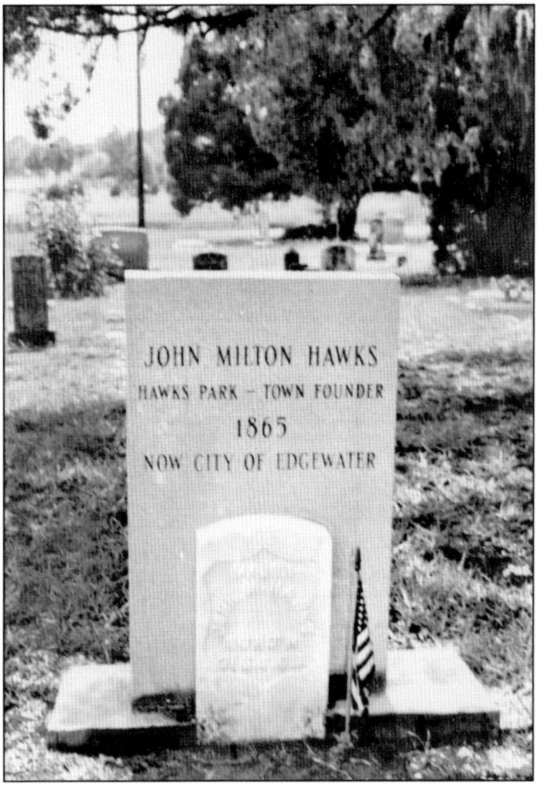

JOHN MILTON HAWKS'S GRAVE, 1990. The old stone marker very simply refers to Dr. Hawks's service to the African American troops during the Civil War. The larger marker, which noted Hawks as the town's founder, was dedicated in 1990. An additional memorial plaque, given by the American Legion, Post 285, now stands in front of the Edgewater Public Library. It states, "Dr. John M. Hawks, His wife, Dr. Esther H. Hawks, Our friends pass from our sight, but we need not say farewell, for our time and the years to follow, their invisible hands will continue to shower blessings upon the people of this community through the inspiration, companionship and solace of books."

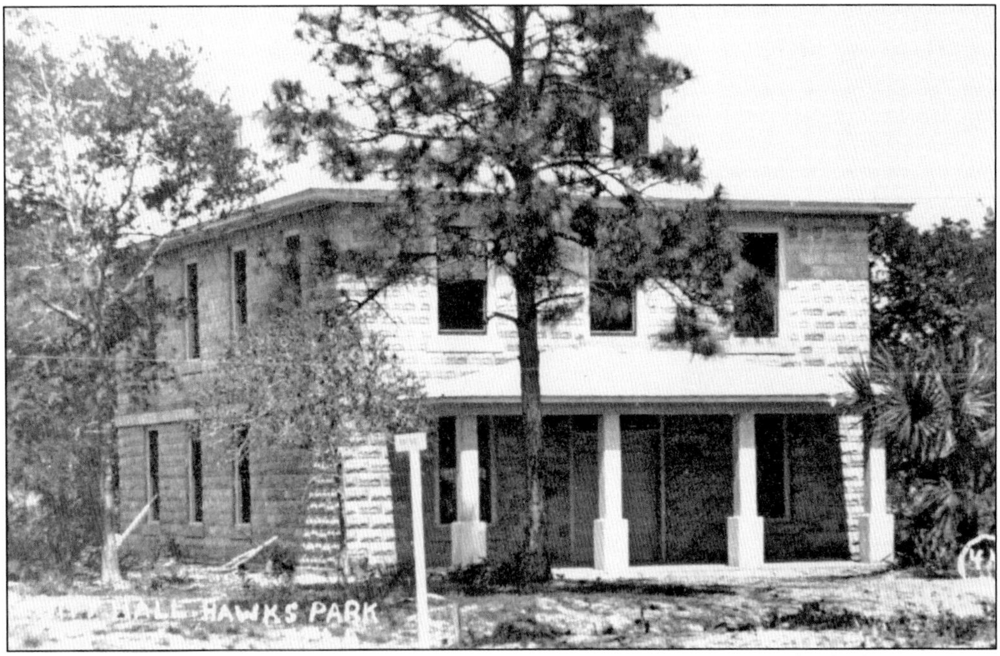

VIA Two-Story Building, 1914. The Village Improvement Association built the new town hall and library in 1914 with the money and land left by Dr. John Milton Hawks and Dr. Esther Hill Hawks. The ground floor would be a town hall and library; the upper floor had a stage, kitchen, and community room for town functions. There was a wooden floor for dancing, and the young boys dreaded taking dancing lessons. Christmas plays were presented and suppers were held outside on a large porch.

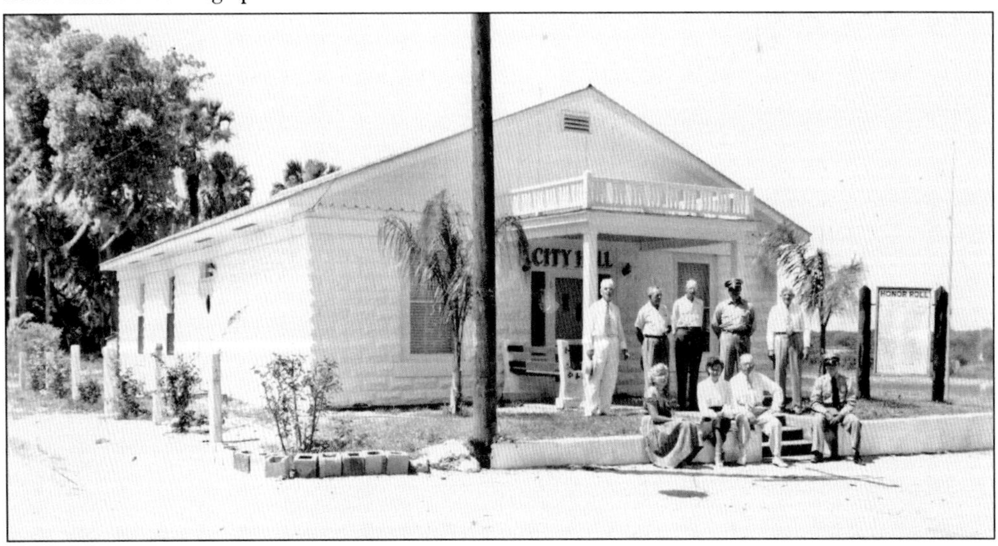

VIA One-Story Building, c. 1960. When a city hall and community center was built in the late 1950s, the top floor of the old VIA building was removed, and it housed the city hall for a short time and then the library. The newer city hall building overlooked a pier being built at the riverside city park, and that park would be enlarged in 1933 with fill from the dredging in the river. The third person from the left in the back row is H. L. Haughton, Hazel Wilkinson's father. The others are unidentified.

Six

PRICES REASONABLE

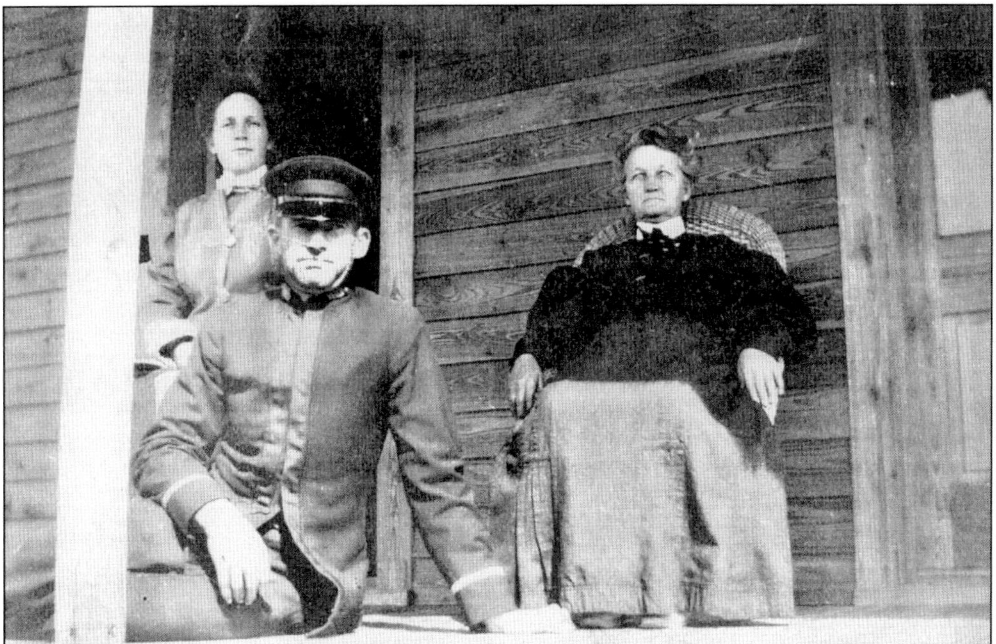

LT. JOHN J. WILKINSON IN WORLD WAR I, C. 1916. Pictured are Lieutenant Wilkinson with his wife, Helen, and her mother. It was a new century, and Hawks Park was about to get a new name and a new government. Some thought Hawks Park sounded too much like "Hog's Park," so in 1924, the name was changed to Edgewater.

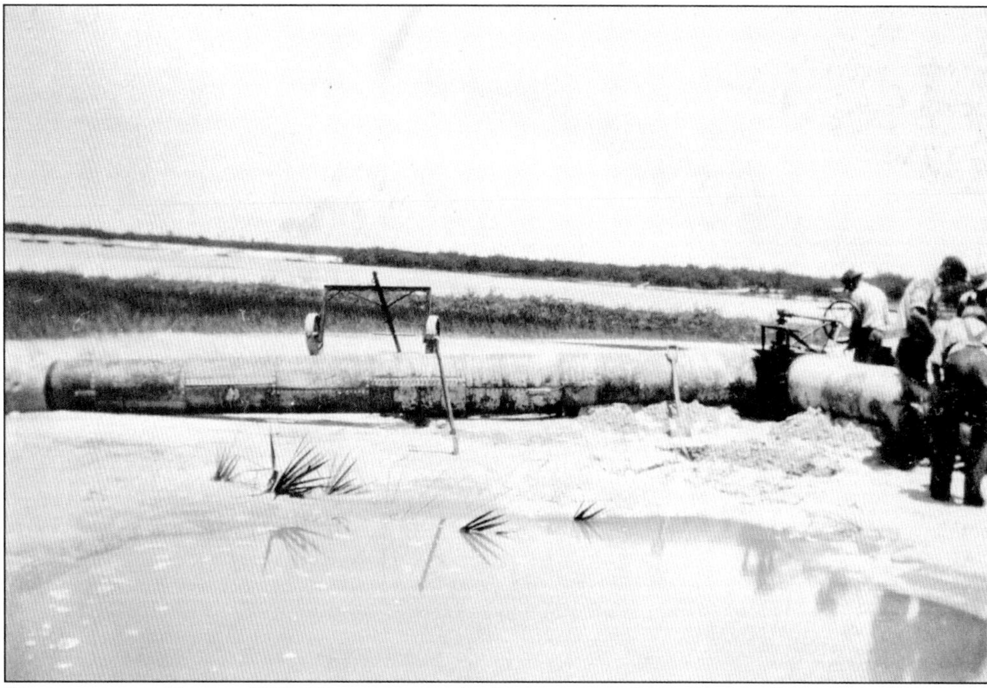

DREDGING THE RIVER, 1933. The river was dredged to create deeper water closer to the Edgewater shore. The dredging material changed the shape of the riverfront, expanding the park near the city hall and library and filling in many mangrove islands. The boys at the time would watch what came out of the dredging pipes. One could find a large shell or lots of interesting things coming from the river bottom. The people are unidentified.

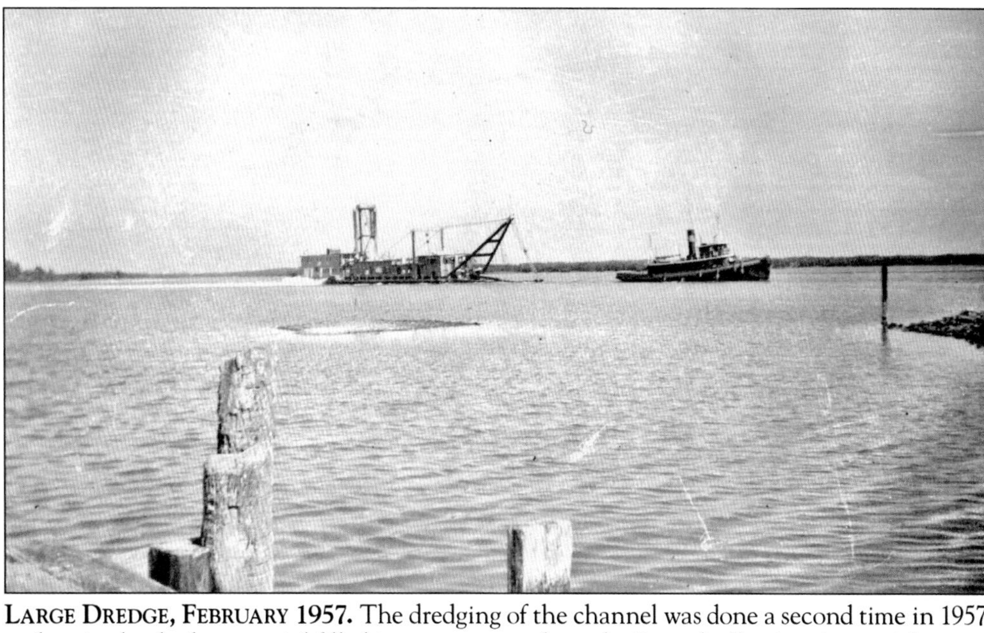

LARGE DREDGE, FEBRUARY 1957. The dredging of the channel was done a second time in 1957, and again the dredge material filled in many coves along the Strand, allowing the straightening and widening of the roadway. Menard-May Park was also enlarged using dredging material. The H. P. Wilkinson dock is in the foreground.

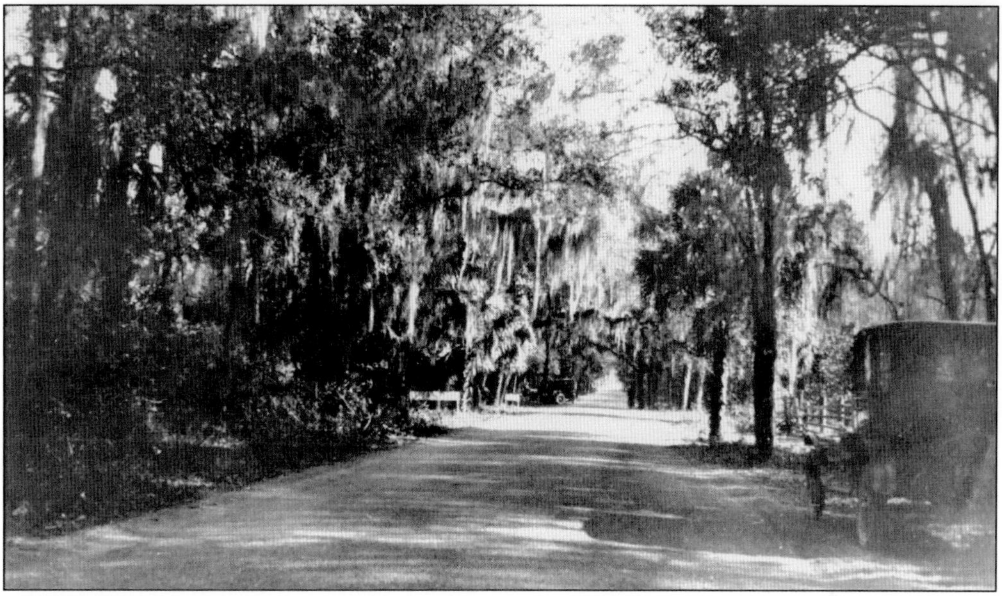

AUTOMOBILE ON RIDGEWOOD AVENUE, 1923. Ridgewood Avenue and the Strand were seeing more and more traffic, so they both were paved with asphalt. Automobile driving would be smoother from then on. This photo was taken looking north.

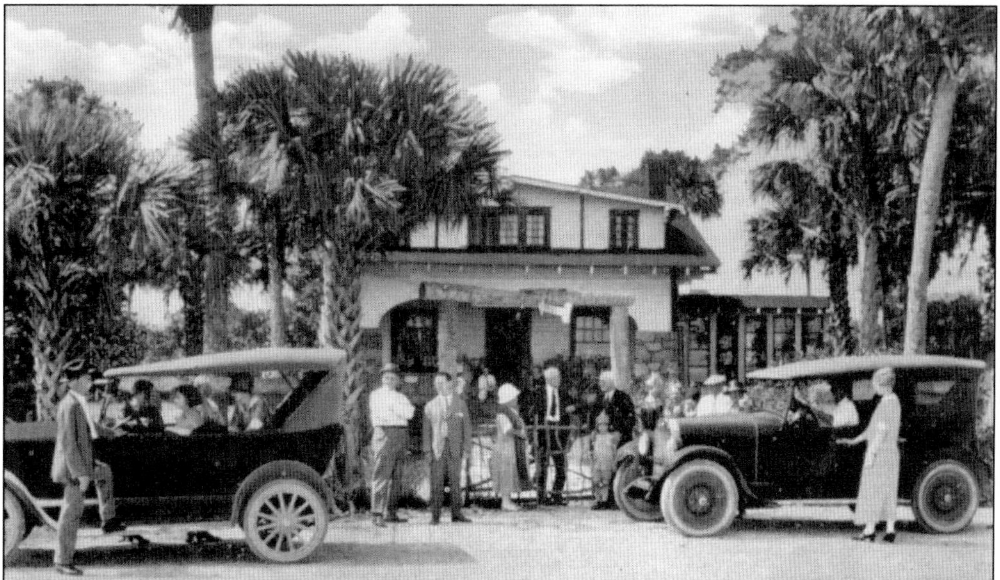

SUNSHINE MANOR, C. 1915. This was a popular boarding house in its day, at a good location along Ridgewood Avenue, nestled in among orange trees. The back of this postcard states, "We have been to Daytona to the movies and stopped to get ice cream. Wish you were here with us." The people are unidentified.

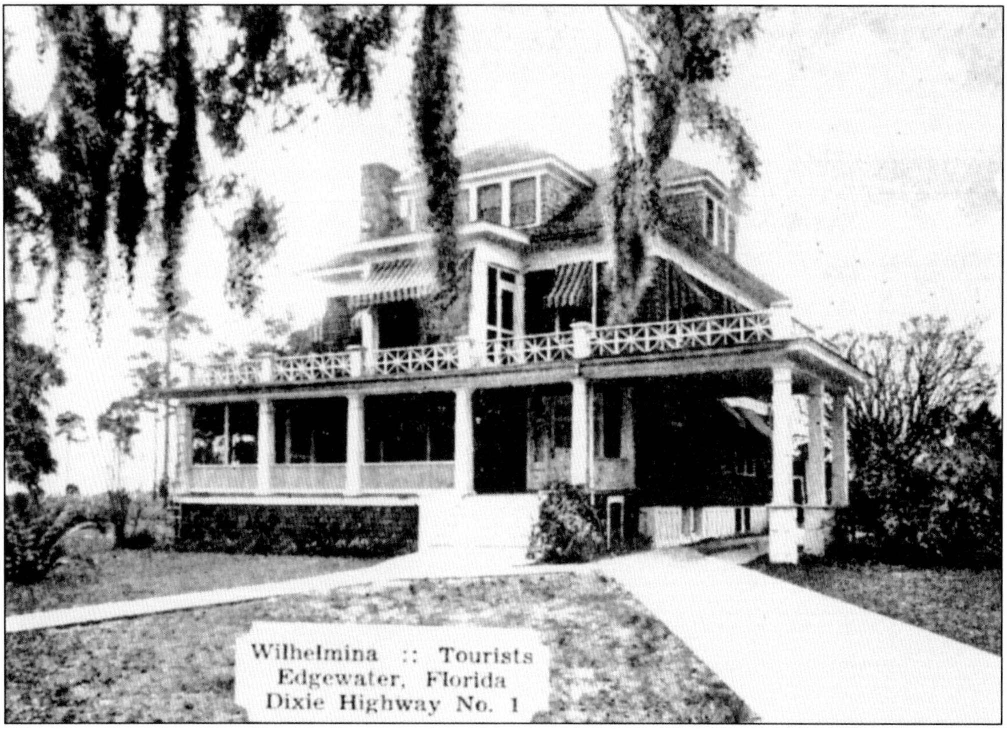

WILHELMINA TOURIST HOME, C. 1950. Cottages, motels, and rooms for rent were found in many areas of Edgewater. Ridgewood Avenue, sometimes called the Dixie Highway, was the location of the Wilhelmina Tourist Home and also the Yelka Terrace Motor Court, among others. Yelka Terrace (not pictured) is still standing today. Edgewater continued to grow as a tourist destination.

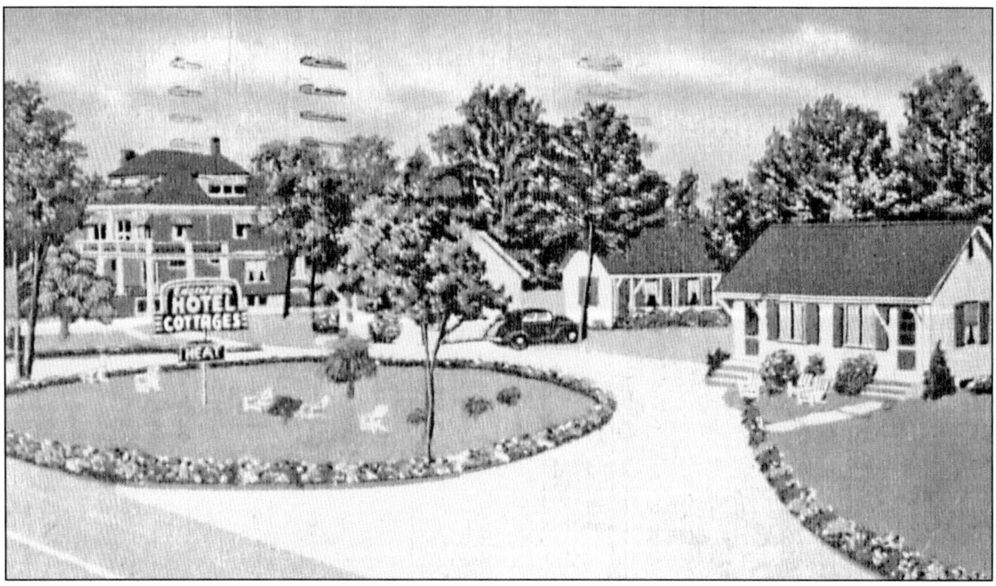

EDGEWATER HOTEL AND COTTAGES, C. 1947. This hotel advertised in the July 4, 1948, fireworks celebration brochure, "Enjoy a cool vacation" "Comfortable, clean and beautiful" "Highly recommended by Duncan Hines – A.A.A." Their telephone number was 449-M. This is a postcard, and the building on the left is likely the Wilhelmina Tourist Home.

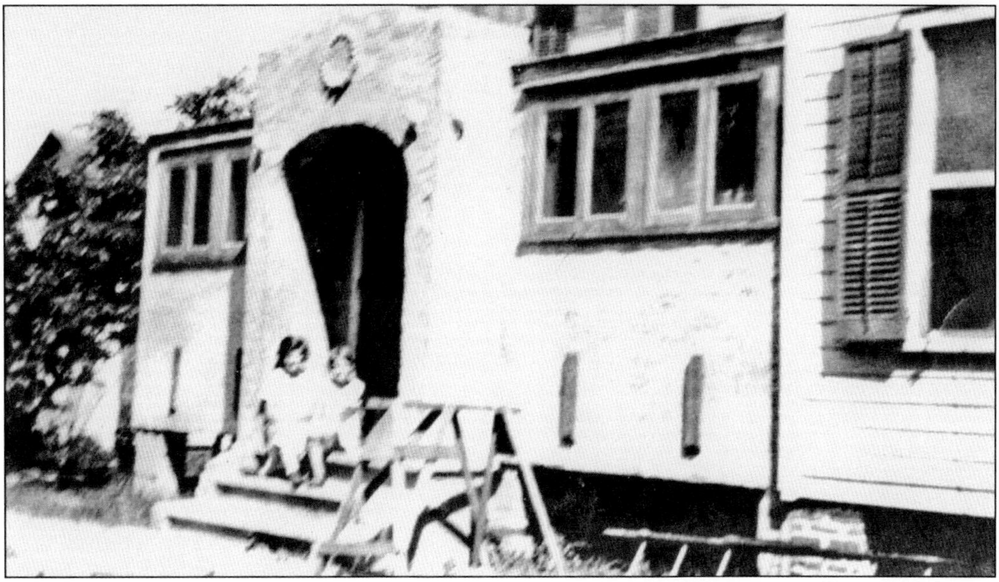

LEEMING HOUSE BEING BUILT, C. 1925. Subdivisions were built for those who wanted to be permanent residents, and some developments had special requirements. Highland Shores subdivision was supposed to be Spanish-style homes. Shown here is a home owned by the Leemings, being constructed in the Spanish style.

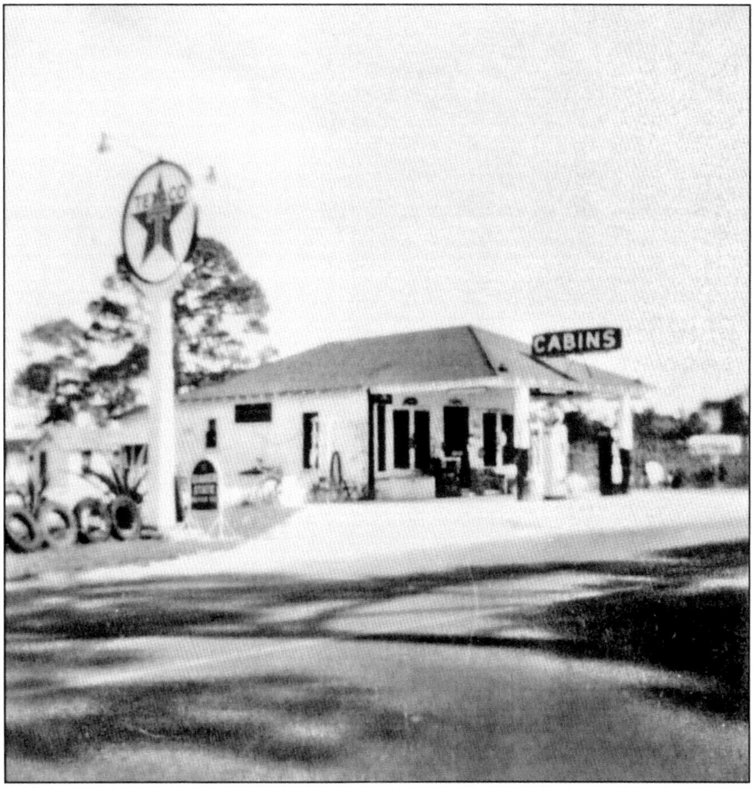

FILLING STATION AT U.S. 1 AND EAST PALM WAY, C. 1950. The automobile was here to stay, and filling stations were an important part of the landscape in the early 1900s. Known as McMurray's Gas Station, this station also had tourist cabins behind the business. Later the building served as a store, and today it is a business plaza with several shops.

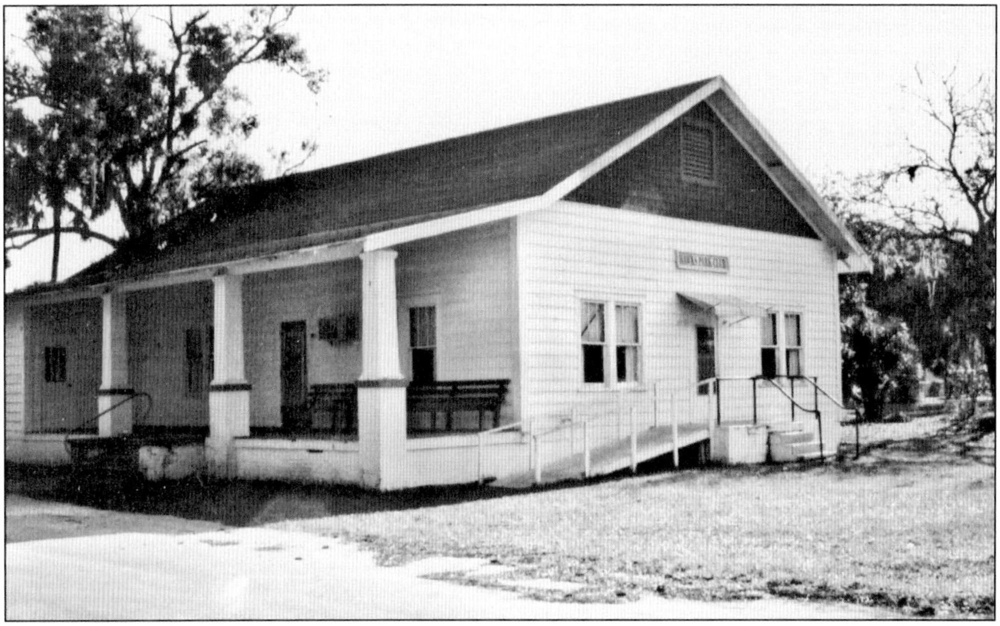

HAWKS PARK CLUB, 1925. Built by Harry Mitchell, this convenient meeting place was located at Woodley Avenue and Fernald. Educational gatherings, musicals, and theatricals were held here. It was at first a women's club, but when the men became interested in the events, it became known as the Hawks Park Club.

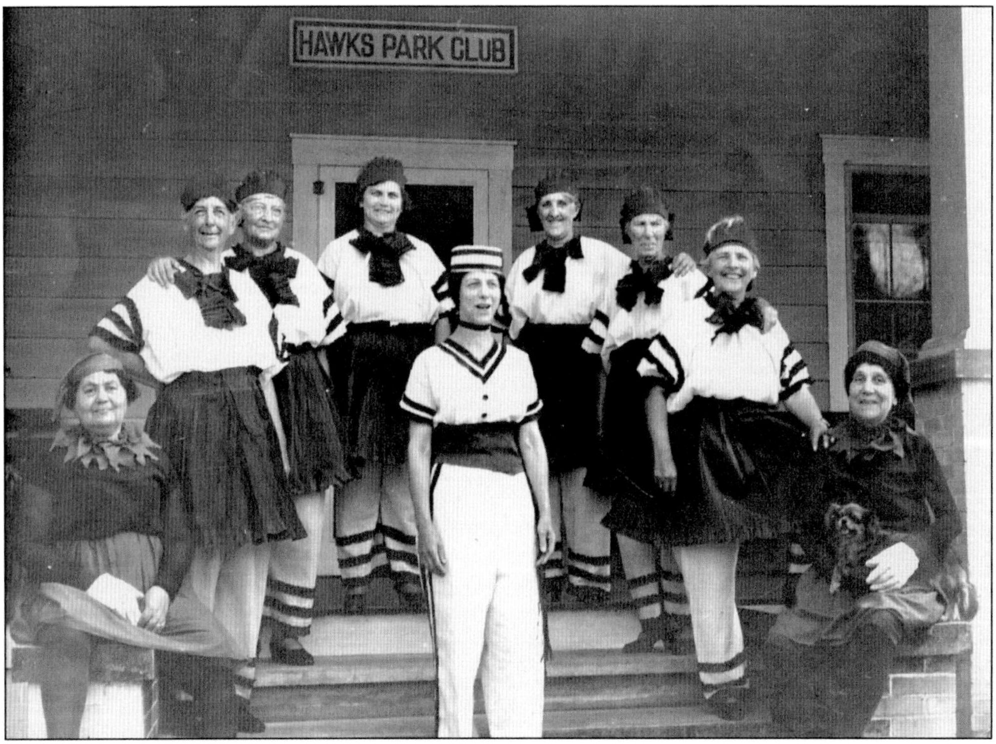

HAWKS PARK CLUB, C. 1950. Evidently this is the cast of one of the theatrical performances at the Hawks Park Club, but unfortunately we no longer have the names of these actors.

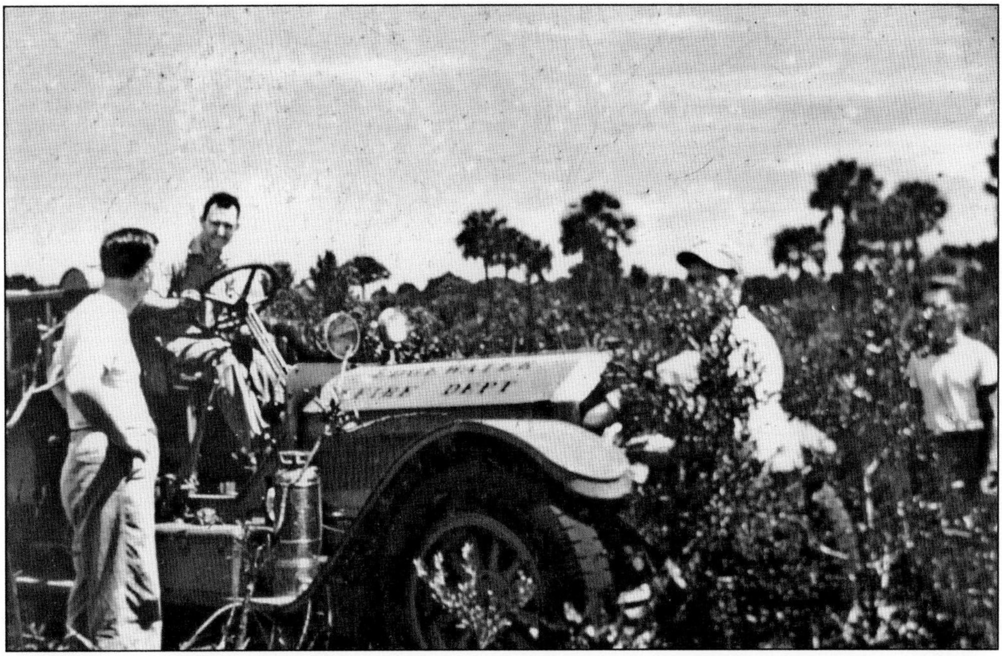

Fire Truck, c. 1949. The old fire truck was a Packard, with solid tires and wooden spokes on the wheels. Pictured are Elmer Bane, chief and driver; Bill Hanson; Richard Hanson; and Jack McMurray. Elmer Bane was also a mechanic, so he helped keep the fire truck going.

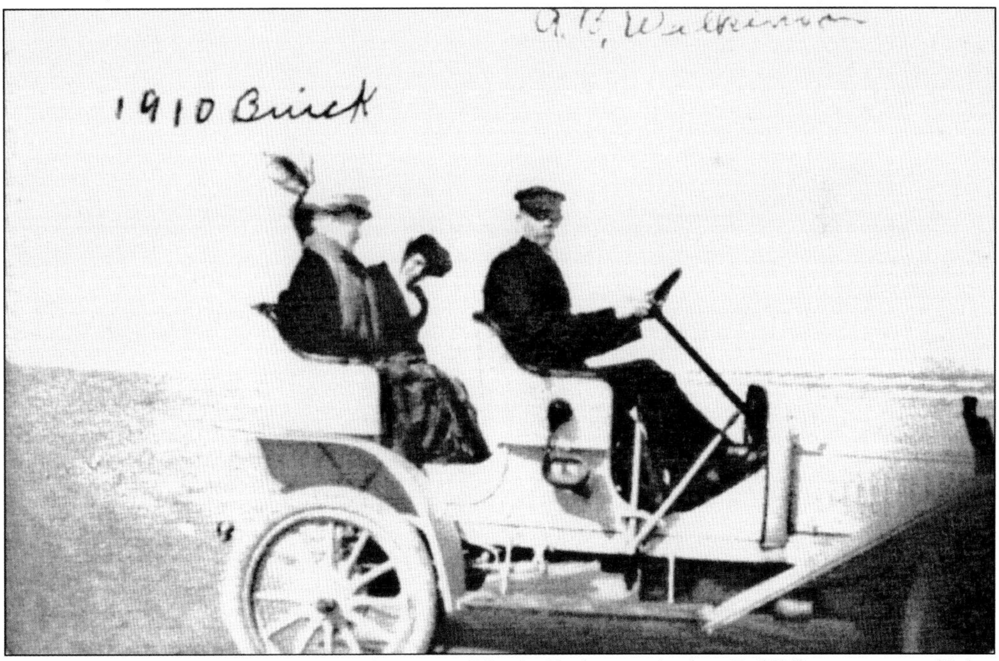

Driving on the Beach, c. 1910. Living in Hawks Park gave Arthur B. Wilkinson, son of John Playters Wilkinson, easy access to the hard sand beaches of New Smyrna and Daytona Beach, and we see him here driving his 1910 Buick. H. P. Wilkinson's sister Gladys might be the girl in the car. Annie Wilkinson is also in the backseat. New Smyrna Beach and Daytona Beach are still known for beach driving.

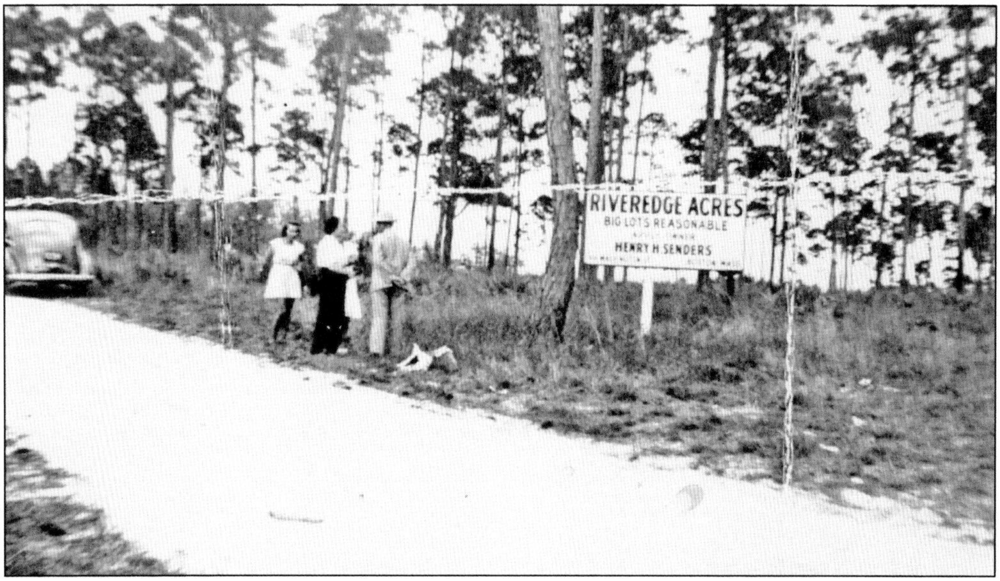

RIVEREDGE ACRES, C. 1940. Located on Ridgewood Avenue, south of Boston Road, Riveredge Acres was a real estate development. Here a realtor is showing lots for sale. The people are unidentified.

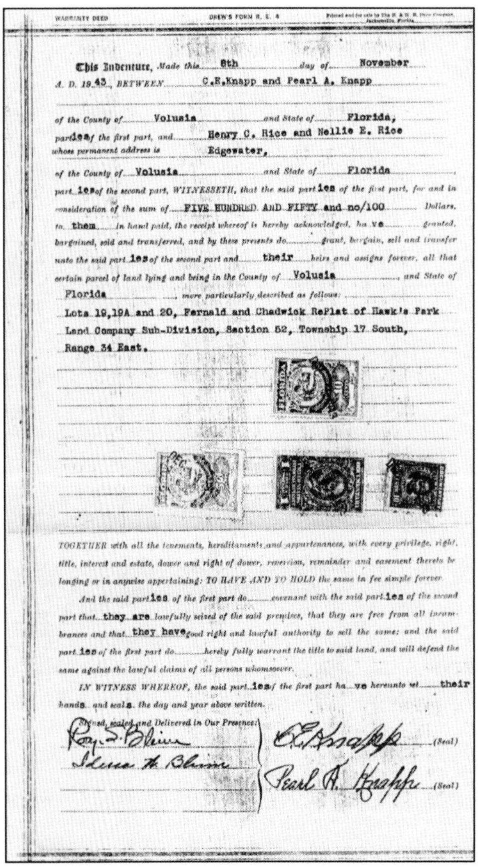

WARRANTY DEED DREW'S FORM R. L. 4

This Indenture, Made this 8th day of November A. D. 1943, BETWEEN C.E.Knapp and Pearl A. Knapp of the County of Volusia and State of Florida, parties of the first part, and Henry C. Rice and Nellie E. Rice whose permanent address is Edgewater, of the County of Volusia and State of Florida, parties of the second part, WITNESSETH, that the said parties of the first part, for and in consideration of the sum of FIVE HUNDRED AND FIFTY and no/100 Dollars, to them in hand paid, the receipt whereof is hereby acknowledged, have granted, bargained, sold and transferred, and by these presents do grant, bargain, sell and transfer unto the said parties of the second part and their heirs and assigns forever, all that certain parcel of land lying and being in the County of Volusia, and State of Florida, more particularly described as follows:

Lots 19,19A and 20, Fernald and Chadwick RePlat of Hawk's Park Land Company Sub-Division, Section 52, Township 17 South, Range 34 East.

TOGETHER with all the tenements, hereditaments and appurtenances, with every privilege, right, title, interest and estate, dower and right of dower, reversion, remainder and easement thereto belonging or in anywise appertaining: TO HAVE AND TO HOLD the same in fee simple forever.

And the said parties of the first part do covenant with the said parties of the second part that they are lawfully seized of the said premises, that they are free from all incumbrances and that they have good right and lawful authority to sell the same; and the said parties of the first part do hereby fully warrant the title to said land, and will defend the same against the lawful claims of all persons whomsoever.

IN WITNESS WHEREOF, the said parties of the first part have hereunto set their hands and seals the day and year above written.

Signed, sealed and Delivered in Our Presence:

C.E. Knapp (Seal)

Pearl A. Knapp (Seal)

WARRANTY DEED, NOVEMBER 8, 1943. In this deed, several lots are being sold for $500. In his ads for Hawks Park, John Milton Hawks wrote, "Do you want a lot that will double in value in a year?" Charles and Henrietta Lincoln had doubled their money in just five days when they sold the Geronimo-Alvarez Grant to Dr. Hawks. Real estate in Florida hasn't changed much!

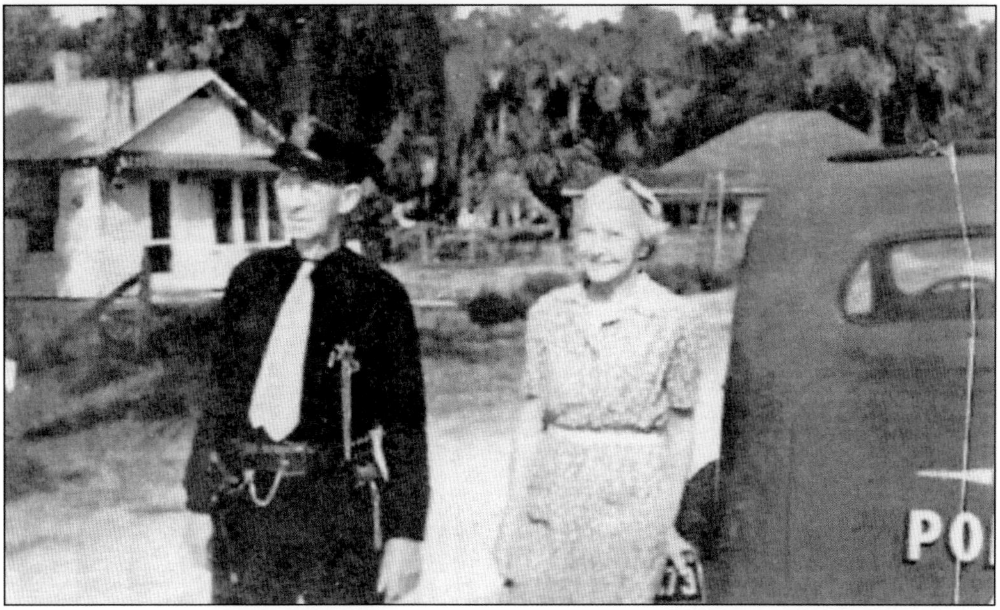

DAVID AND JESSIE THOMAS WITH POLICE CAR, C. 1945. In 1938, David and Jessie Thomas were traveling to Miami to live when they had car trouble in Edgewater. It took three days to get the car fixed, so they stayed at the Blue Gables Motel, where they met several people from the town. On mentioning that he was a retired policeman from New York, Thomas was asked to be town marshall for Edgewater. He said yes and remained on the job until 1951.

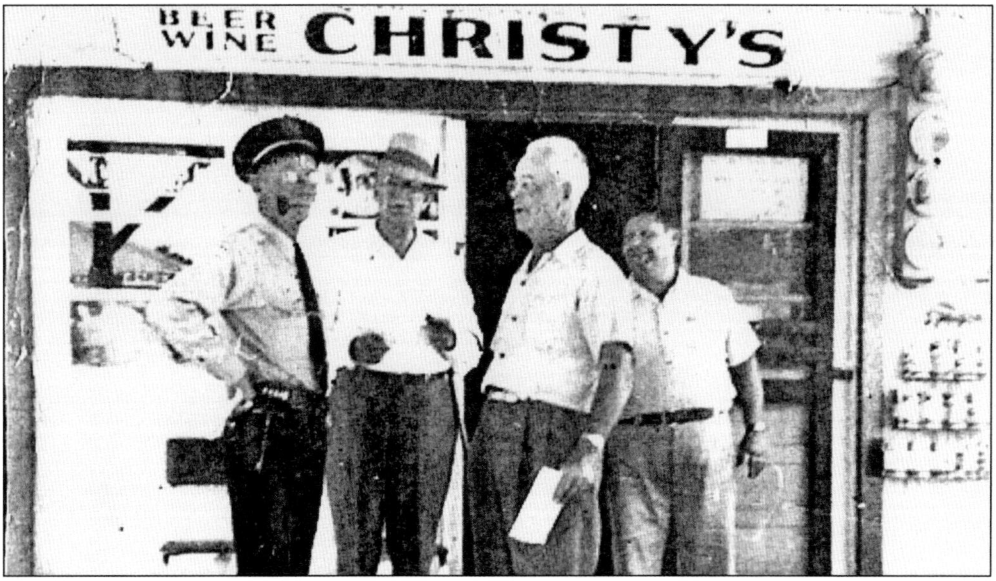

DAVID THOMAS AT CHRISTY'S, C. 1945. Christy's was where one could get a "fat ham sandwich," among other items. Here, from left to right, Marshall Thomas stands with an unidentified man, mayor Henry Gibbs, and the owner of the store, Mr. Christy. Some of David Thomas's duties were to preserve peace and order at all gatherings, enforce the ordinances of the town, inspect the construction of all septic tanks and file copies of inspection reports with the town clerk, patrol the streets, act as fire chief, inspect all old and dangerous buildings, and attend all meetings of council. Thomas Street was named after David Thomas.

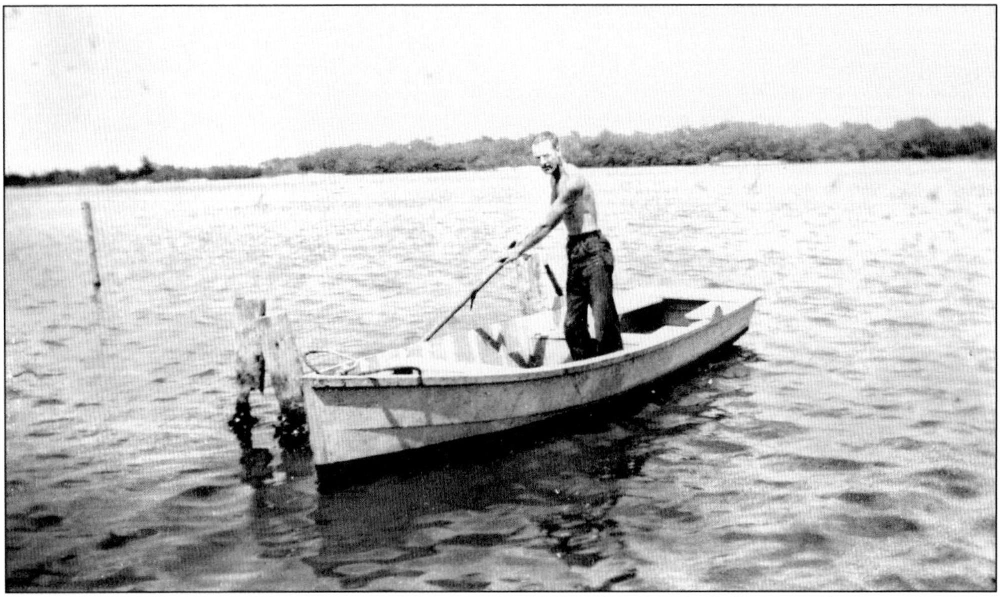

DAVID DINNEN IN HIS NEW BOAT, APRIL 1939. After being out fishing in the waters of the Indian River, David Dinnen was coming back to shore with his catch.

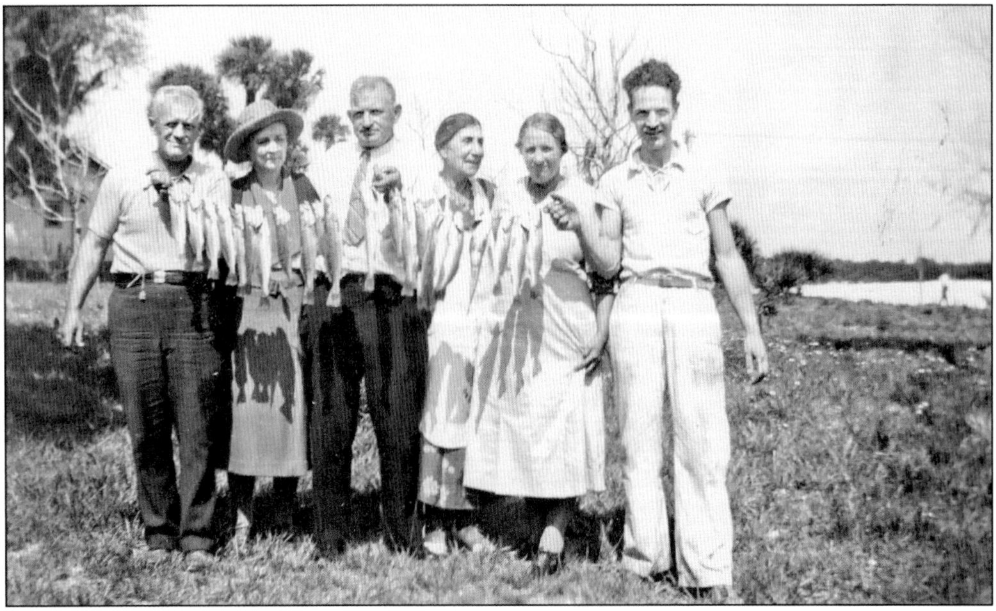

TWENTY-TWO TROUT, MARCH 15, 1936. Standing in the Huettich front yard, this group is proudly showing the catch of the day. On the left is Rudolf Huettich, the four people next to him are unidentified, and on the right is David Dinnen, who caught all the fish.

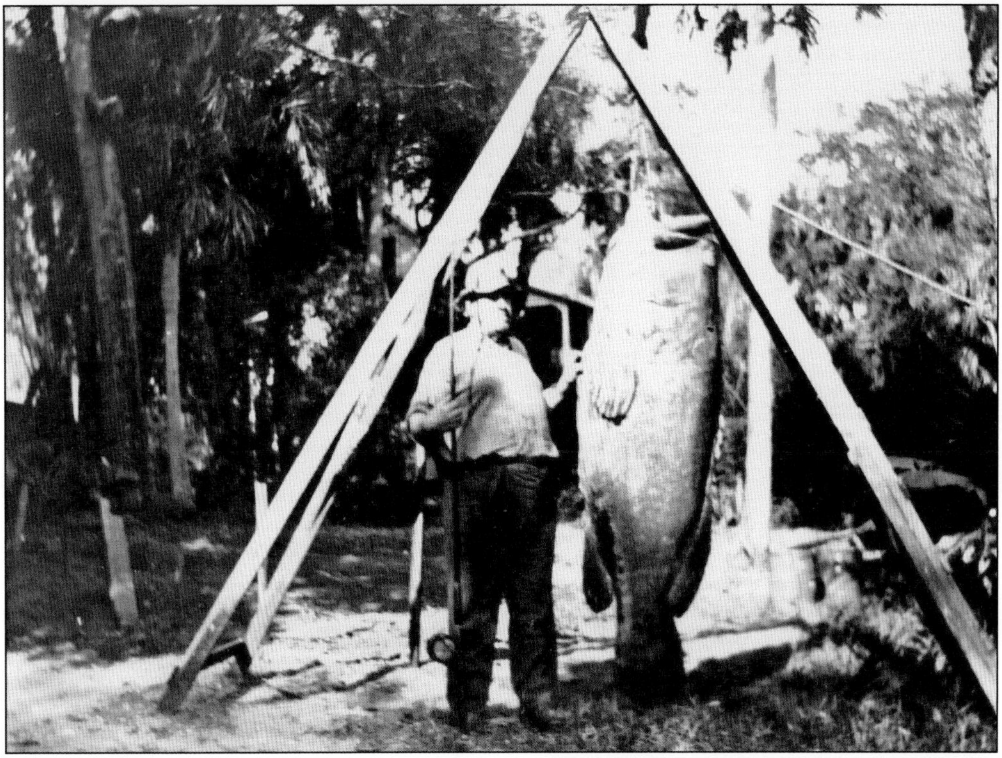

FIVE-HUNDRED-POUND JEW FISH, DECEMBER 6, 1936. Fish were still plentiful in the 1930s. Mr. Bartlett is standing with the Jew fish. The huge catch was 7 feet and 2 inches long and weighed over 500 pounds. It was caught in the Indian River near the long dock.

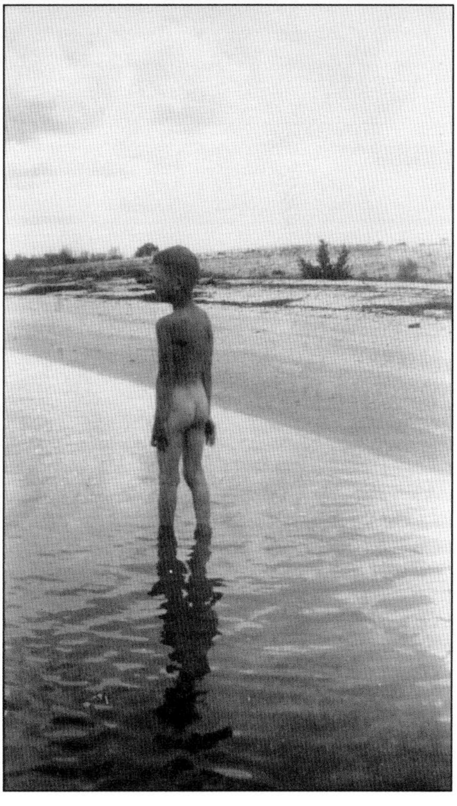

SKINNY-DIPPING, APRIL 1939. This photo is identified as "Roddy in bathing, old channel, front of house." This was typical attire for young boys swimming in those days. Note the very clear Florida tan line.

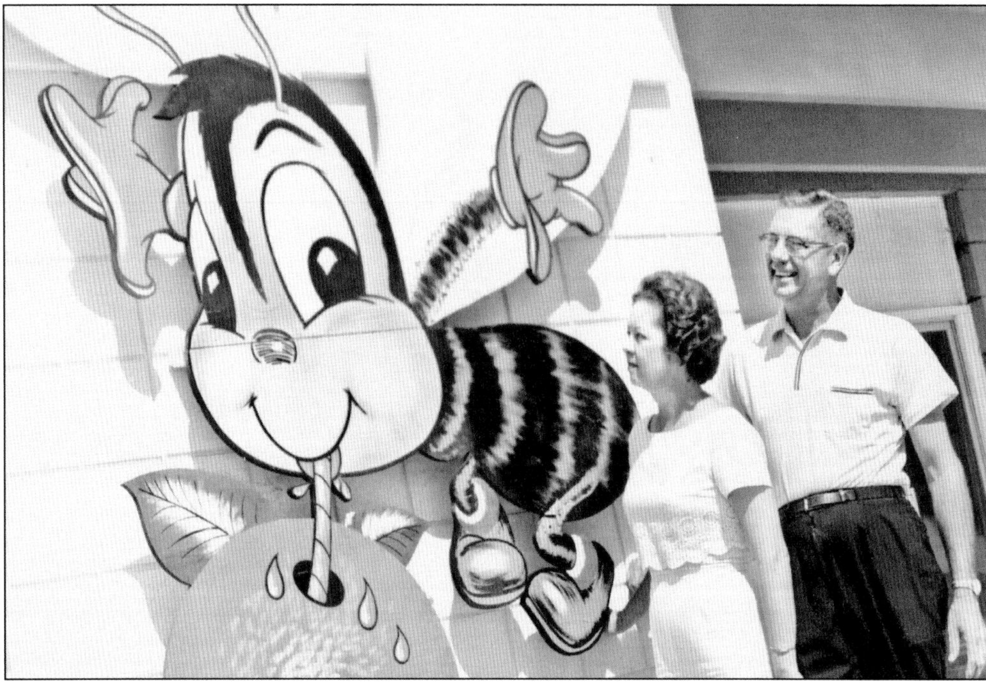

David and Helen McGinnis, c. 1950. This young couple traveled south from West Virginia to start new careers. David and Helen began selling honey and citrus to fruit stands and trailer parks from New Smyrna to Ormond Beach, and their business gradually expanded. They bought the building on the corner of Ridgewood and Park Avenues and sold citrus, honey, and Florida novelties to people traveling through the area.

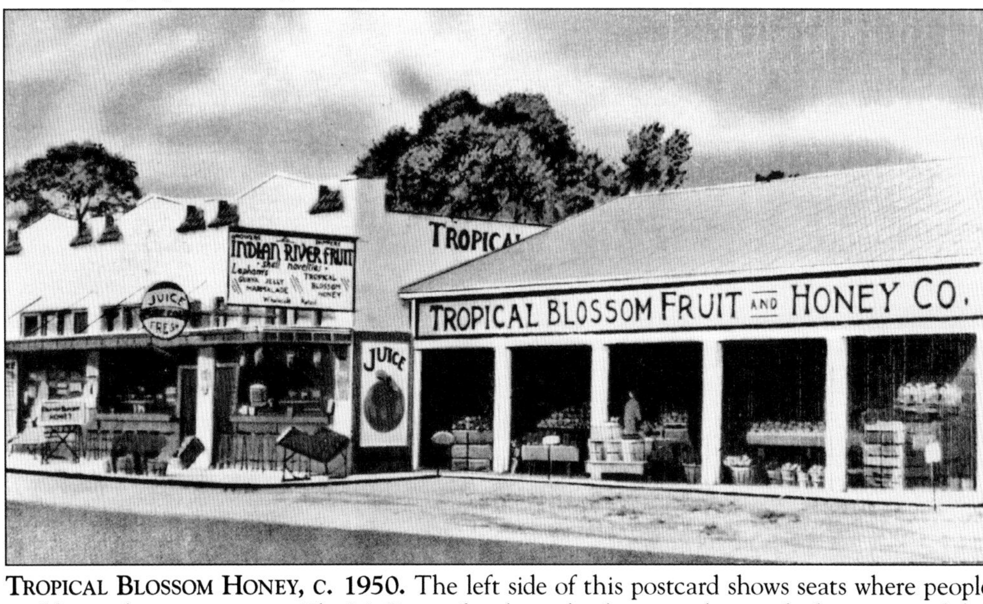

Tropical Blossom Honey, c. 1950. The left side of this postcard shows seats where people could sit and sip orange juice. The McGinnis family used to live next door to the business, and this building used to have a whistle out front. In the event of a fire, the children had to run up to blow the whistle to alert the volunteer firemen. Tropical Blossom Honey Company is still in business along Ridgewood Avenue. They have a honey museum and ship honey all over the world.

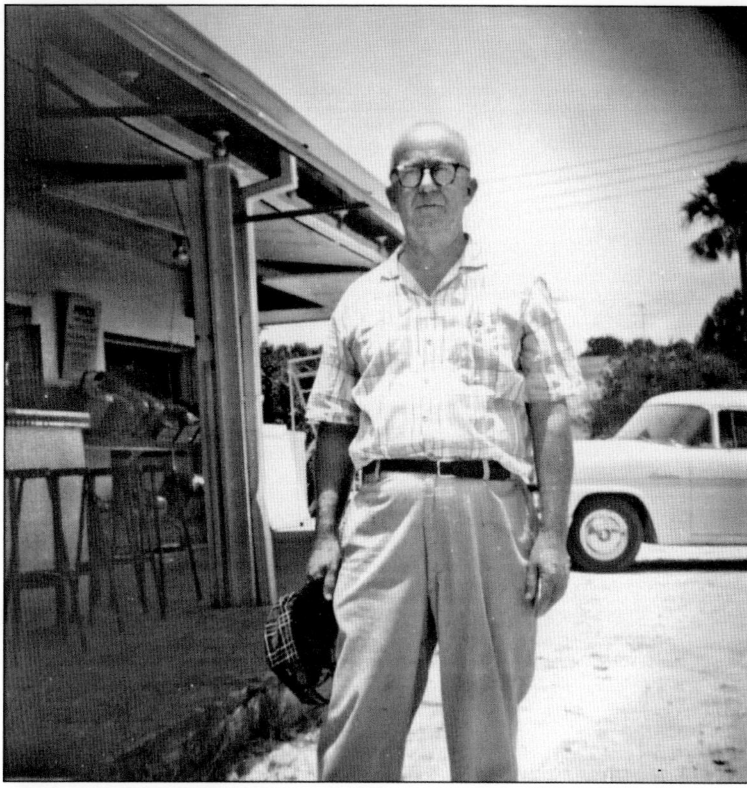

PERCY LOVELAND, 1960. Percy N. Loveland of Chicago came south and saw the possibilities in citrus sales. In 1946, he bought some land and started Loveland Groves. His son Thomas helped and later bought the business, and they began shipping all over the United States.

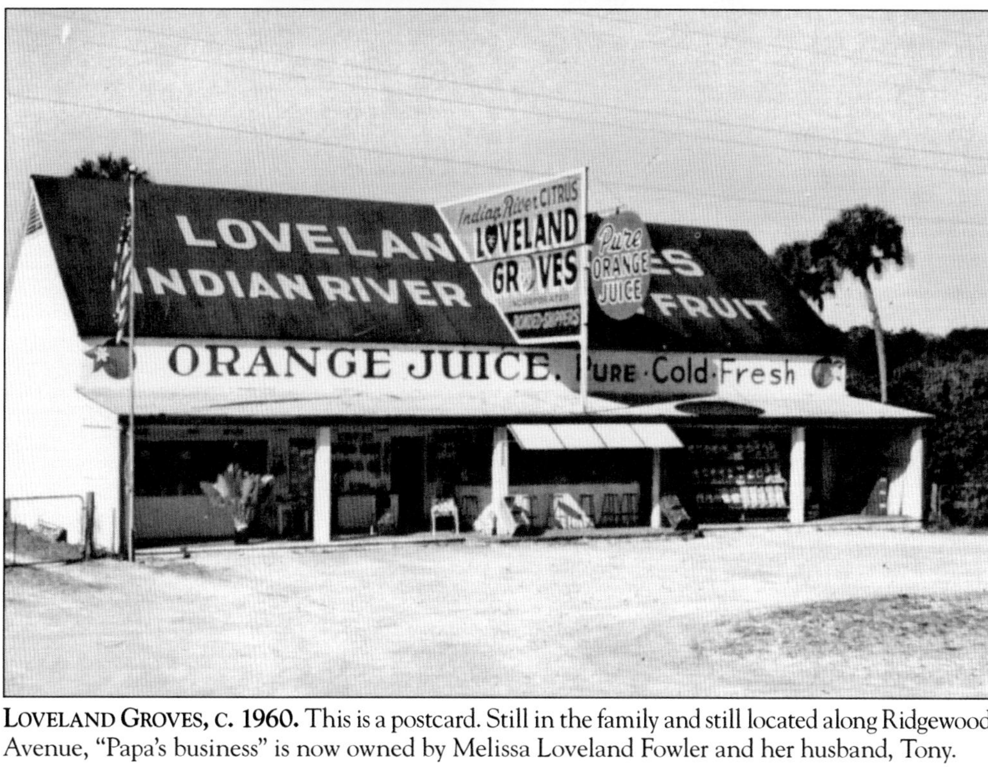

LOVELAND GROVES, C. 1960. This is a postcard. Still in the family and still located along Ridgewood Avenue, "Papa's business" is now owned by Melissa Loveland Fowler and her husband, Tony.

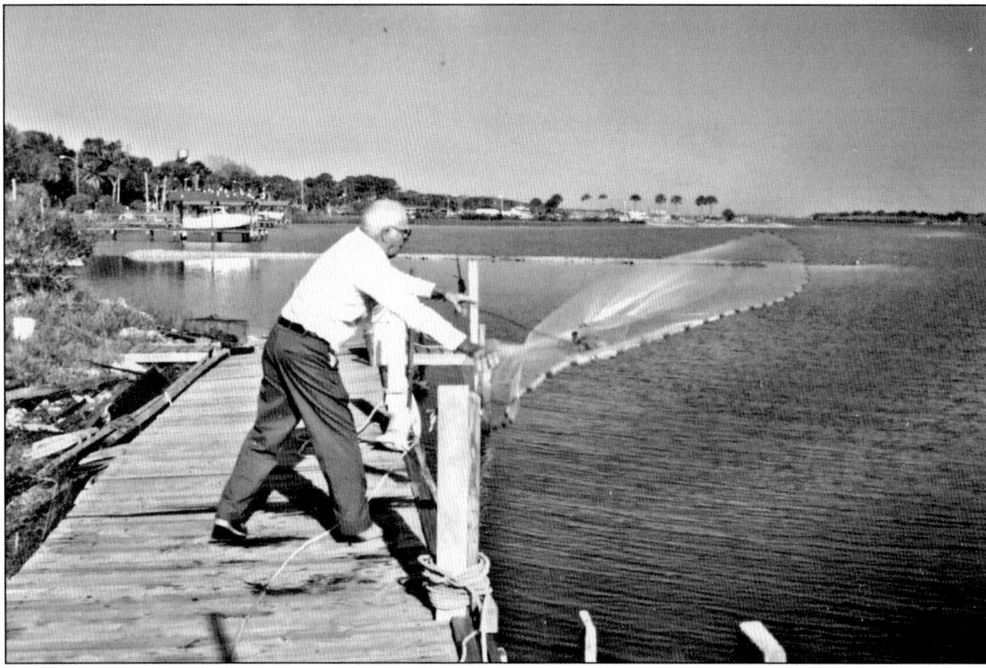

H. P. Wilkinson Getting Some Bait Fish, c. 1995. The fishing still continues to be good through the years, and here H. P. Wilkinson is shown throwing out a cast net. He was 90 years old when this photo was taken.

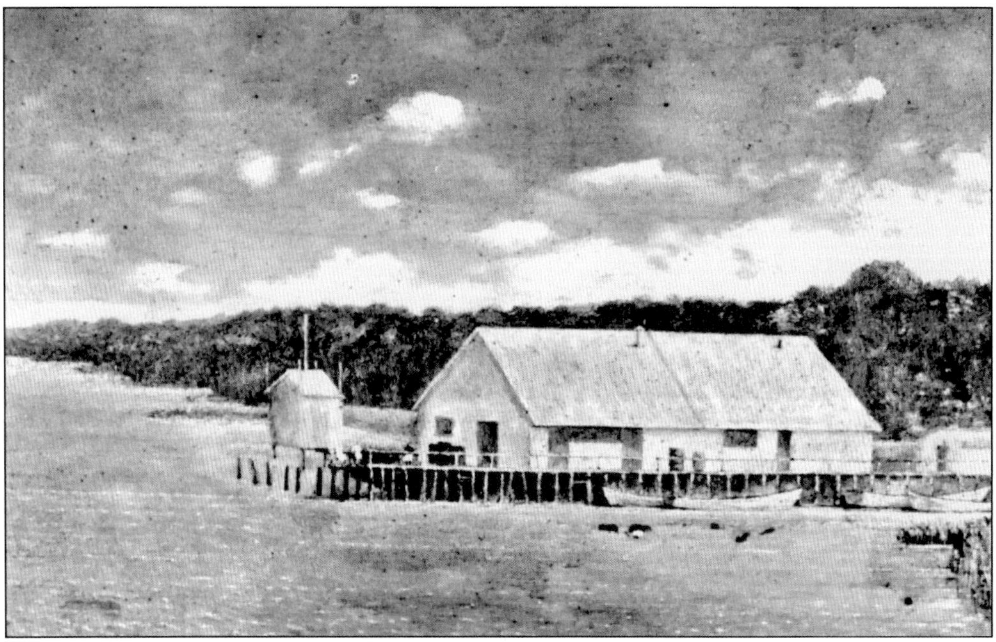

Floreco Crab Company, c. 1950. The Floreco ("Florida East Coast") Crab Company was located right on the riverfront at the intersection of the Strand (now South Riverside Drive) and Turgot Street. It was owned and operated by E. P. Fuller and was an active business for more than 20 years. The building was set on pilings out over the river. The "crabbers" could simply pull their boats up to the long dock and unload. The photograph is from a painting.

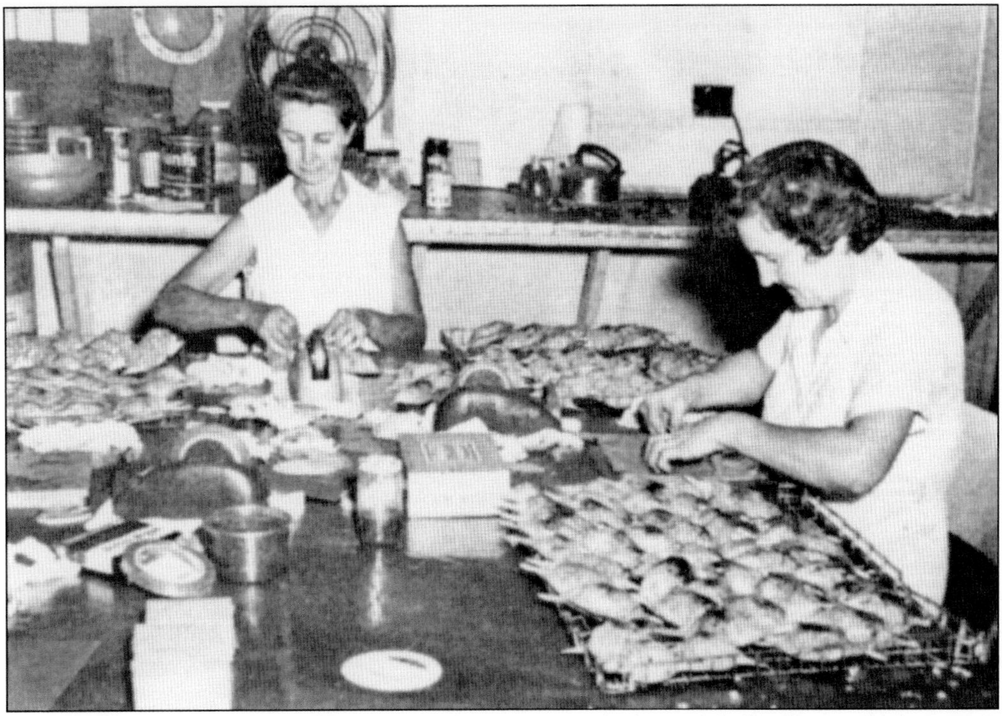

MAKING DEVILED CRAB, C. 1950. The crab meat was picked out of shells, then cooked, canned, or mixed with seasoning and made into deviled crab, as seen here. The Floreco Crab Company advertised "Fresh Crab meat every day" in one of their ads. Their phone was 504-J in early Edgewater. The workers are unidentified.

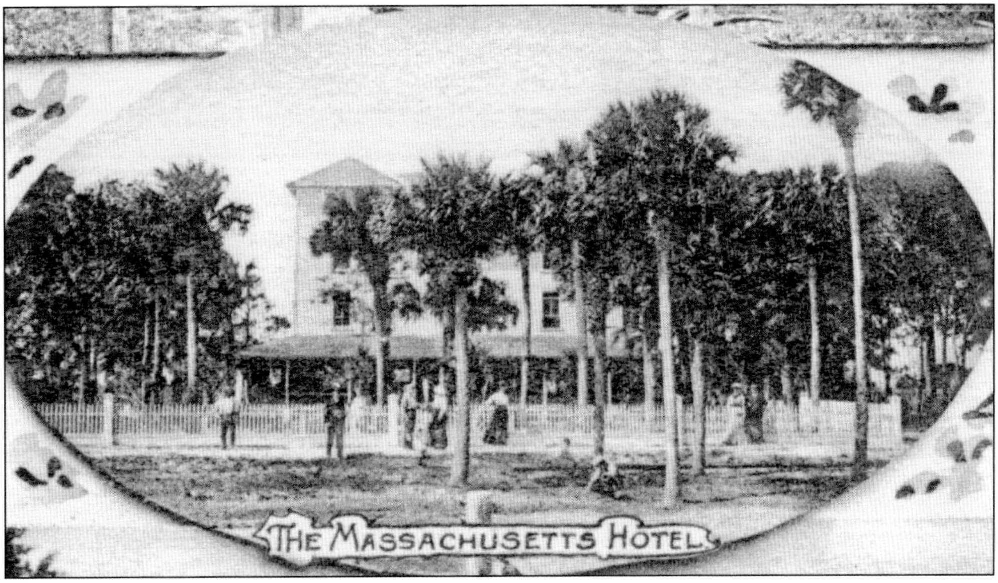

MASSACHUSETTS HOTEL, 1910. Structures along the river were being built higher and higher. First built as the Massachusetts Hotel, the four-story building shown here was bought by Dr. Davis Forster for use as a hospital in January 1912. He called his hospital the Shelter. The people are unidentified.

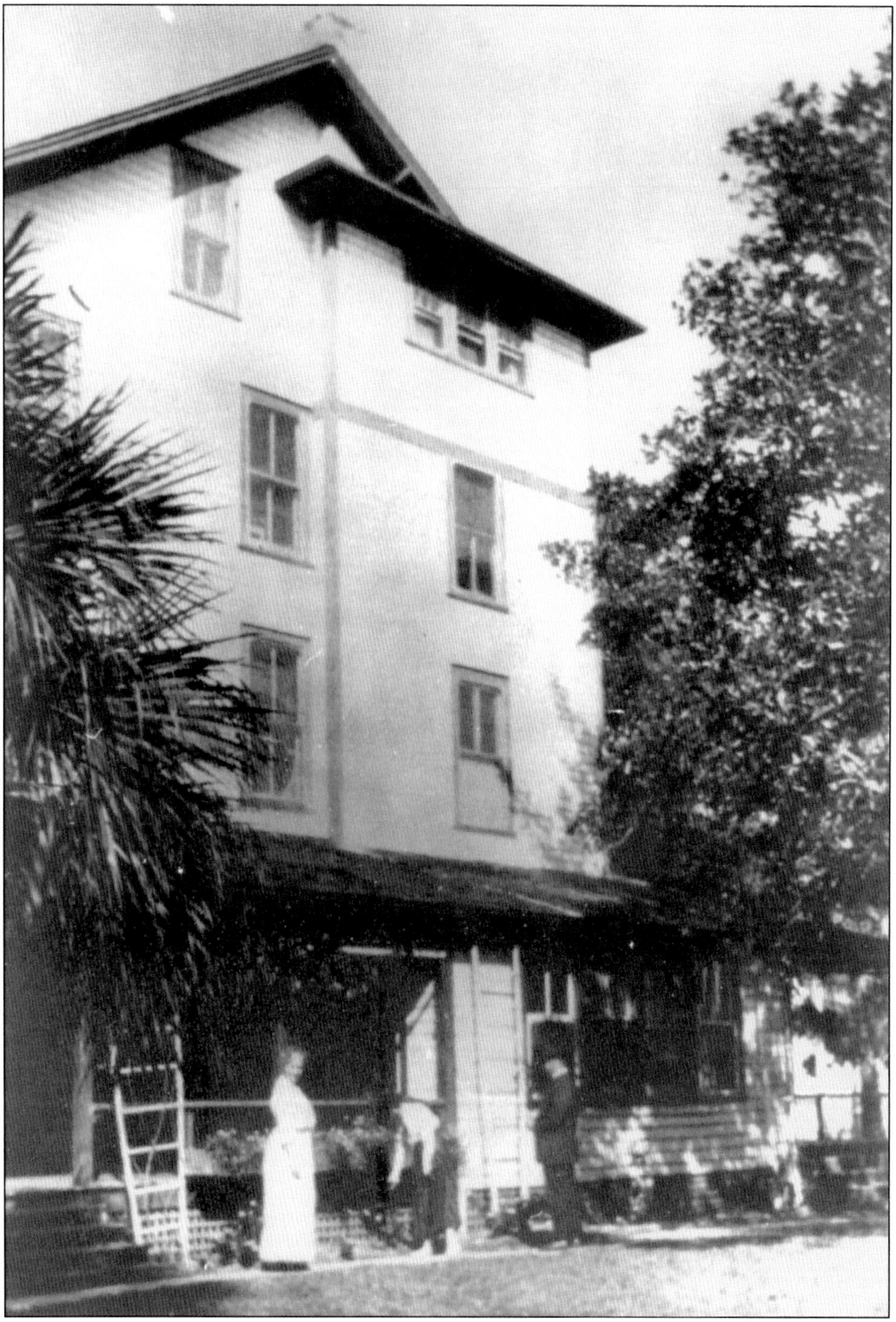

THE SHELTER, C. 1915. The Shelter was the largest building and the only hospital along the east coast between St. Augustine and Key West. Dr. Forster even had some patients come from Miami for treatment. Many patients came by boat to the Shelter's own dock. Located between Hotel and New Hampshire Avenues, along the Strand, the Shelter had seven acres of land. The people are unidentified.

Seven

Town Regularly Laid Out

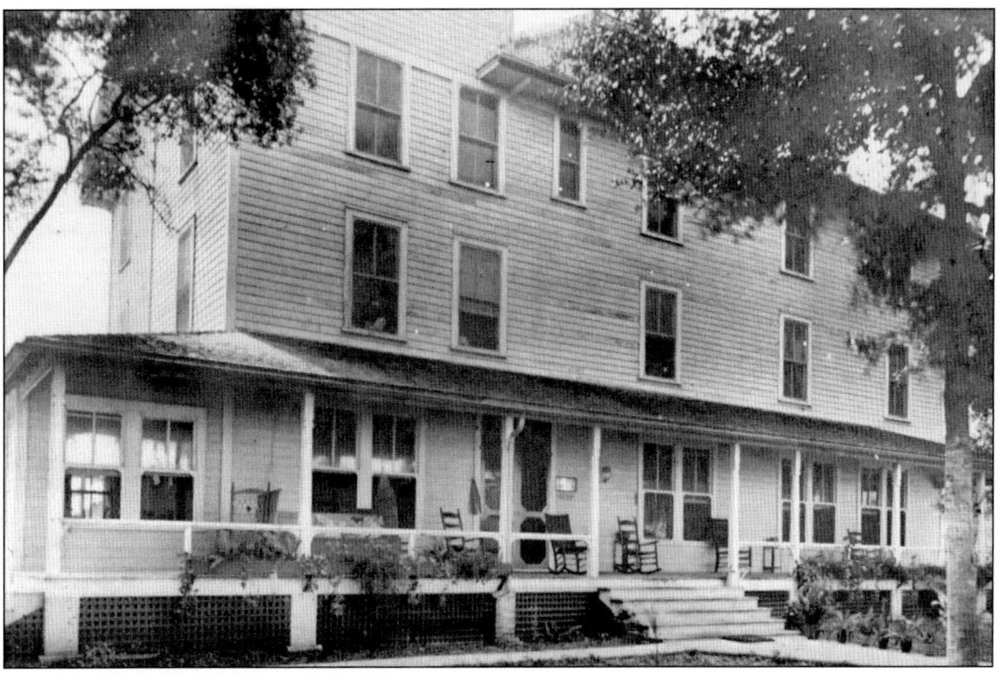

Porch of the Shelter, c. 1915. The porch shows the homey atmosphere of this early hospital. A New Smyrna Beach resident who was born at the facility remembers that her mother paid $50 for a two-week stay at the Shelter. "Rates, including nursing and medical attention, $25 a week in advance. Surgery and consultations extra." There were 33 rooms in the building.

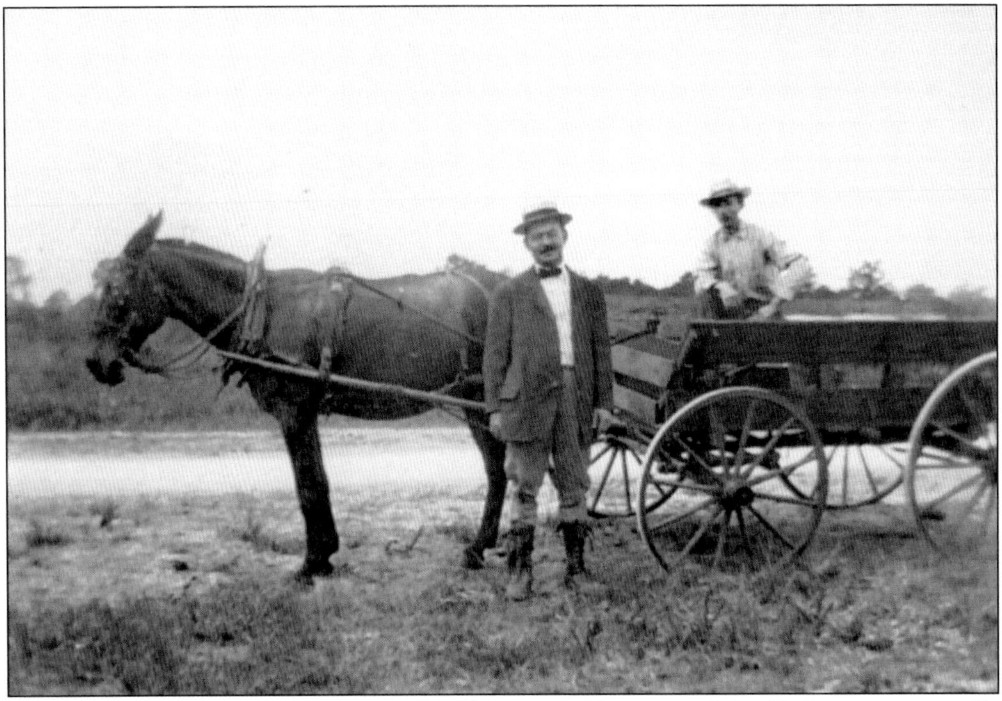

Dr. Davis Forster, c. 1915. Dr. Forster, physician and surgeon of the Shelter, was originally from St. Louis, Missouri. He was the only regular full-time staff doctor at the facility and even made house calls. Other doctors may also have practiced at the facility occasionally. The man on the wagon is unidentified.

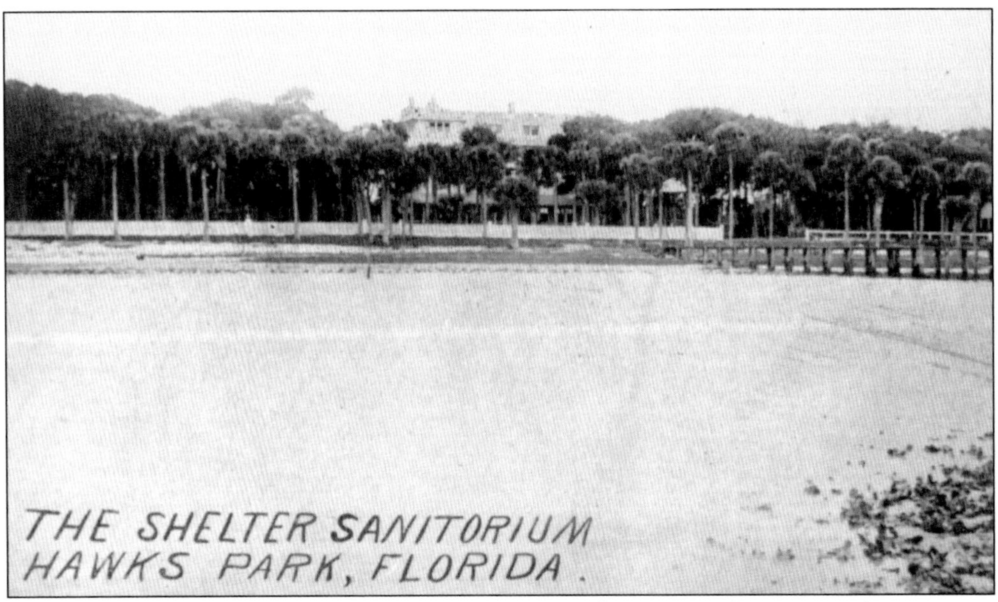

The Shelter from the River, c. 1915. There was no electricity at this time, so the operating room was on the top floor. A skylight was made in the roof so that natural light could be used. That meant, however, that on cloudy days there could be no surgery. There was no indoor stairway from the fourth to the third floor. The Shelter hospital was later called the Shelter sanitorium.

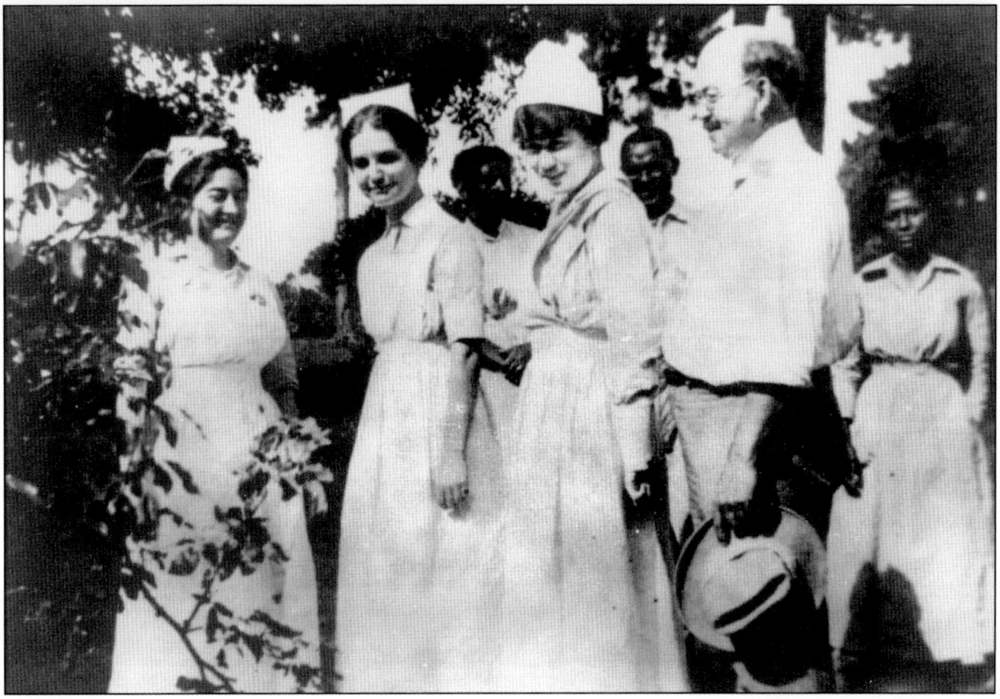

Dr. Forster and Nurses, c. 1915. Forster, second from right, was a specialist in obstetrics and gynecology and had gone for training in Berlin, Germany. Babies were still often delivered by midwives, but many newer residents were born at the hospital. The nurses were well trained. The others are unidentified.

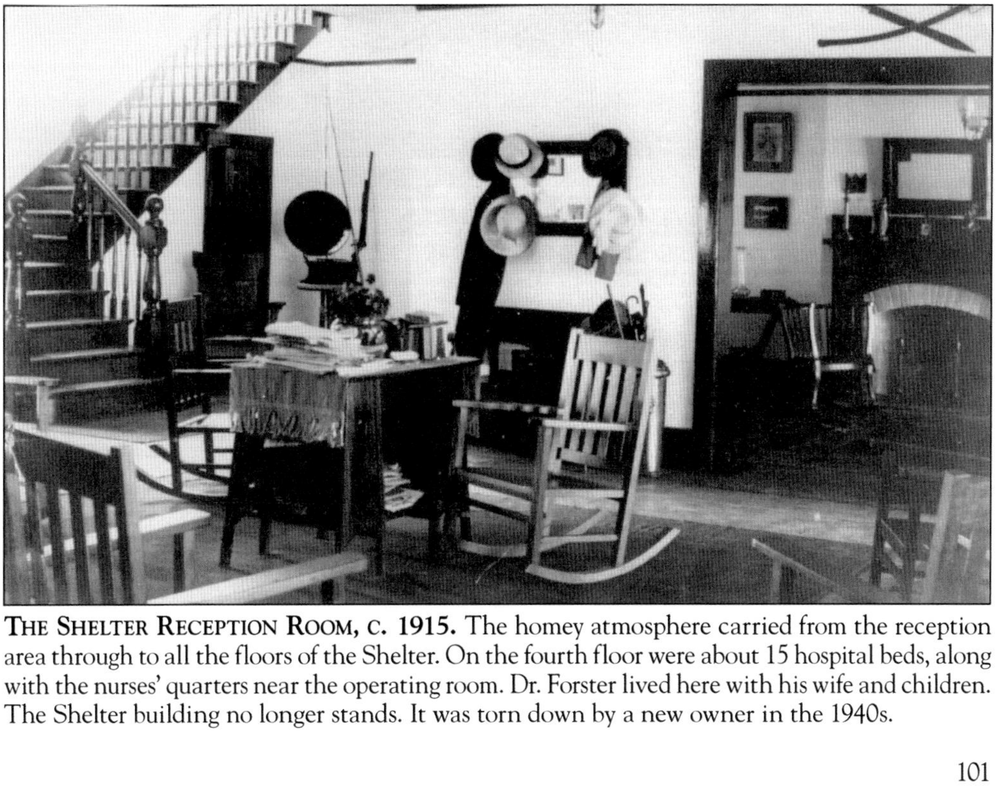

The Shelter Reception Room, c. 1915. The homey atmosphere carried from the reception area through to all the floors of the Shelter. On the fourth floor were about 15 hospital beds, along with the nurses' quarters near the operating room. Dr. Forster lived here with his wife and children. The Shelter building no longer stands. It was torn down by a new owner in the 1940s.

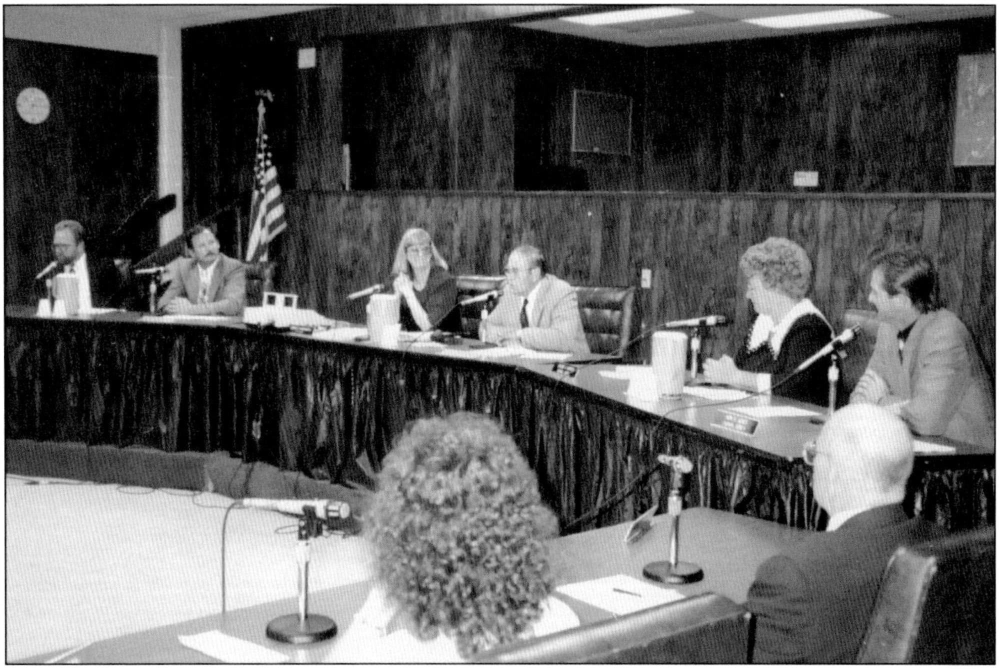

CITY COUNCIL IN SESSION, C. 1992. On July 25, 1951, the city of Edgewater was incorporated, and the city council is shown here in 1992. Pictured clockwise from top left are David Mitchum, Mike Hays, Susan Wadsworth, mayor Jack Hayman, Louise Martin, Kirk Jones, George McMahon, and Kristi Storey. Today Edgewater has a city manager type of government with a mayor and five council members.

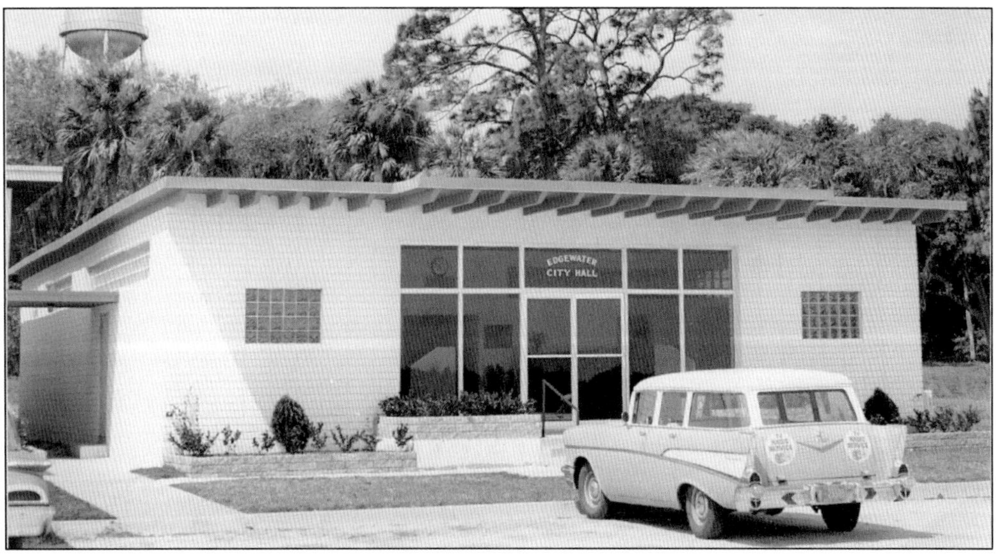

CITY HALL, C. 1962. Before this new city hall was built, the 1948 Fourth of July celebration took place here, on the corner of Park Avenue and Riverside Drive. Sponsored by the volunteer fire department, the day-long celebration included fireworks for the first time, ball games, boxing matches, children's races, and a fish fry, ending with a dance in the evening. The New Smyrna Saddle Club also played a game of palmetto polo on horseback with a large ball and a long palmetto stick.

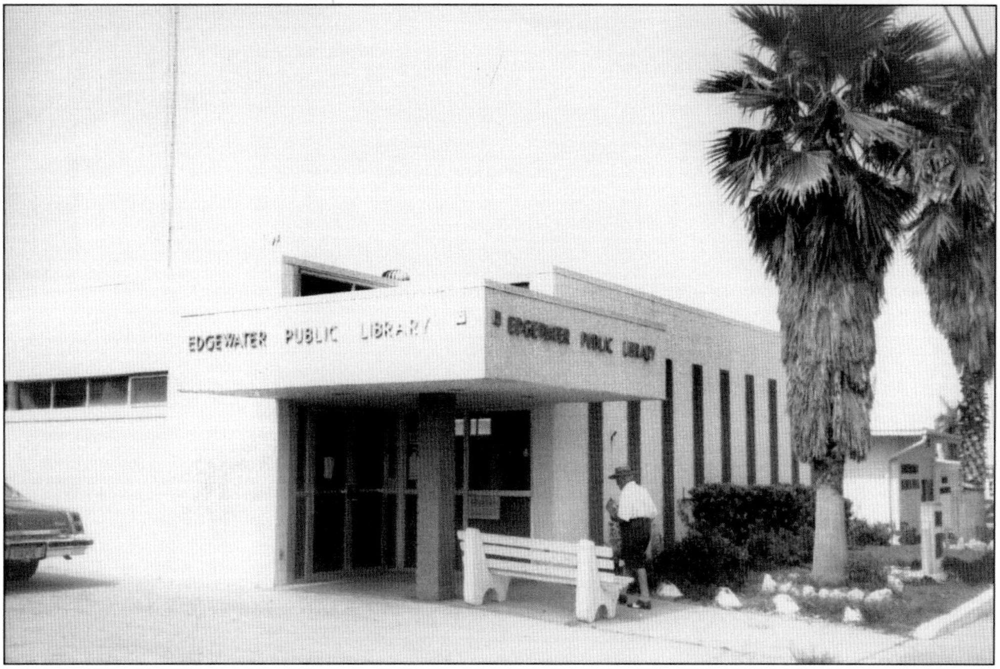

EDGEWATER LIBRARY, C. 1965. A new library was built in the 1960s, and Edgewater Library had become part of the Volusia County Library system. The building was enlarged in the 1970s because of the rapid growth of the community. The town was thriving, and with so many young people, more room was needed for children's programs. By 1967, the library had more than 10,000 volumes in its collection. Gayle Harmon was appointed head librarian in 1971. The person is unidentified.

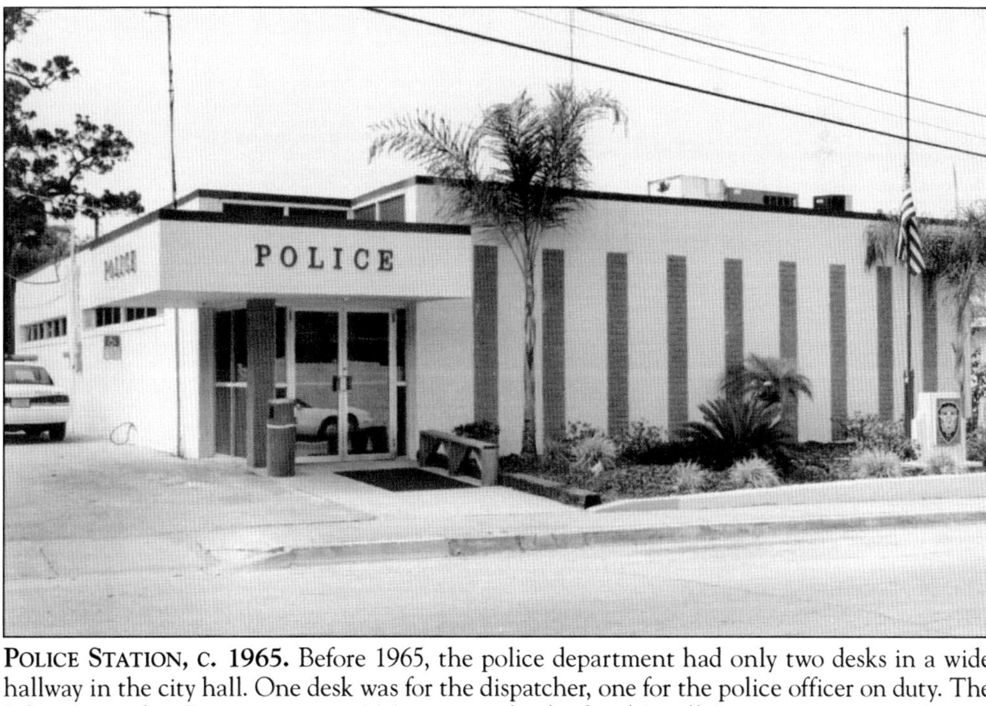

POLICE STATION, C. 1965. Before 1965, the police department had only two desks in a wide hallway in the city hall. One desk was for the dispatcher, one for the police officer on duty. The Edgewater Police Department in 2005 consists of a chief and 32 officers.

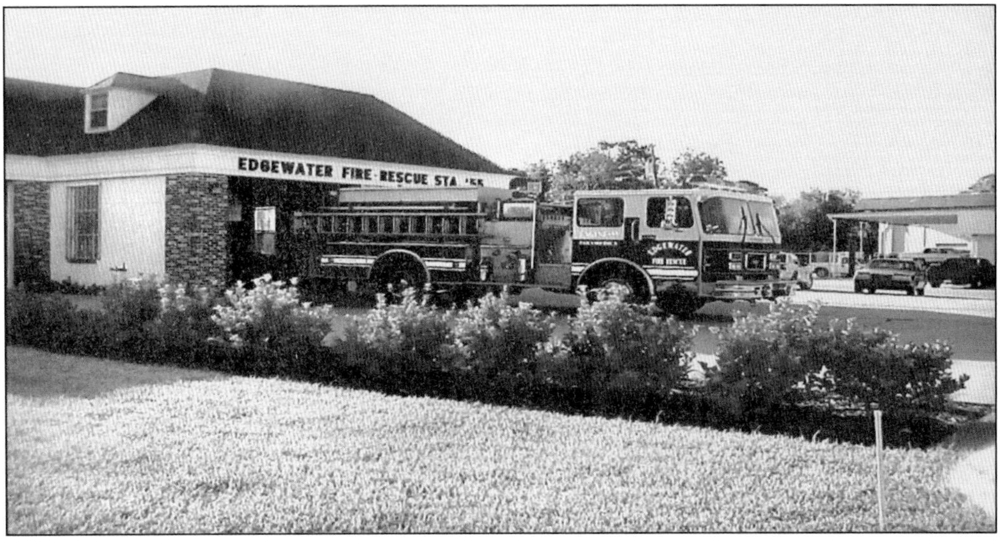

FIRE STATION 55, 1975. A grand opening celebration was held when a new fire station was built on South Ridgewood Avenue in Edgewater. A parade wound from the old firehouse on Park Avenue to the new one and included a marching unit from Orlando, the Stingray Band from the middle school, and local Boy and Girl Scout troops. Started with volunteers, Edgewater's department now has 27 paid firefighters trained as emergency medical technicians.

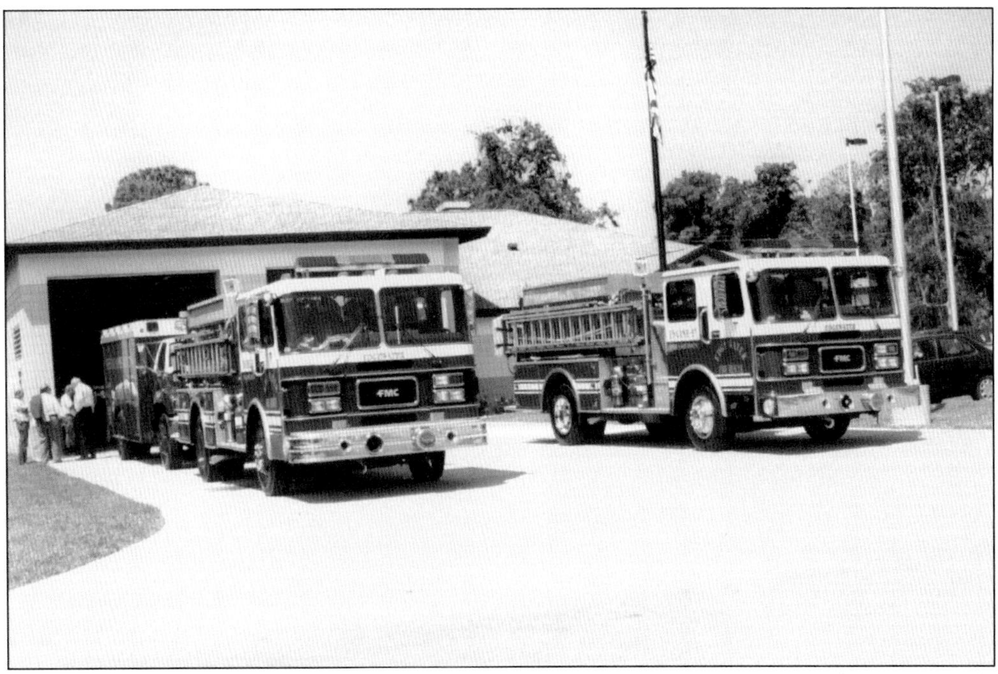

FIRE STATION 57 ON HIBISCUS DRIVE, APRIL 1999. A fire station was needed in the Florida Shores area, and this one was located on Hibiscus Drive. Another asset to the community was EVER, the Edgewater Volunteer Emergency Rescue. EVER was formed in 1975 to provide emergency service until an ambulance arrived. This independent, volunteer group of well-trained citizens was separate from the fire department.

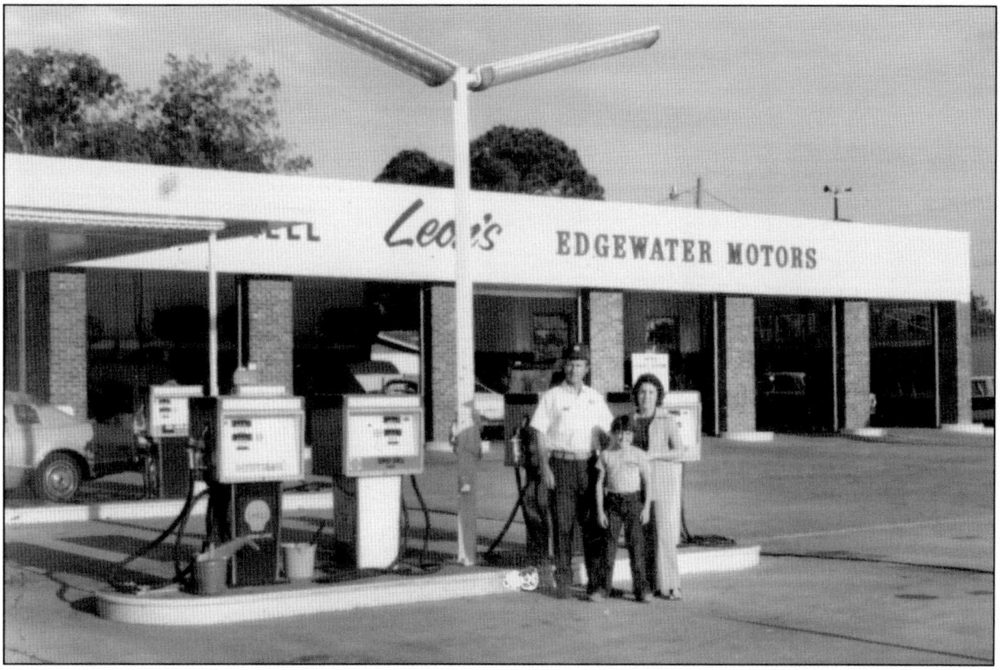

LEON'S EDGEWATER MOTORS, C. 1980. Leon and Frances Robitzsch bought a gas station and garage along Ridgewood Avenue in May 1978. He had no idea the area would grow as fast as it did. For several years, he could count four or five cars every half hour coming east. Leon Robitzsch has retired, but his son, Mark Robitzsch, now carries on the family business, with the help of mechanics who have stayed with the business for a long time. Shown are Mr. and Mrs. Leon Robitzsch and their son Grant.

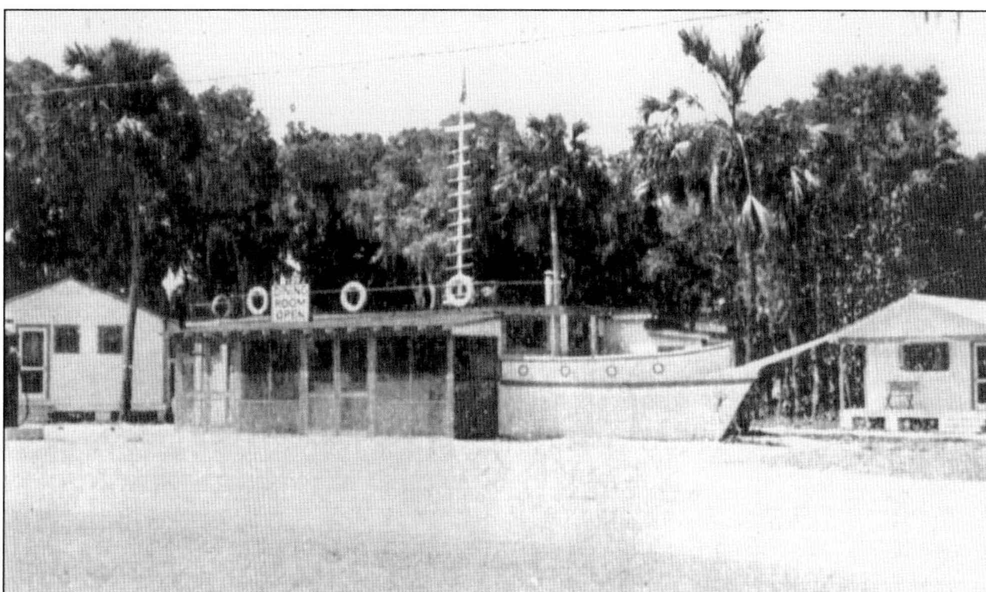

OLD SHIP RESTAURANT, C. 1945. For many years this was a restaurant along U.S. 1. Decorated with a nautical theme, it gave customers the feeling of walking into a ship. It was a delightful stop for ice cream on a hot day.

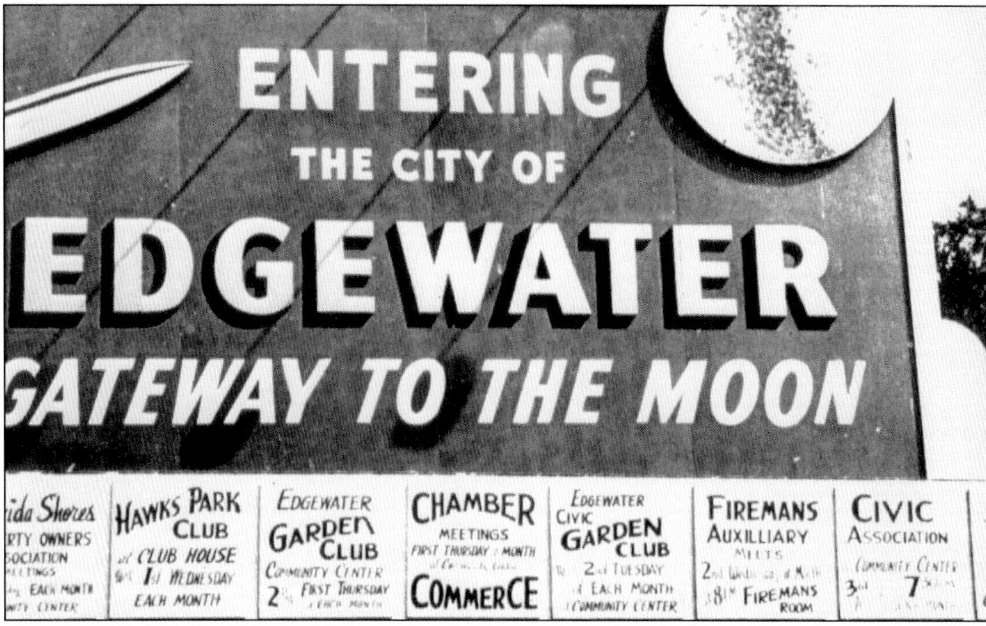

EDGEWATER: GATEWAY TO THE MOON, C. 1956. The world's attention had turned to space, so a billboard was put up stating, "Entering the City of Edgewater—Gateway to the Moon." The building of Kennedy Space Center about 35 miles south of Edgewater opened the way for tremendous growth. The city now had a post office with home delivery, a water system, and lighted streets.

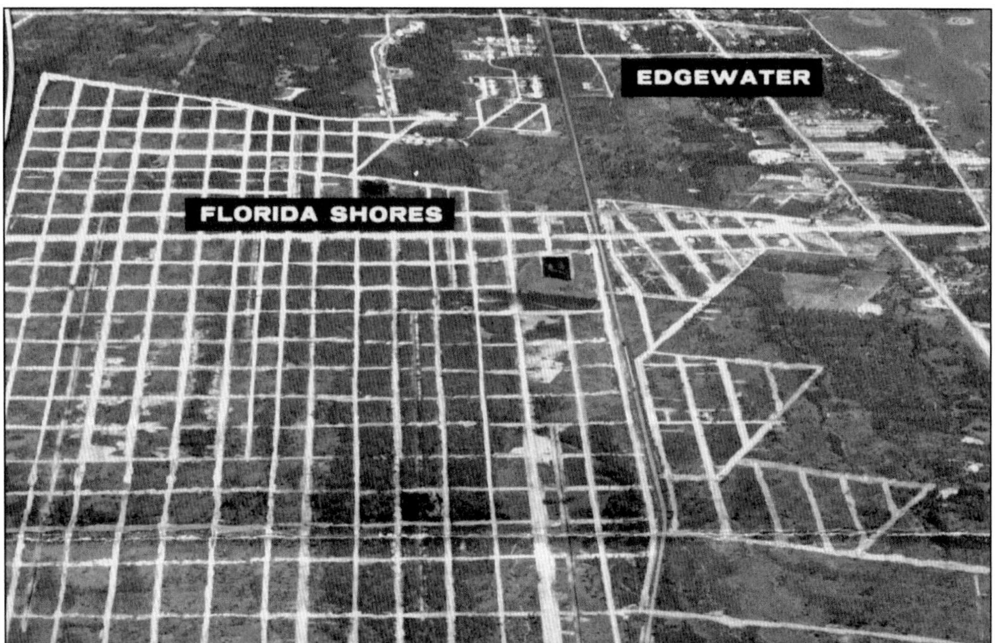

FLORIDA SHORES, 1957. The annexation of the Florida Shores subdivision by a special election tripled the size of Edgewater. The building of homes in the subdivision had been started much earlier, and other subdivisions followed, including Silver Ridge and Edgewater Landing. By the 1960s, a water and sewer system was completed, and Edgewater had a population of 2,051.

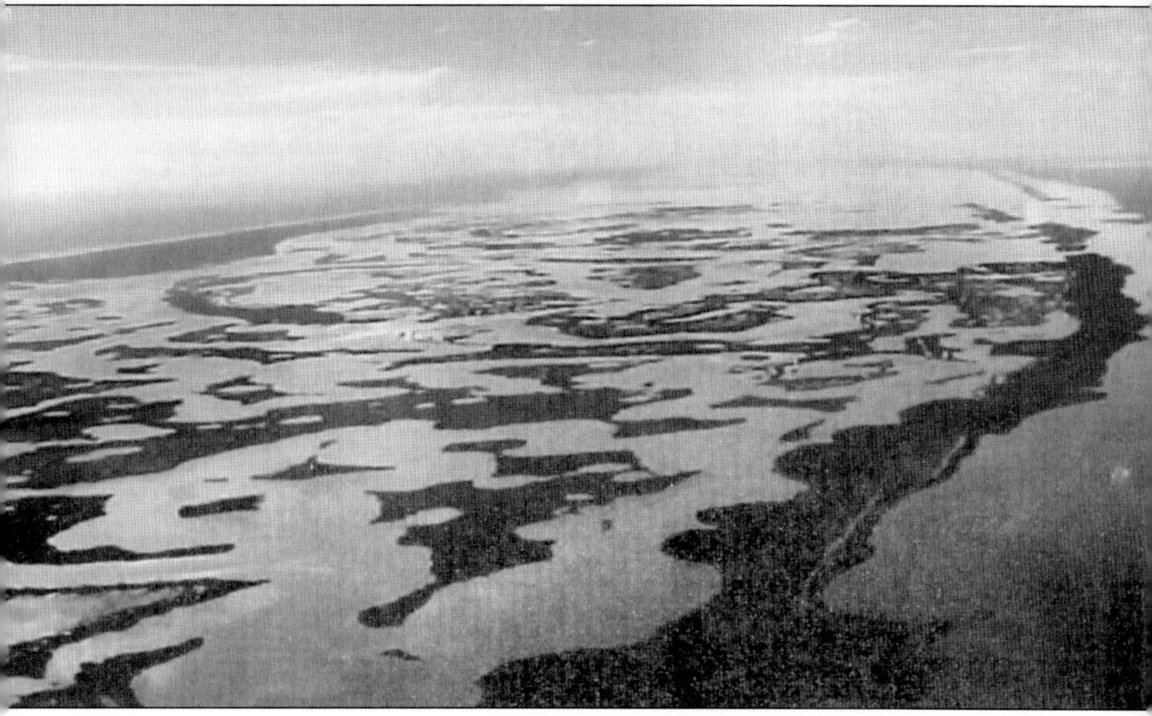

INDIAN RIVER LAGOON, 2003. Dr. John Milton Hawks described the area: "The river is interspersed with mangrove islands." Edgewater is part of the Indian River Lagoon estuary, where salt water from the ocean mixes with fresh water. The result is an environment teeming with plant and animal life. The lagoon is a spawning and nursery habitat for ocean and river fish and a large variety of birds. It is located on the Atlantic Flyway, a "biological highway" for many species of birds between the tropic and temperate zones.

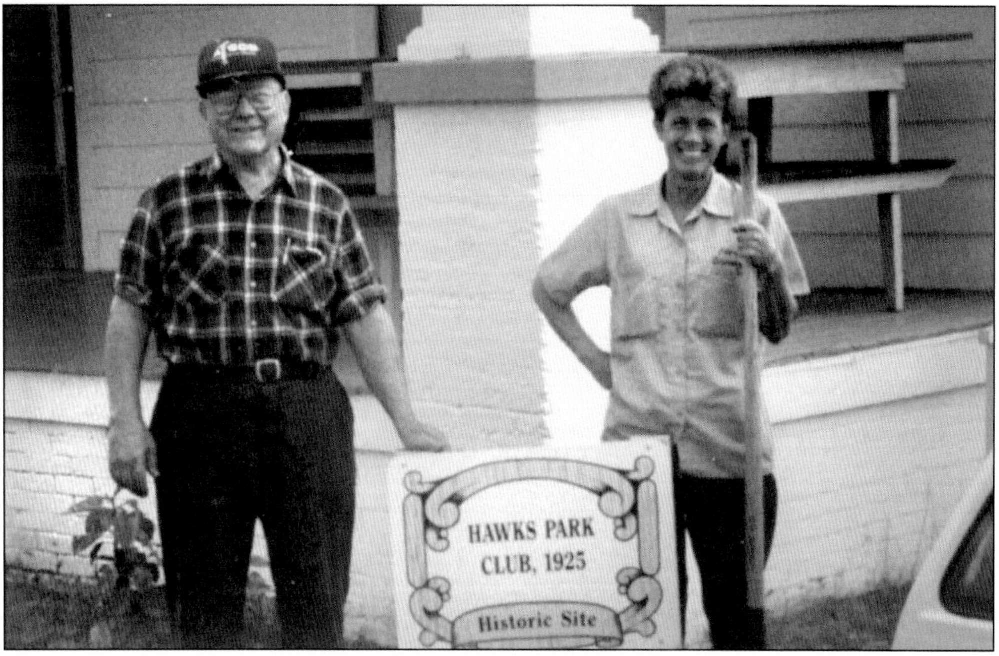

HISTORICAL SITE MARKERS, 1990. Showing pride in its past, the city provided funding for signs designating historic sites. Shown here are Henry Knapp and Gloria Greenwood at the placement of the marker at the Hawks Park Club. Others were placed at the first town hall and library, the site of the Betsy Ross School, the Union Church, the flow well, and the steamboat wharf. By 1990, there was also a beautification committee in Edgewater.

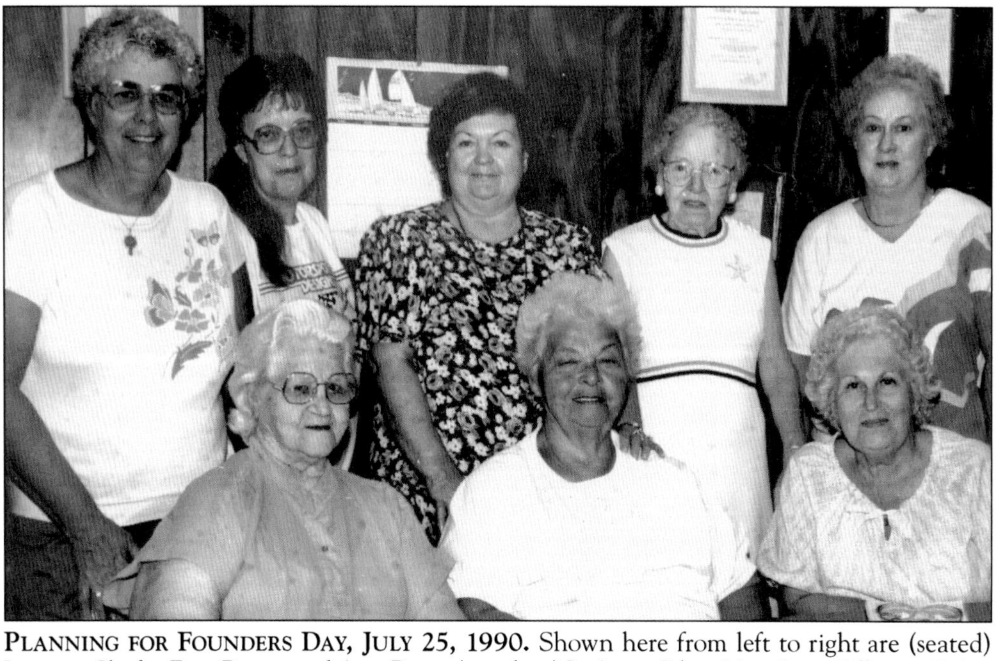

PLANNING FOR FOUNDERS DAY, JULY 25, 1990. Shown here from left to right are (seated) Lauretta Shafer, Fran Byrne, and Ann Ryan; (standing) Jo Anne Sikes, Nora Jane Gillespie, Peggy Wolsfelt, Dorothy Silva, and Lelia Wilsey. The main speaker for the festivities was Prof. Gerald Schwartz, who edited Dr. Esther Hawks's diary, *A Woman Doctor's Civil War.*

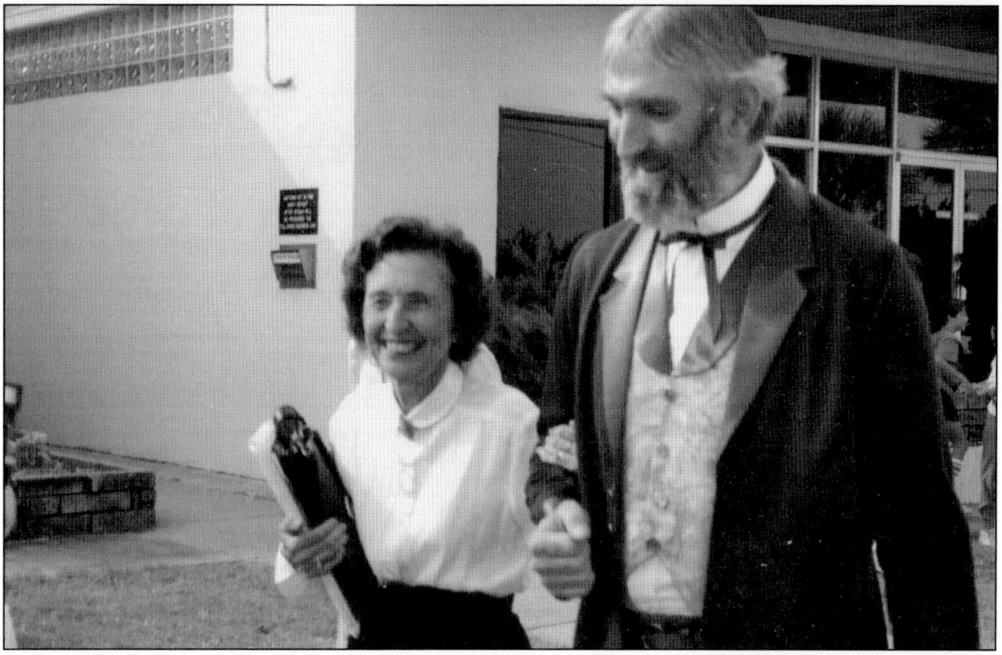

FOUNDERS DAY CELEBRATION, NOVEMBER 17, 1990. Celebrating the founding of Hawks Park, Marie Goodrich and Chuck Storey donned period clothes to portray Dr. Esther Hill Hawks and Dr. John Milton Hawks. On that day, the aforementioned new marker was also placed at John Milton Hawks's grave.

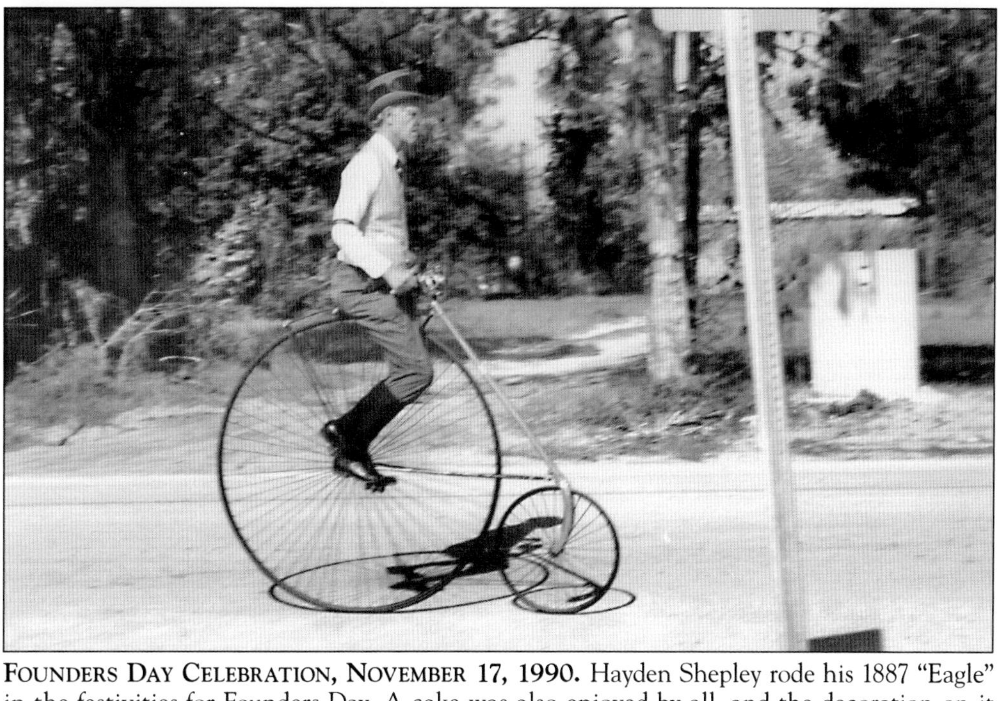

FOUNDERS DAY CELEBRATION, NOVEMBER 17, 1990. Hayden Shepley rode his 1887 "Eagle" in the festivities for Founders Day. A cake was also enjoyed by all, and the decoration on it showed a miniature map of the river shore, with the flow well, steamboat landing, and Dr. Hawks's home.

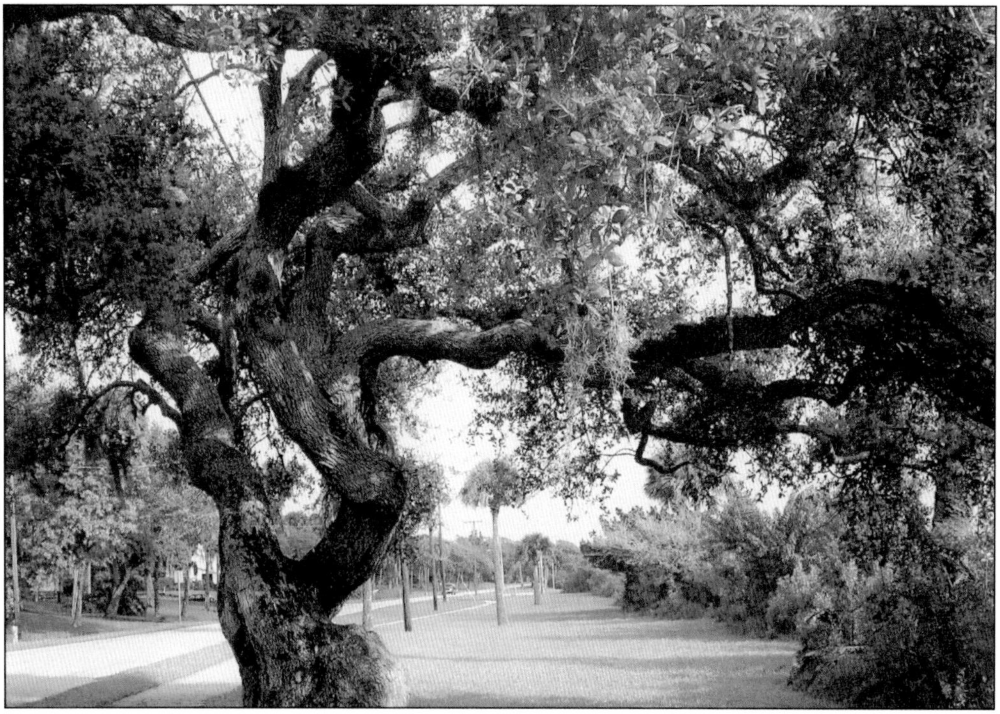

RIVERWALK BY DAY, 1998. Edgewater has a "Tree City U.S.A." designation, and Riverwalk is a walking/cycling path between Riverside Drive and the Indian River. Joggers and walkers enjoy the three-mile pathway, watching the seasons of the year change by the sumptuous yachts that glide by on the Intracoastal Waterway. In the fall, the boats head south, looking for safe haven from the cold. In the spring, sailboats and yachts head back to harbors in the north.

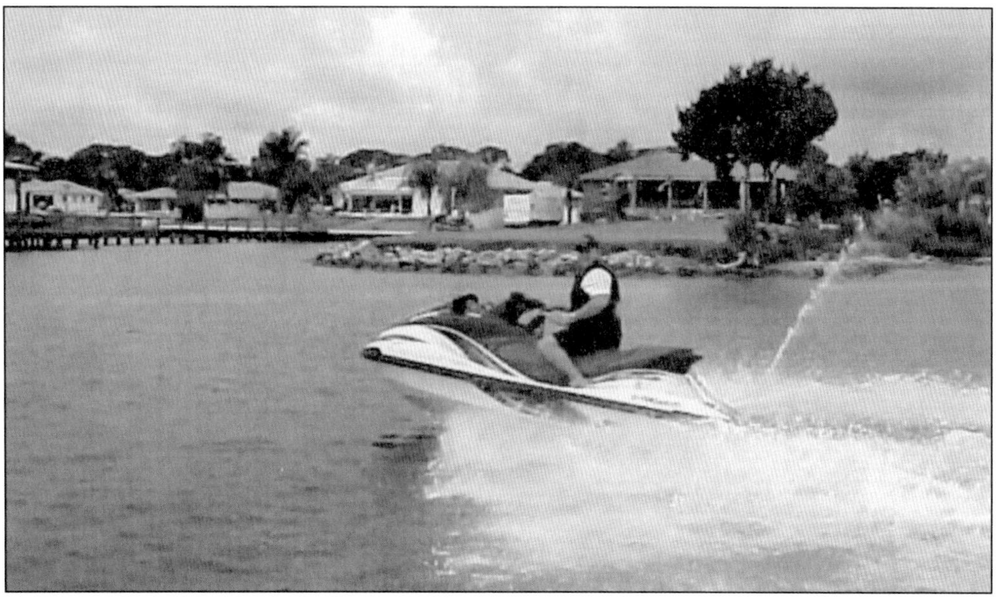

OFFICER CLARK ON SKI-DOO, C. 1998. The Edgewater Police Department has its own Jet-ski, shown here, protecting the river. Alan Clark is on duty in the picture, but pleasure water sports abound on the river in Edgewater, for whatever you "wantah" do!

Eight

School of 30 Pupils

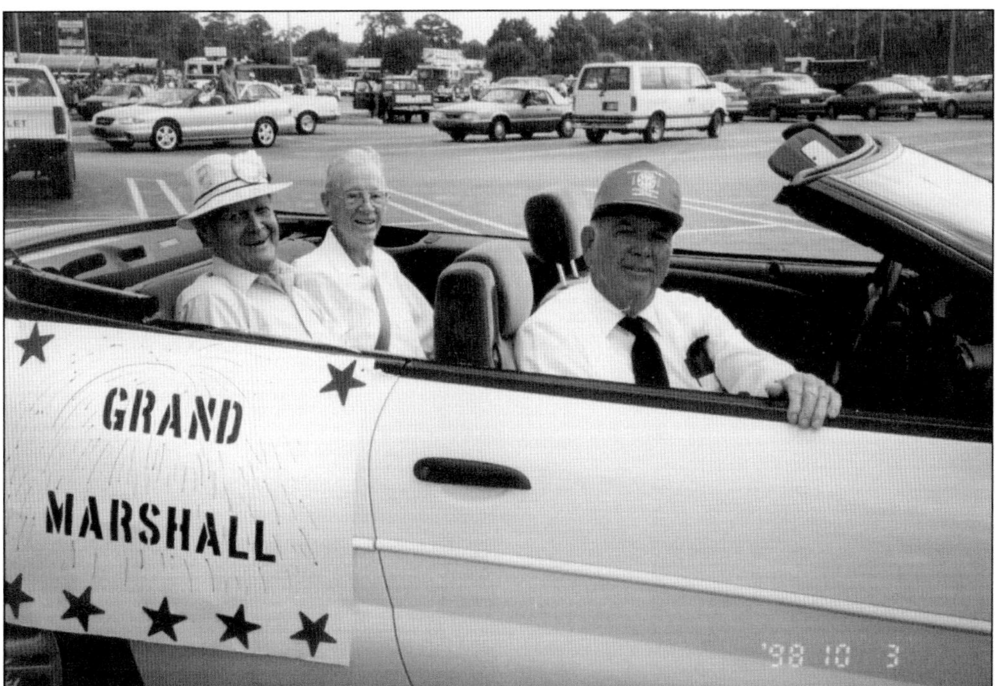

Grand Marshall of the Parade, 1998. Leading the 1998 Fourth of July parade in Edgewater, the grand marshall's car included David McCallister in the front seat, Bob Poland with the hat on in the back, and Harry Broga.

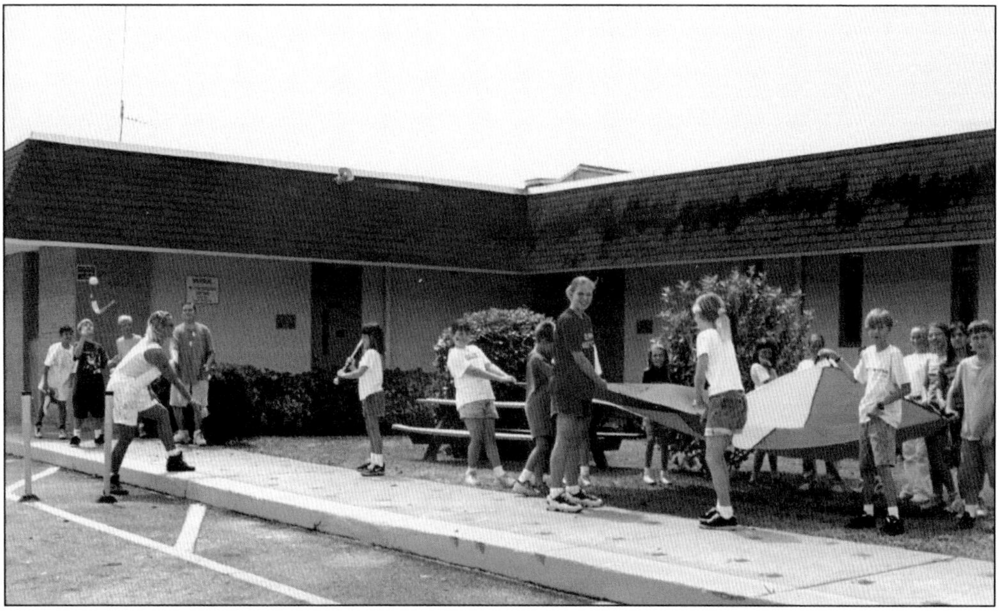

EDGEWATER PUBLIC SCHOOL, 1998. Located on Old County Road, this school opened its doors in 1966 with 268 students. The school was built on palmetto-covered land and it was loaded with rattlesnakes. One teacher remembered throwing logs at a huge rattler, hoping to kill it. The land was soon cleared of the palmettos. Today the school has more than 650 students. The students here are unidentified.

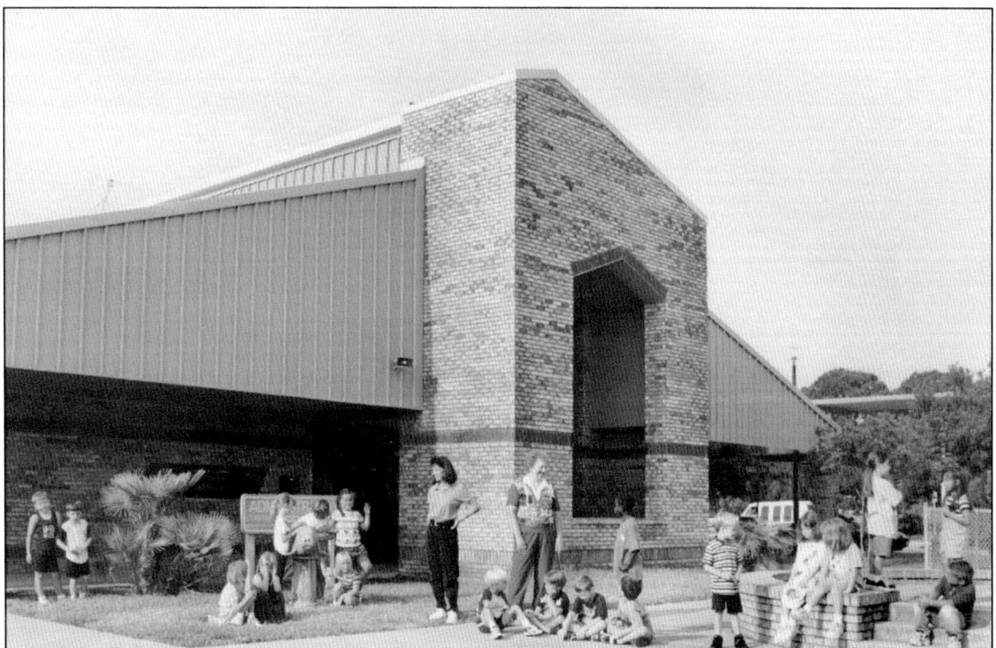

INDIAN RIVER ELEMENTARY SCHOOL, 1998. Named for its proximity to the Indian River, this second elementary school to be built in the city of Edgewater is located on Roberts Road. The school now has over 700 enrolled, and the students have a time capsule that they filled in 1991 to be opened in 2011. The people are unidentified.

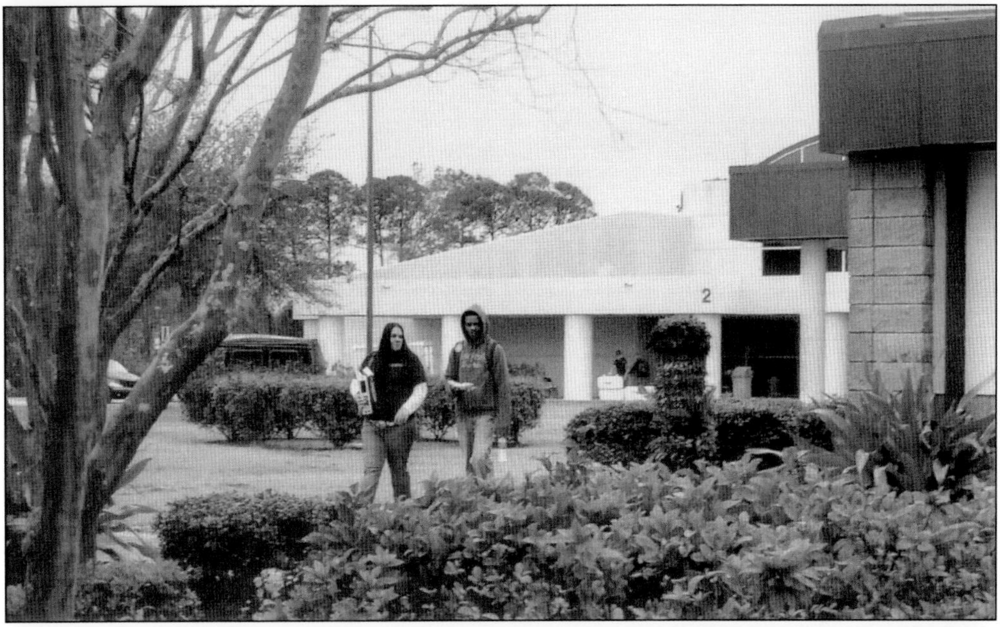

DAYTONA BEACH COMMUNITY COLLEGE, 2005. The New Smyrna/Edgewater campus of DBCC, located on Tenth Street in Edgewater, is convenient to students in southeast Volusia County. Classes started in August 1994 with the completion of its second building at this location. Now with more than 1,900 students, DBCC offers basic undergraduate classes, with laboratories, computer rooms, a library, and bookstore. The students are unidentified.

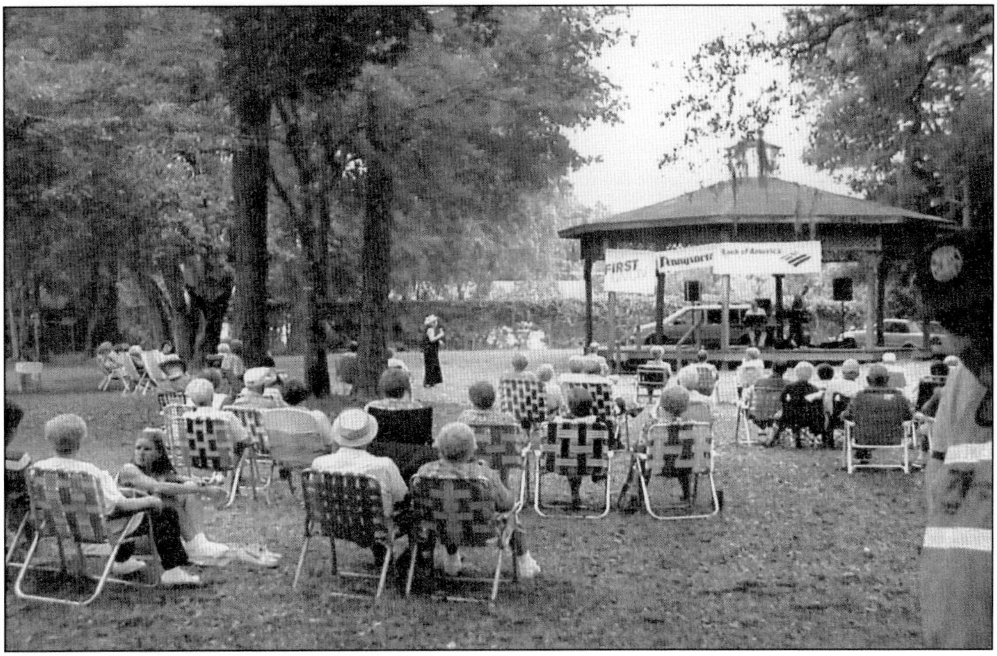

CONCERT IN ROTARY PARK, 2003. Edgewater is no longer a community to spend only the winter months or retirement years. It is growing as more people move here to make it their home. The Atlantic Ocean, the Indian River, and the Florida sunshine are natural assets to this area and attract more people each year. This is Florida at its finest! The people are unidentified.

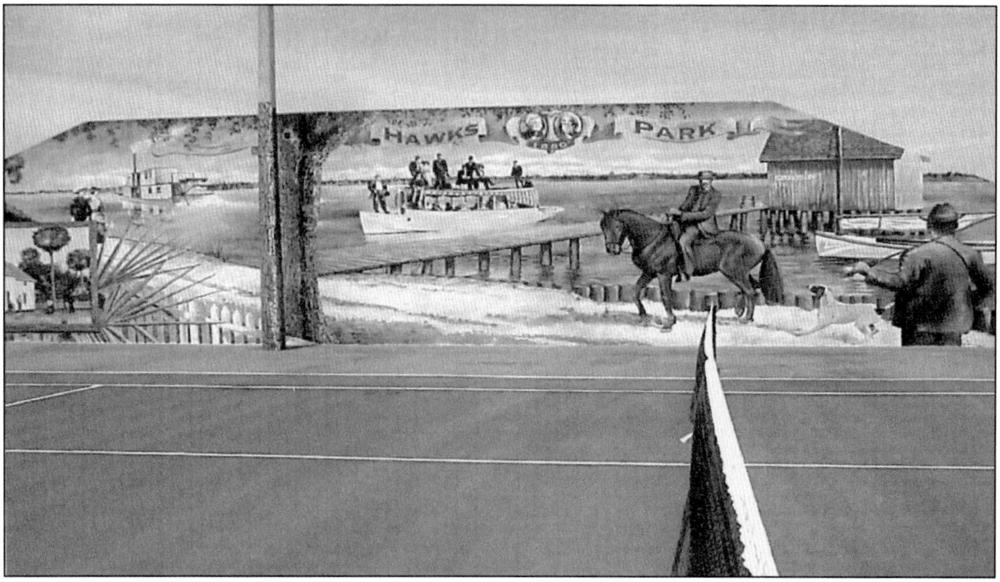

MURAL AT KENNEDY PARK, 2003. Again celebrating the rich history of Edgewater, this mural was painted by Courtney Canova in 1999 on the wall by the tennis courts in Kennedy Park. The design was chosen from historic Hawks Park photos. The park, just across the street from city hall, was named for fire chief George M. Kennedy, who was killed when fireworks malfunctioned during a Fourth of July celebration.

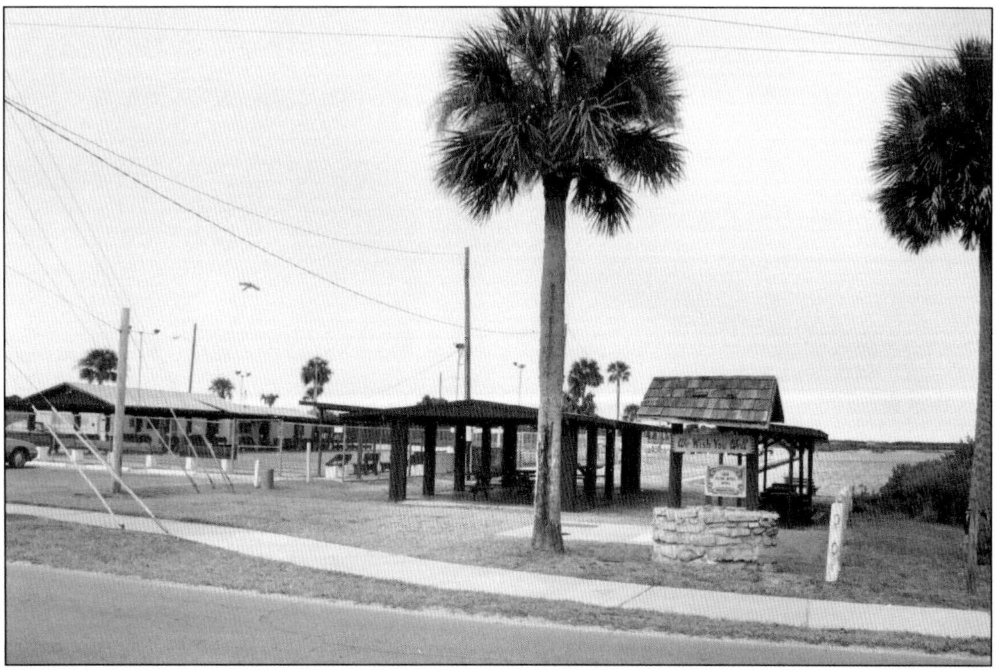

SHUFFLEBOARD AND TENNIS COURTS, KENNEDY PARK, 2003. George M. Kennedy Park had been an active place, with tennis, handball, and shuffleboard courts. Shuffleboard tournaments had been held there for many years, but the mural and the shuffleboard courts were destroyed by a hurricane in 2004. Note the old flow well in the right foreground.

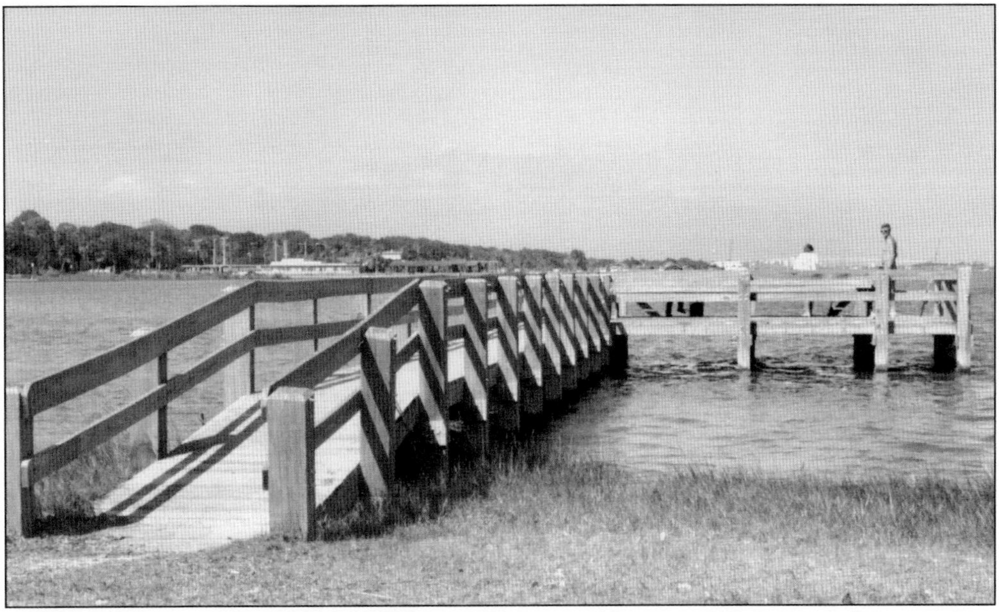

FISHING DOCK AT MENARD-MAY PARK, 2003. Located between Merrimac and Connecticut Avenues along Riverside Drive, Menard-May Park now juts out into the Indian River as a four-acre recreation area. Manatees, dolphins, and many kinds of sea and land birds still inhabit the area where the long dock had been in Hawks Park. Some of the land was donated by the Menard and May families. The people are unidentified.

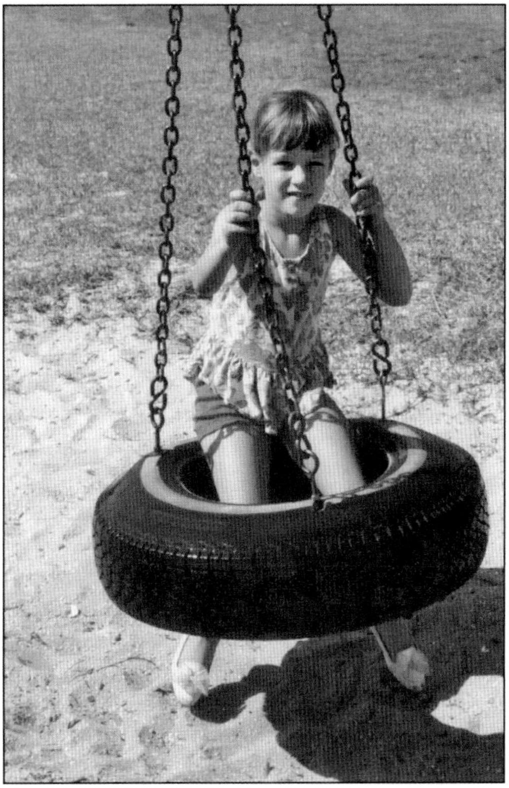

GIRL ON SWING IN MENARD-MAY PARK, C. 1995. Hawks Park may have started with one central park around which the town was built, but today Edgewater has many parks. Swings, picnic pavilions, basketball, tennis, and racquetball courts can all be found in Edgewater's parks today. The girl shown here is unidentified.

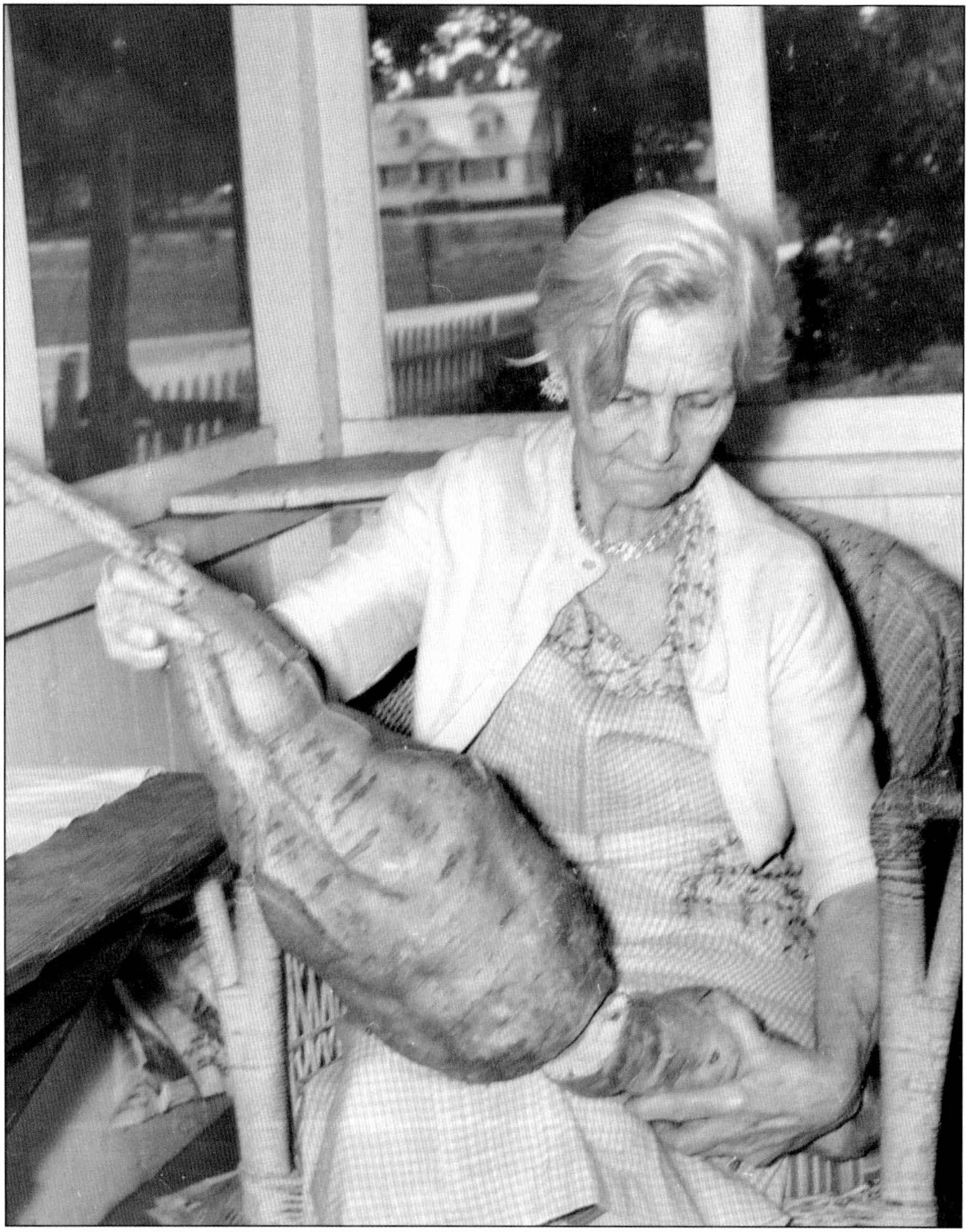

A Bumper Crop! c. 1963. Dr. Hawks said, "Sweet potatoes are a profitable crop," but even he could not have counted on this harvest. This woman, who may be Lottie Bittinger, grew one of the largest sweet potatoes seen in Edgewater.

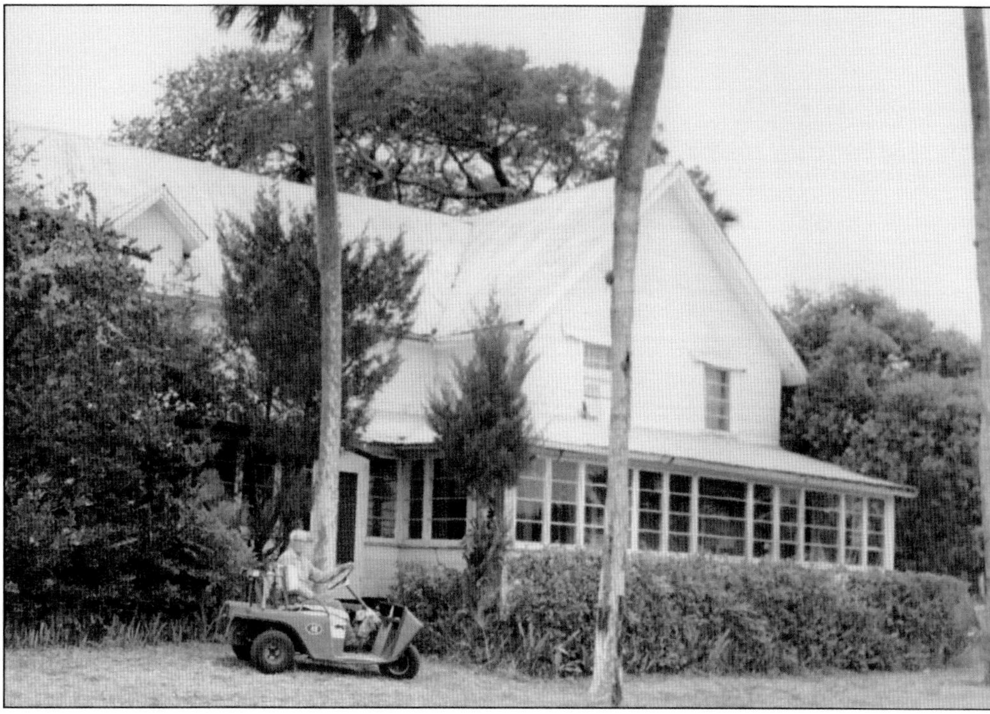

WILKINSON HOME ON RIVERSIDE DRIVE, 1998. H. P. Wilkinson is shown on his golf cart in front of the home he owns on the road that used to be the Strand, now busy Riverside Drive. This home was the old Mendell Boarding House in Hawks Park days.

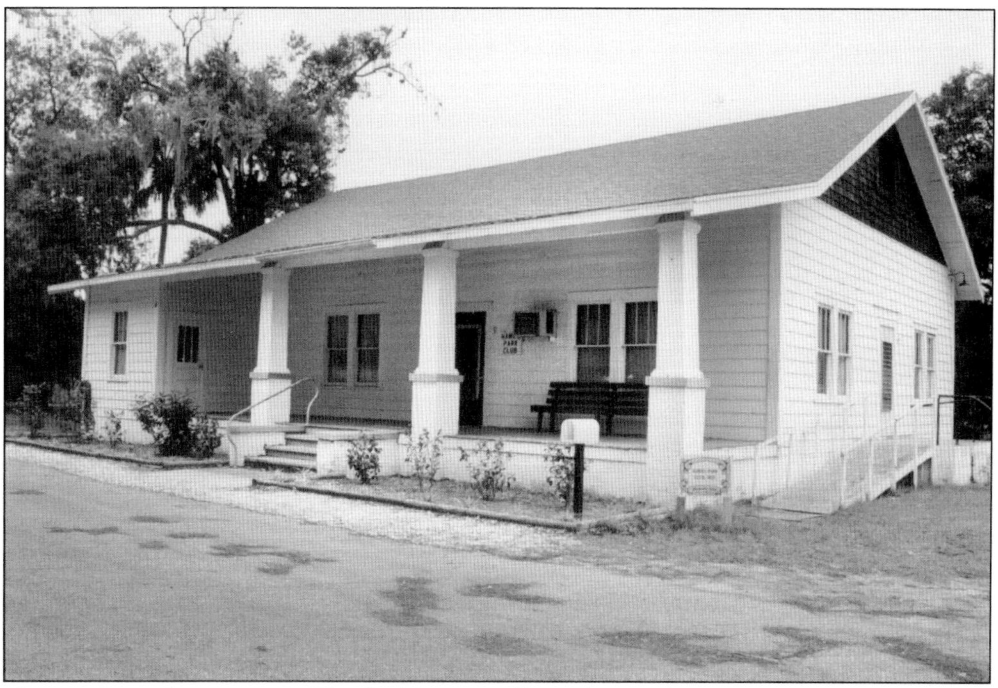

HAWKS PARK CLUB, 2005. This building is still standing with its historical marker proudly displayed. A variety of meetings are still held here.

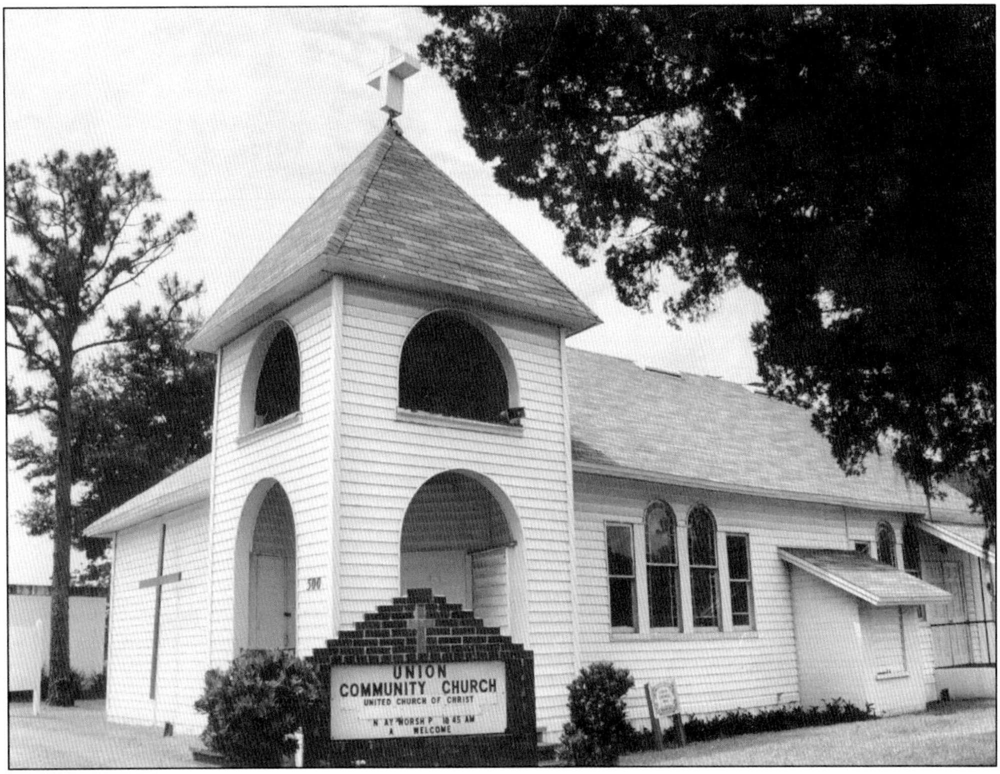

UNION CHURCH, 1998. Still a very active church at the corner of West Ocean and Ridgewood Avenues, the Union Church bell rings every Sunday morning in today's Edgewater. Several times this historic landmark has been remodeled, and when a ceiling was installed in the 1950s, the minister's sermon could easily be heard. The church women's organization is now called the Willing Workers.

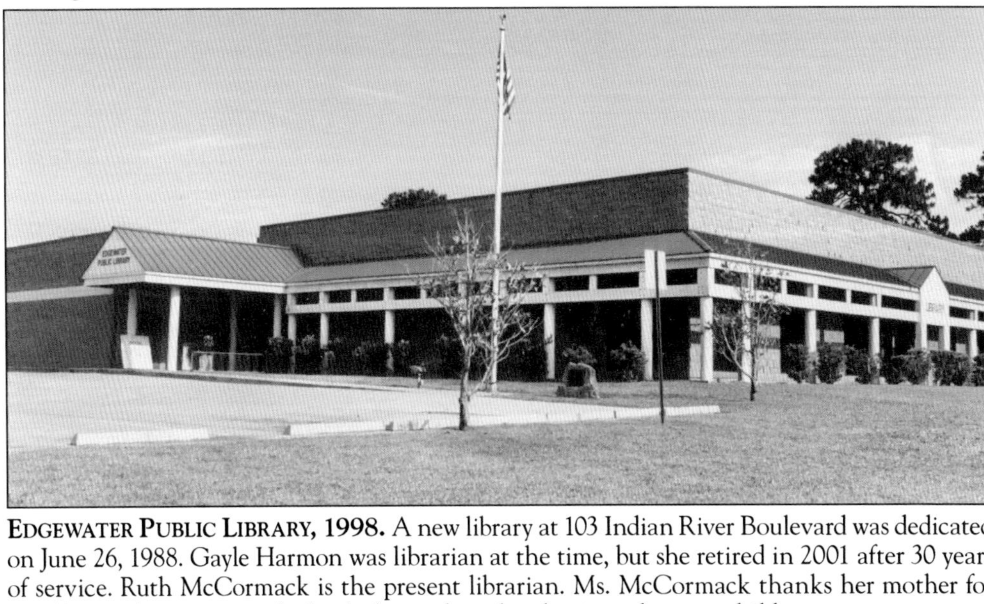

EDGEWATER PUBLIC LIBRARY, 1998. A new library at 103 Indian River Boulevard was dedicated on June 26, 1988. Gayle Harmon was librarian at the time, but she retired in 2001 after 30 years of service. Ruth McCormack is the present librarian. Ms. McCormack thanks her mother for instilling in her a passion for books by reading the classics to her as a child.

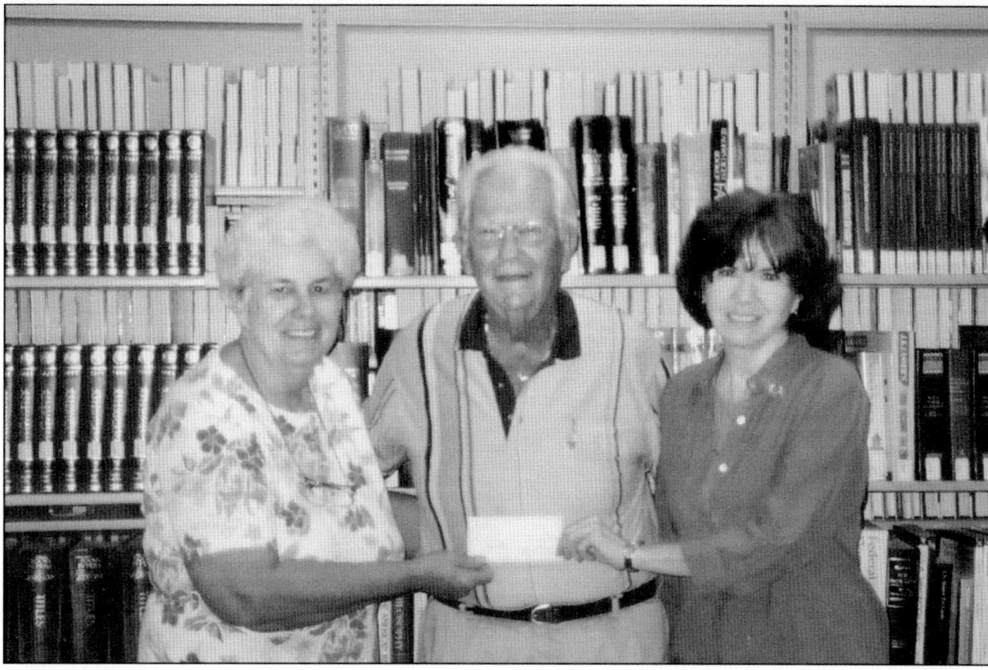

EDGEWATER PUBLIC LIBRARY, NOVEMBER 2003. Pictured from left to right in the new library, on Indian River Boulevard near U.S. 1, are Jo Anne Sikes, a member of the Edgewater Library Board and Friends of the Library at the time; Bob Richards; and Ruth McCormack, head librarian. Bob Richards was presenting a bequest from Mary Rice, establishing the Friends of the Library Endowment Fund.

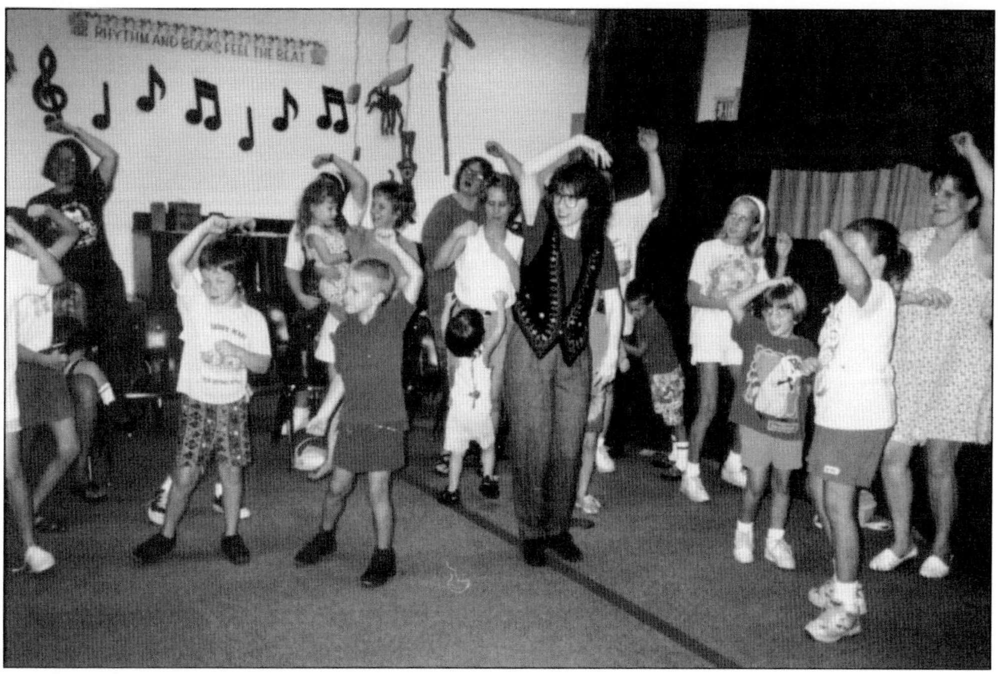

EDGEWATER PUBLIC LIBRARY, 1996. Ruth McCormack had been the children's librarian and is shown participating in a program with the children.

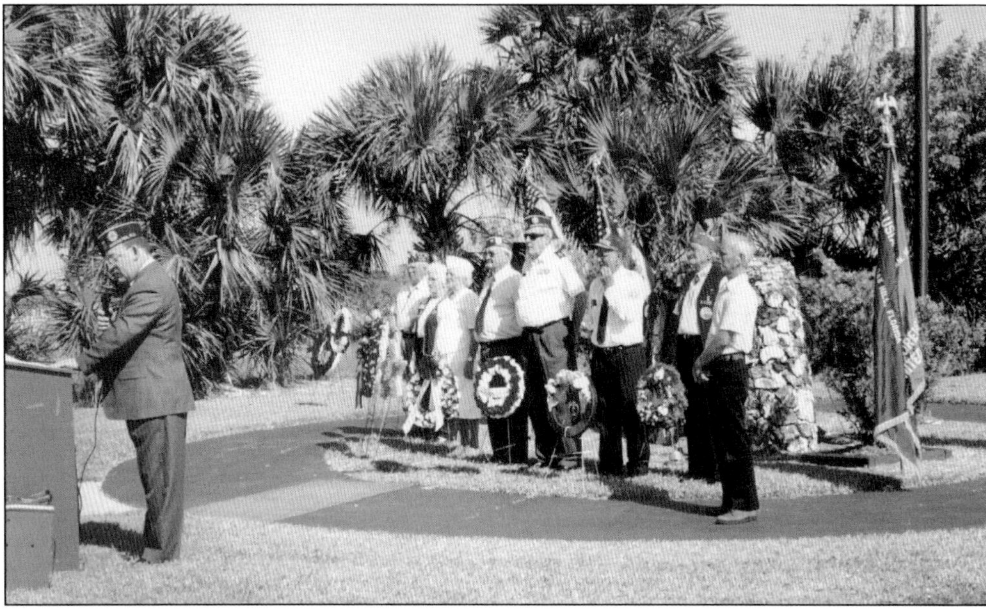

VETERANS' PARK CELEBRATION, 1994. Veterans' Park, along Riverside Drive, is the scene of many celebrations of remembrance. At this Memorial Day service, representatives from the American Legion, Veterans of Foreign Wars, Gold Star Mothers, Disabled American Veterans, and others attended. The speaker is unknown. Others are Alfred Gray, Helen Miller, and some unidentified people, with councilman James Brown on the far right.

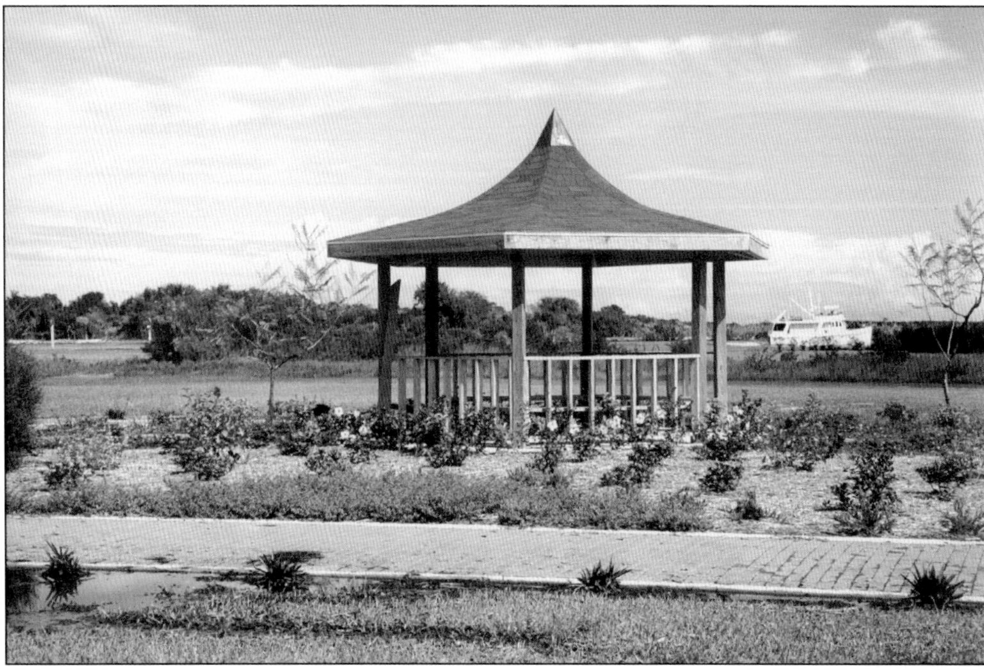

RIVERWALK GAZEBO BY DAY, 1998. Photographer Marie Goodrich chronicles Edgewater's recent history, and this gazebo, near the northern end of Riverside Drive, is a convenient stop along the Riverwalk that follows the Indian River. Joggers, cyclists, and walkers of all ages still enjoy the land and water birds, the dolphins and manatees, and the elegant yachts going by.

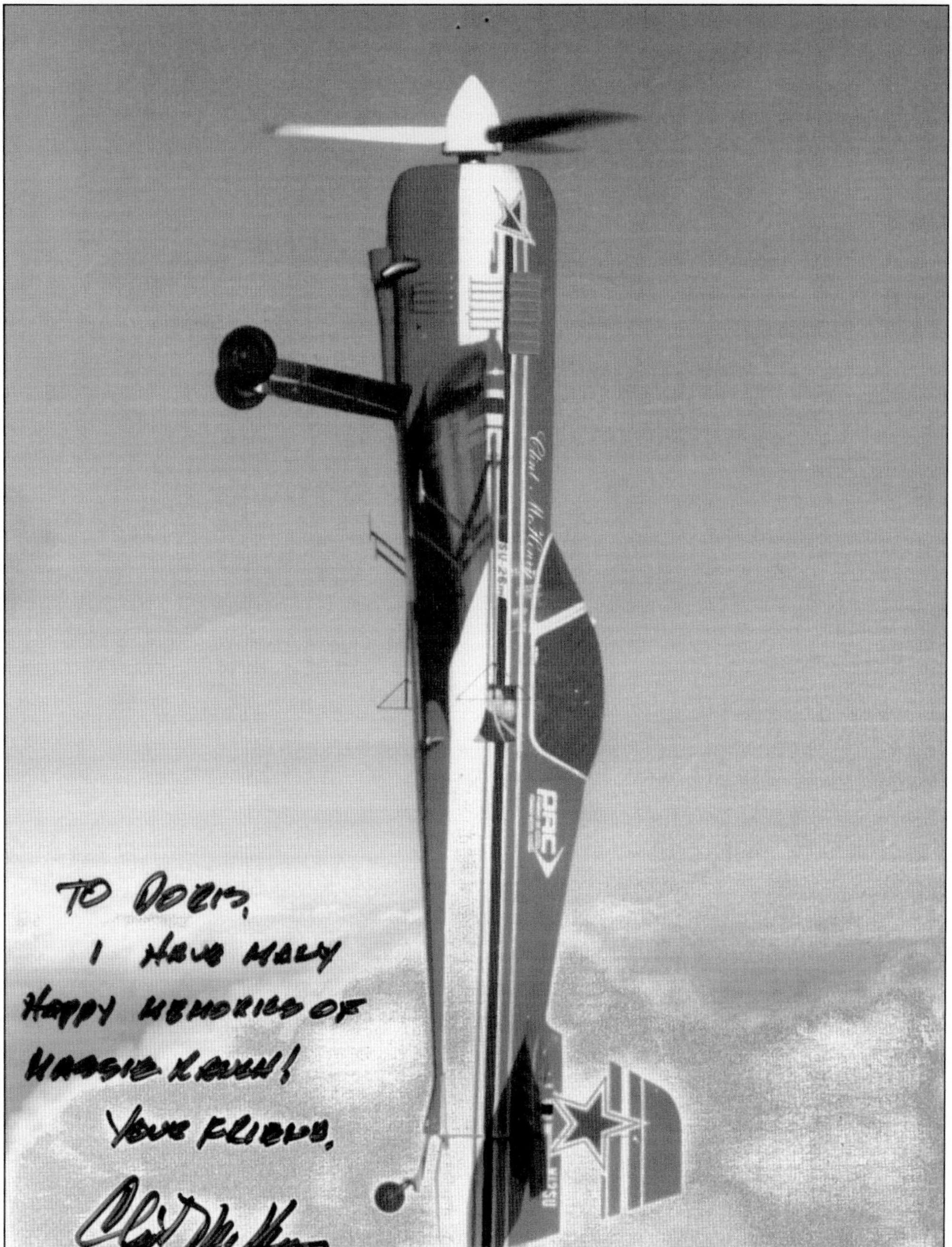

MASSEY RANCH AIRPARK, C. 1990. Clint McHenry was a stunt flier who gave Edgewater audiences a thrill when he did his aerobatics over Massey Ranch Airpark. The airpark was started by the Massey family in 1950 as a sod field. In 1957, it became a public licensed airport, and in 1998, the runways were paved. Still a family-owned business, the airpark now offers fly-in homes, complete with hangar.

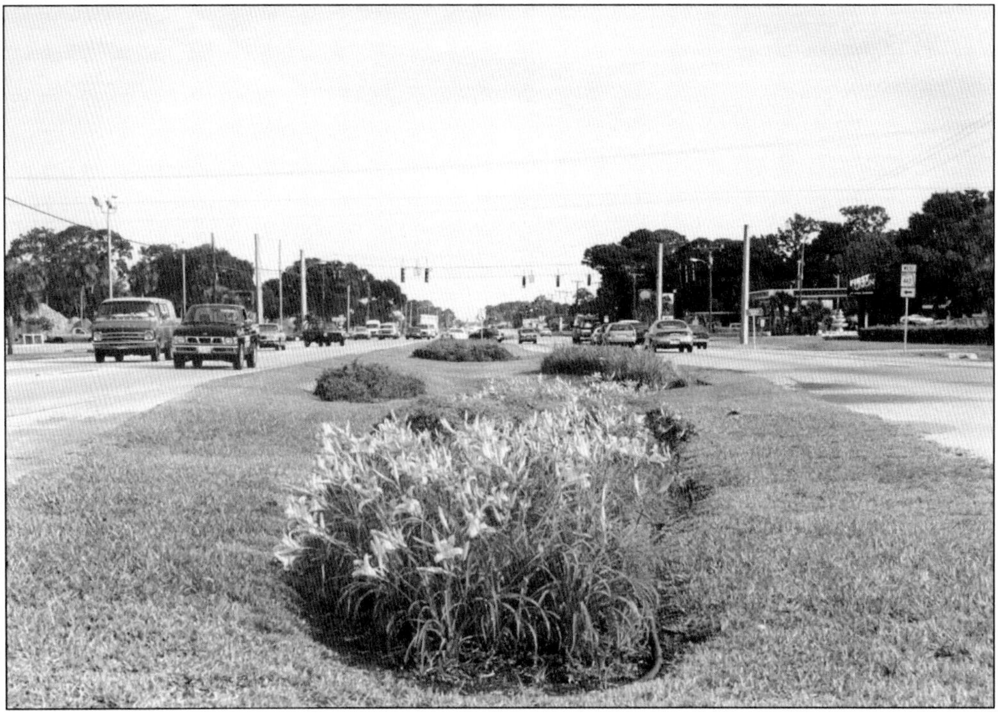

RIDGEWOOD AVENUE/U.S. 1, 1998. The New County Road to New Smyrna now is part of U.S. 1, on which one can travel from Key West to eastern Maine. In 1979, bus service to the other area communities was also available. The City of Edgewater keeps the medians landscaped for all to enjoy, even if they are just passing through.

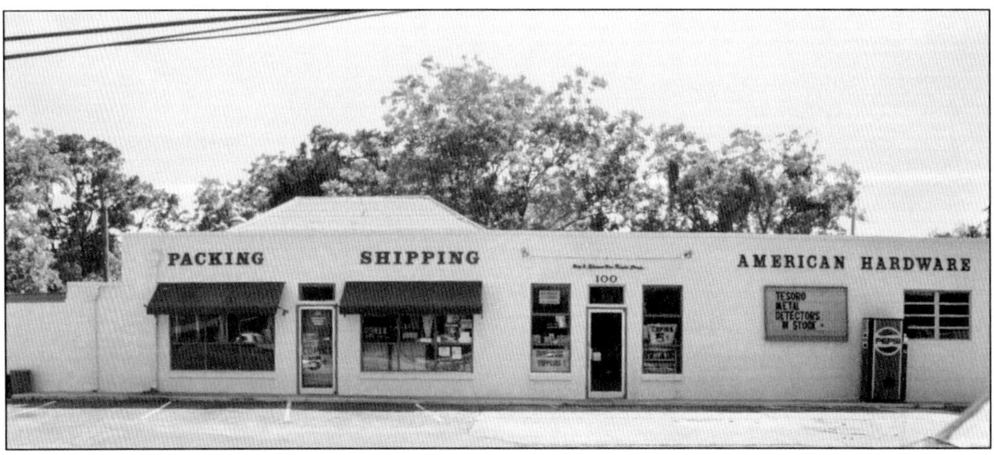

AMERICAN HARDWARE STORE, 1998. Located at the busy intersection of U.S. 1 and Park Avenue, the American Hardware store still shows the distinctive roof from another structure. The hardware store was built around and still includes the roof and some walls from the old Betsy Ross School from Hawks Park days.

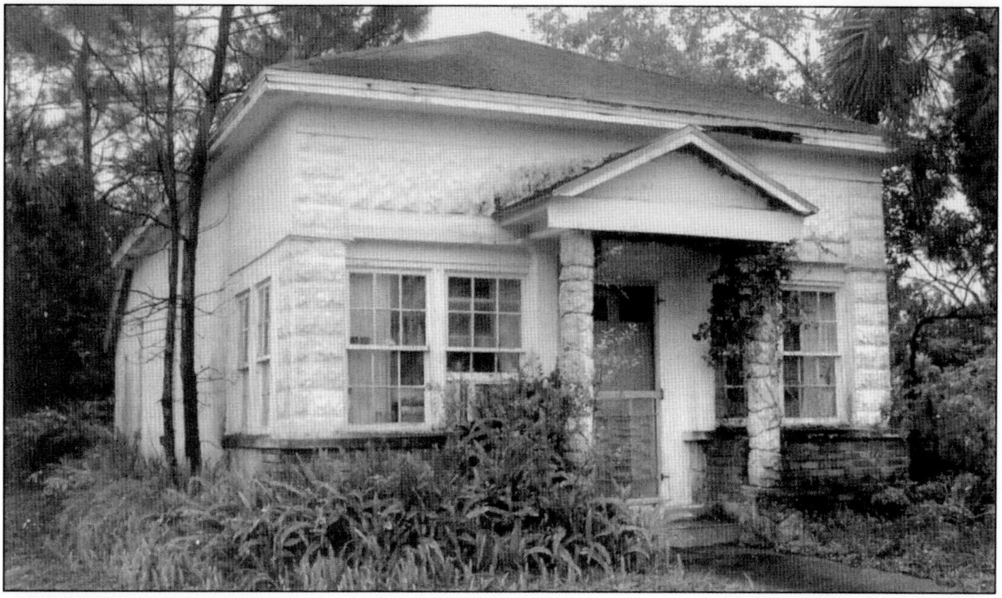

HAWKS PARK GROCERY STORE, 2005. Many grocery stores have opened and closed their doors since the early Hawks Park grocery was built, but this old structure still stands on Ocean Avenue where it was originally located.

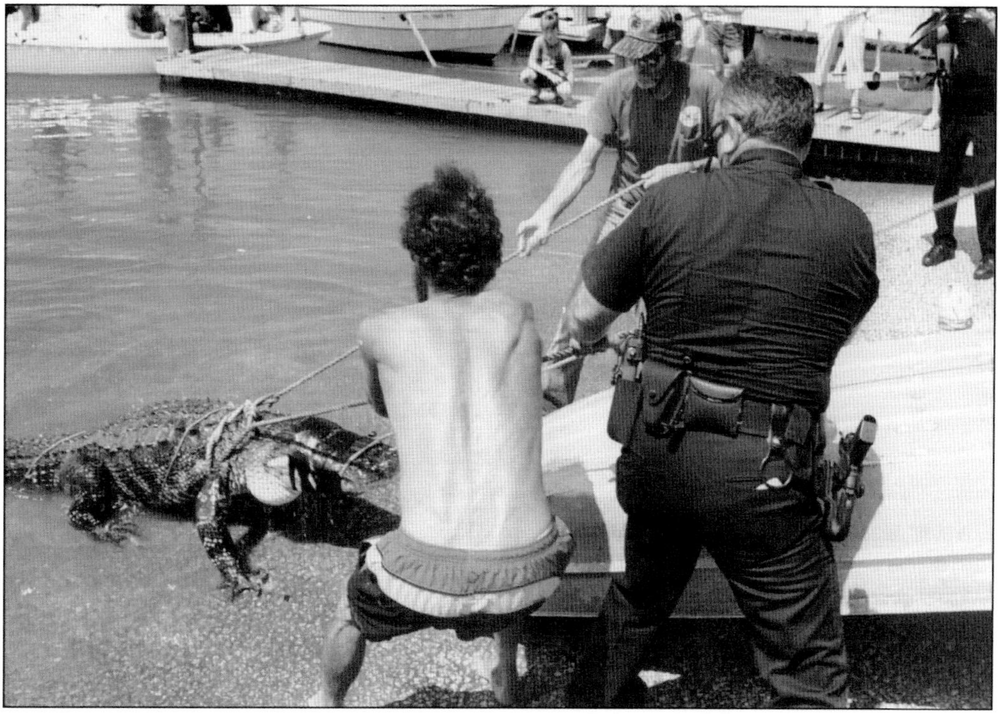

POLICE TAKING A GATOR FROM THE RIVER, 2003. Marie Goodrich, a local photographer, caught this image showing that alligators sometimes are still seen in the river, just as they were in the days of John Milton Hawks. In 2001, a 10-foot alligator was lurking near some docks and did not leave. The gator was captured and taken in a trapper's "Gators to Go" truck. The people are unidentified.

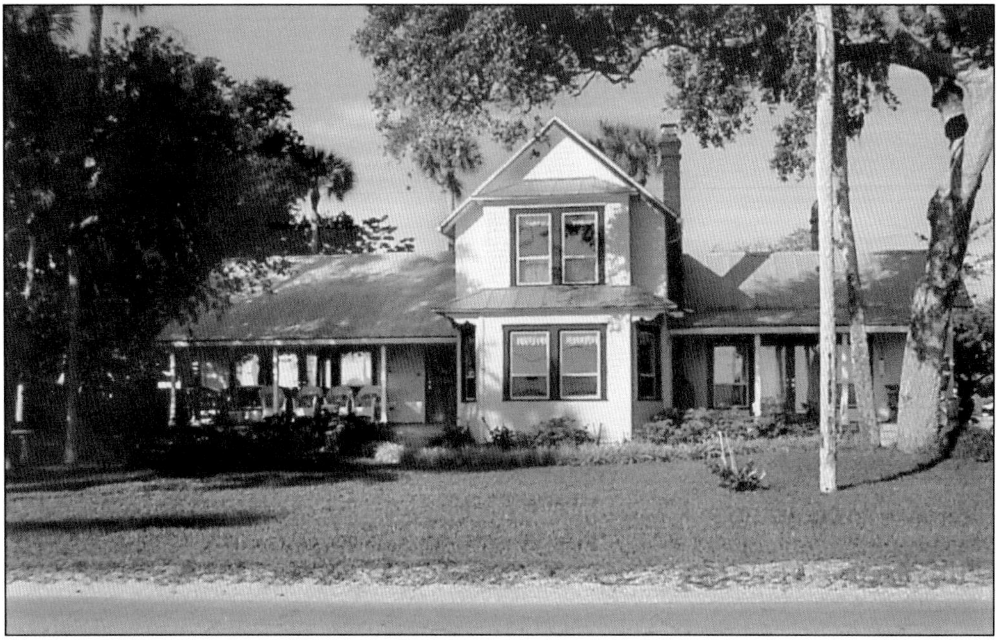

HARRY MITCHELL HOME, 1998. This home still stands, thanks to many years of careful preservation, at Woodley Avenue and South Riverside Drive, just a short distance from the Hawks Park Club.

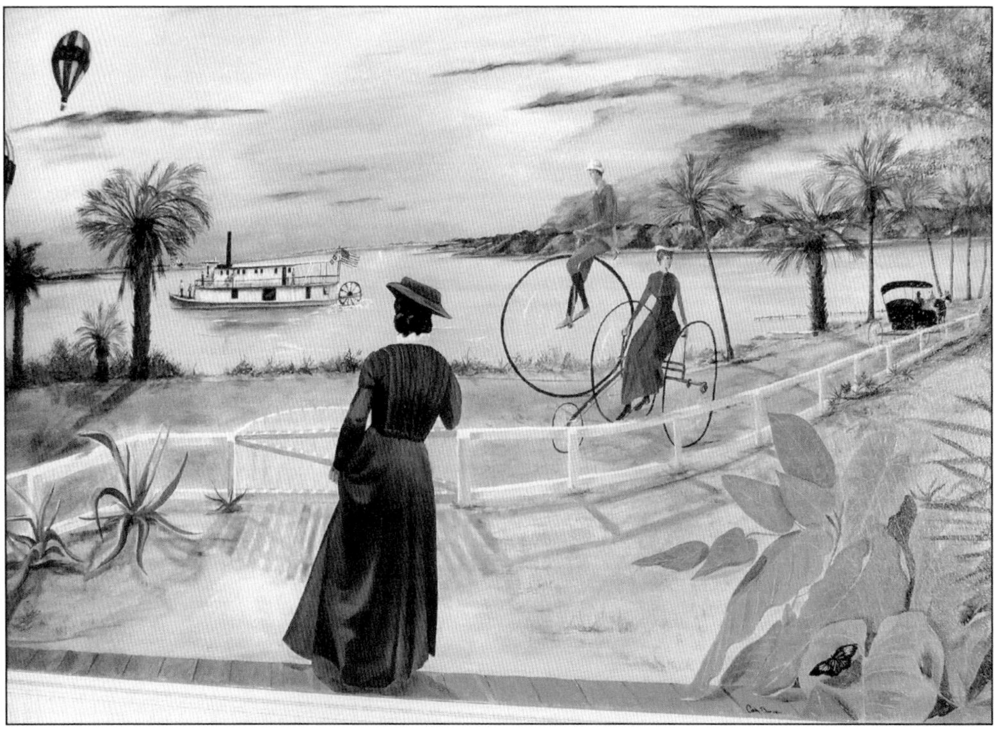

HARRY MITCHELL HOME MURAL, 2005. The current owners were pleased to find a mural in the bathroom that had been part of the house for many years. It depicts scenes of old Hawks Park including the long dock, a horse and buggy, and hot air balloons!

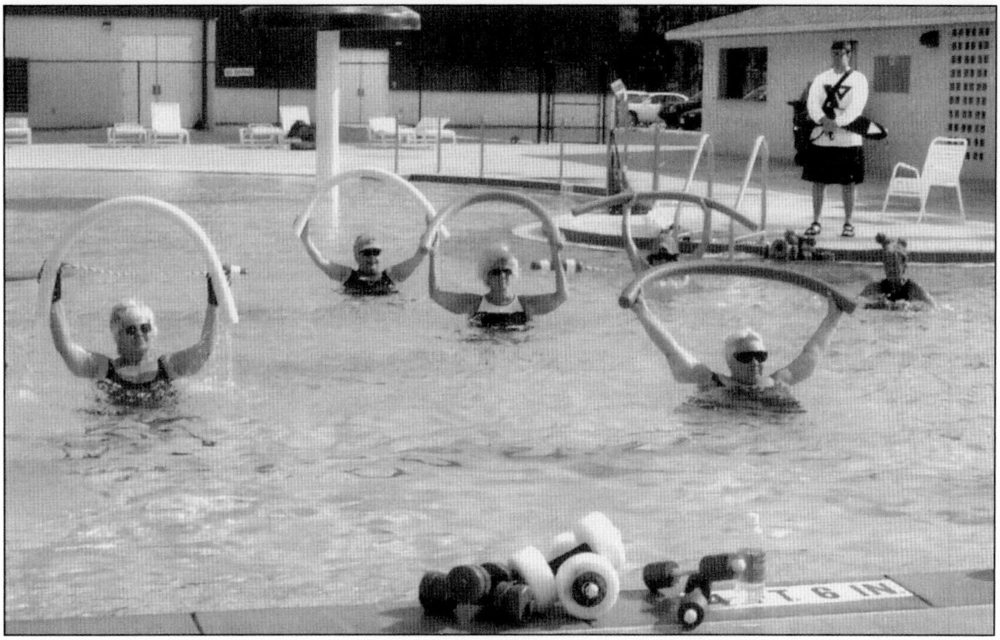

YMCA, 2005. The first large community center built in Edgewater was built in the 1950s by the townspeople. Today there is also a YMCA with many facilities, including a pool. The grand opening of the pool was in July 2002, and it is well used. The people are unidentified.

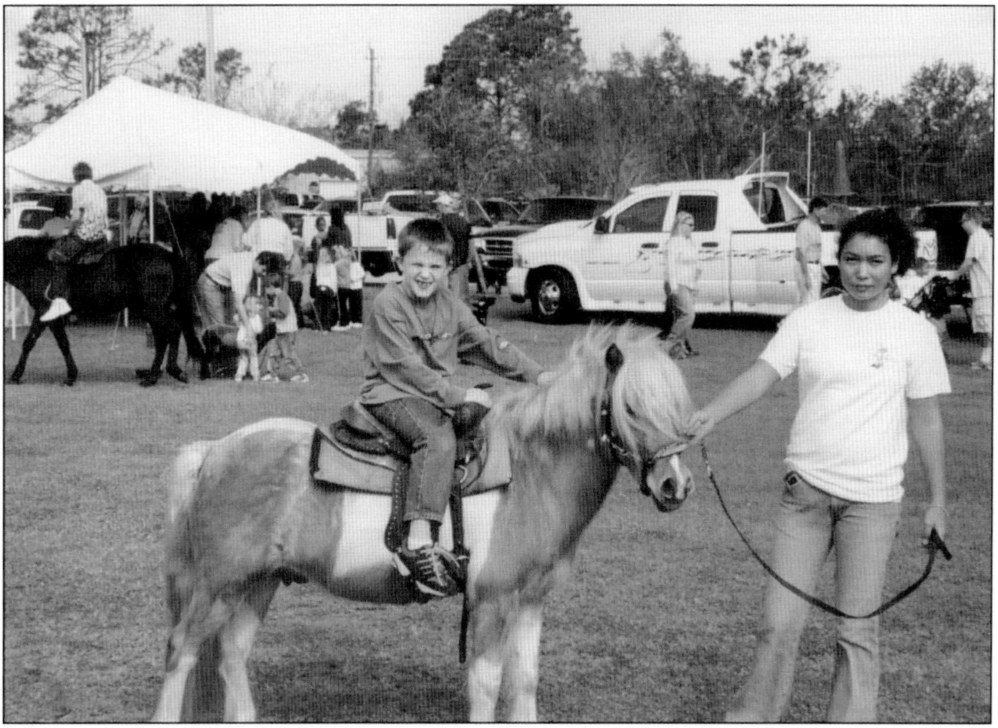

HAWKS PARK RECREATIONAL COMPLEX DEDICATION, JANUARY 2005. Thousands participated in the gala dedication for the recreational complex named for the original town. Here Calvin Sammons rides a pony during the festivities. The other people are unidentified.

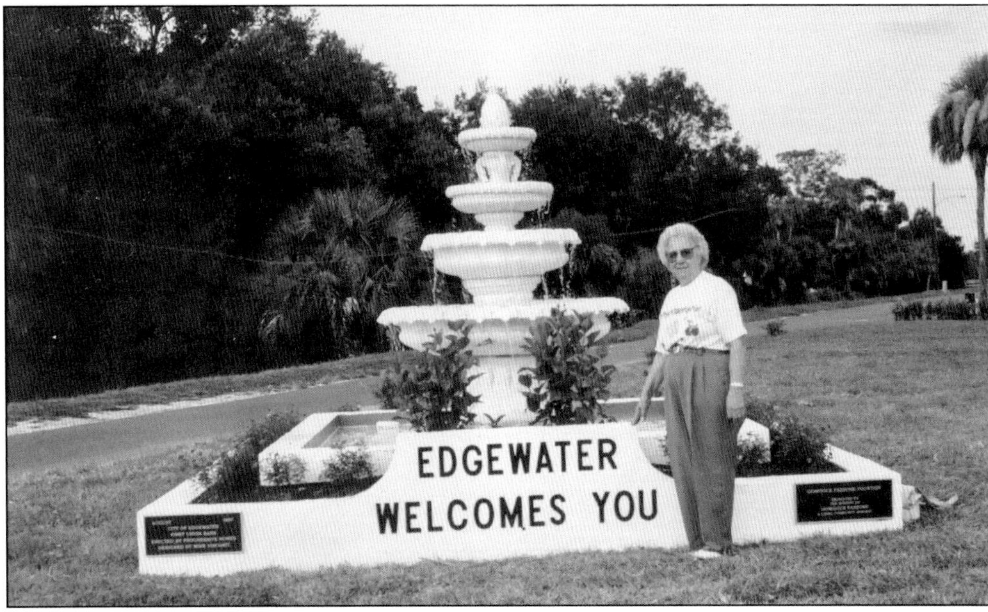

FOUNTAIN AT INDIAN RIVER BOULEVARD AND U.S. 1, 1998. Mrs. Bridget Visconti stands beside a fountain at the intersection of two major roads in modern Edgewater. In 1998, the city's beautification committee dedicated the fountain in memory of Dominick Fazzone and his many years of volunteer work for the city. The fountain no longer stands. It was decided in 1999 to remove it to allow for expansion of the roadway.

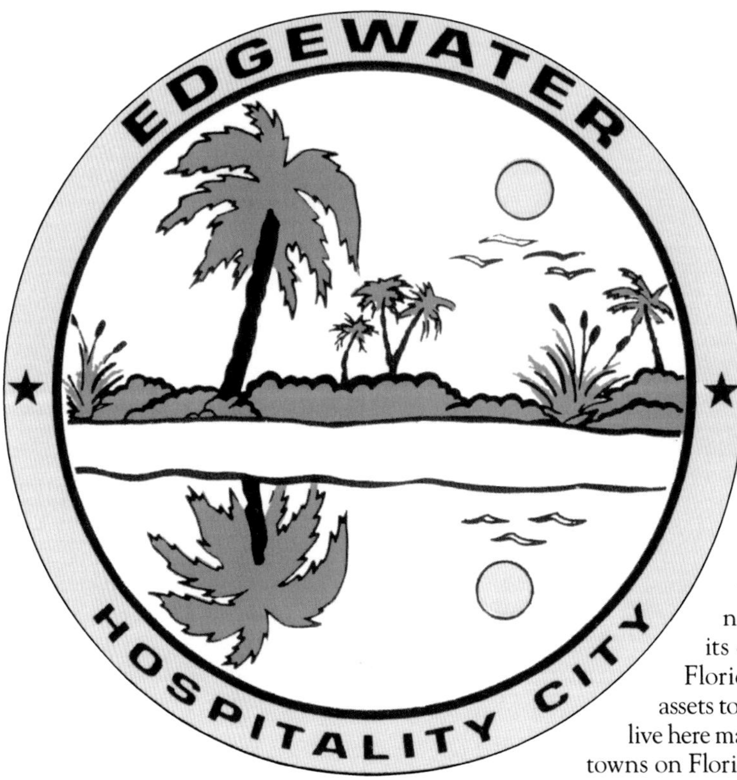

HOSPITALITY CITY SEAL, C. 2000. Many other early settlements in Florida failed, but Hawks Park grew and prospered into a city with over 20,000 people, with only a name change along the way. The Atlantic Ocean nearby, the Indian River at its doorstep, and the bright Florida sunshine are natural assets to the area. The people who live here make it one of the friendliest towns on Florida's east coast.

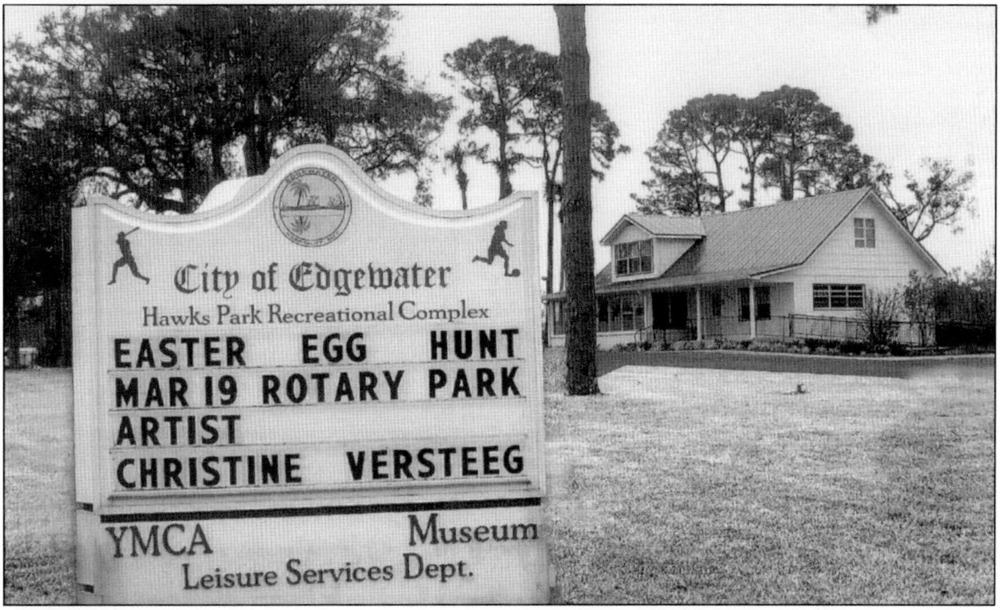

EDGEWATER MUSEUM AND LEISURE SERVICES BUILDING, 2005. In October 2002, the City of Edgewater bought the 1940s home of Ralph and Thelma Miller along U.S. 1 for use as a historical museum, art museum, and offices for the Leisure Services Department. Lynne Plaskett is the museum curator. Many visitors enjoy the artifacts from the past, such as Native American arrowheads, a drying crate for saw palmetto berries, and much, much more.

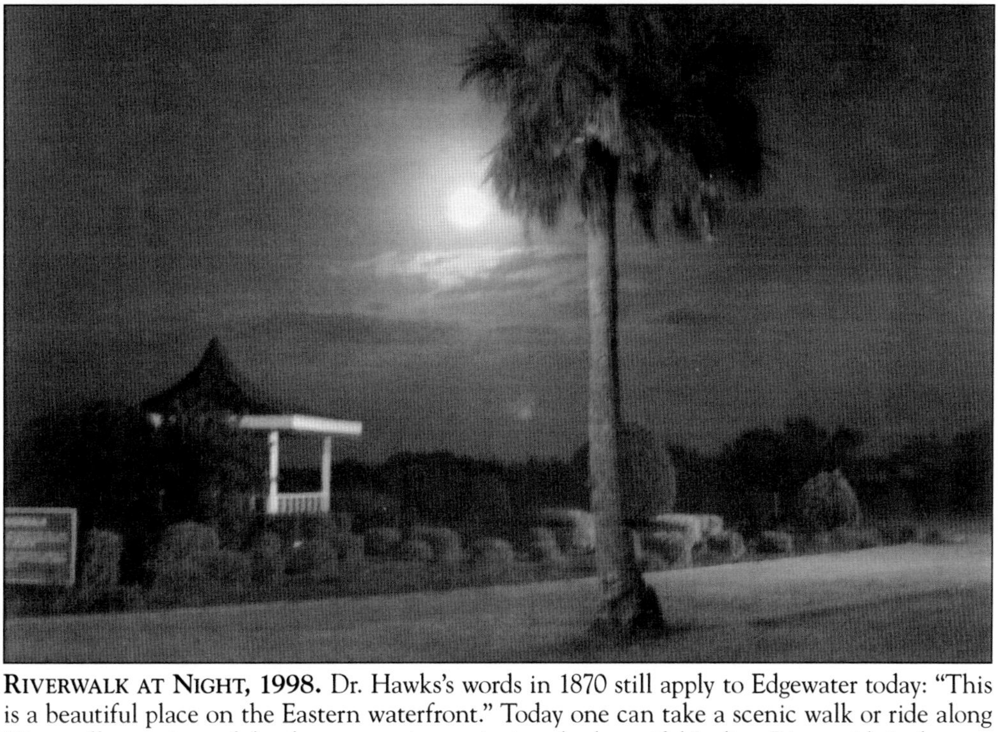

RIVERWALK AT NIGHT, 1998. Dr. Hawks's words in 1870 still apply to Edgewater today: "This is a beautiful place on the Eastern waterfront." Today one can take a scenic walk or ride along Riverwalk any time of the day or evening, enjoying the beautiful Indian River with its homes, parks, dolphins, manatees, waterbirds, and other wildlife.

Bibliography

Ancient and Modern New Smyrna, Fla. And Vicinity: Facsimile reprint of Royal Hubbell's 1906 photo book. Introduction by A. Stephen Patrick. Annotated by Gary Luther. New Smyrna, FL: Luther's Publishing, 1997.

Fitzgerald, T. E. (Thomas Edward). *Volusia County: Past and Present*. Daytona Beach, FL: *The Observer Press*, 1937.

Hawks, J. M. (John Milton). *The East Coast of Florida: A Descriptive Narrative*. Lynn, MA: Lewis & Winship, 1887. A facsimile reproduction of the 1887 edition was sponsored by Larry Sweett *c*. 1995.

Hubbell, Royal. *Ancient and Modern New Smyrna, Fla. And Vicinity*. Hawks Park, FL: Self-published, 1906.

Memorial Addresses on the Life and Character of Dr. Esther Hill Hawks. Lynn, MA: Boys Club Press, 1906.

Sammons, Sandy, and Jo Anne Sikes. *Two Early American Doctors*. Edgewater, FL: Self-published, 2003.

Schene, Michael. *Hopes, Dreams, and Promises: A History of Volusia County*. Daytona Beach, FL: News-Journal Corporation, 1976.

Schwartz, Gerald, ed. *A Woman Doctor's Civil War: Esther Hill Hawks' Diary*. Columbia, SC: University of South Carolina Press, 1984.

Volusia County Schools. *The Odyssey of an American School System: Volusia County Schools 1854–2000*. DeLand, FL: Self-published, 2000.